SERVING FAMILIES AND CHILDREN THROUGH PARTNERSHIPS

A How-To-Do-It Manual

Sandra Feinberg and Sari Feldman

HOW-TO-DO-IT MANUALS FOR LIBRARIANS

NUMBER 65

NEAL-SCHUMAN PUBLISHERS, INC.
New York, London

Published by Neal-Schuman Publishers, Inc.
100 Varick Street
New York, NY 10013

Printed and bound in the United States of America.

Library of Congress Cataloging-in-Publication Data

Feinberg, Sandra, 1946–
   Serving families and children through partnerships / by Sandra Feinberg
and Sari Feldman.
      p.   cm.—(A How-to-do-it manual for librarians ; 65)
   Includes bibliographical references and index.
   ISBN 1–55570–227–9
1. Libraries—Services to families—United States.   2. Libraries—Services
to preschool children—United States.   3. Public libraries—United
States.   I. Feldman, Sari, 1953– . II. Title.   III. Series: How-to-do-it
manual ; no. 65.
Z711.92.F34F453   1996
027.6—dc20   96–10177

DEDICATION

To Richie, Jake and Ted Feinberg
To Matt, Meg and Bridget O'Dwyer

CONTENTS

ACKNOWLEDGEMENTS

Special acknowledgement is given to Barbara Jordan, Middle Country Public Library, for her contributions to our manuscript. Her knowledge, expertise, and involvement in collaborative ventures are exemplary and greatly appreciated by the families of the Middle Country district and professionals throughout Suffolk County (NY) and New York State.

Recognition is also extended to the entire Middle Country Children's Department for initiating and developing family centered services and programs. In addition, appreciation is given to the colleagues and friends involved with the Suffolk Coalition for Parents and Children and the children's librarians in Suffolk County who supported efforts in the development of library-based family services.

Appreciation is also given to the entire staff of the Onondaga County Public Library with particular thanks to Tracey Durham, Janet Park, and Martha Morgan for their support in conceptualizing the Parent Information Resource Library.

Thank you to Virginia Mathews for her contribution on the Head Start/Library Partnership Project and her editorial comments and suggestions in the development of our book. Special acknowledgement is also extended to the Newburgh Public Library for sharing materials related to family support services, to Mary Viggiano for her excellent desk top publishing which appears throughout the text and in the appendixes, and to Beth Vella and Jennifer L. Brown for their contributions on Internet resources.

A special thank you to Dr. Margaret Monroe for instilling an understanding of public library partnerships.

FOREWORD

Most people, when they think of libraries, envision a place filled with rows and rows of books, a reading area for newspapers and magazines, video collections, and a reference desk. It may also include rooms for community events, children's story hour, and a literacy program. While always an important part of family and community life, today's libraries have an even greater potential to play a significant role in responding to and meeting the broader needs of children, youth, and families. Toward that end, Sandy Feinberg and Sari Feldman have been pioneers in shaping library programs that fully integrate the library into the community through partnerships and collaborations with other community services and providers. These partnerships place the library in a central position as a life development support center offering a broad range of family-centered services.

Serving Families and Children Through Partnerships presents a clear vision of ways in which libraries can focus services on the needs of families with young children and to collaborate effectively with other community partners. The book challenges libraries to look within their own resources as well as outside of their own walls into the broader service community to address the diverse and complex needs of today's families. The approach that is described by Feinberg and Feldman is built on the philosophy that all families need support and the best way to provide support is to empower parents, enabling them to help themselves and their children. The goals of a family support approach are to prevent problems rather than correct them; to strengthen the caregivers' capacity to nurture children and maximize the development of all family members; to integrate fragmented services and make them accessible to families; and to encourage and facilitate families' efforts to solve their own problems.

The family support movement is spreading across the nation, spurred on by the knowledge that healthy and involved families are critical to a child's future success. Of course, a parent is the most influential person in a child's life, but it takes every community member and organization to build a strong environment for the child to thrive fully. This means that schools, neighborhood service providers, churches, libraries, and businesses have a responsibility to provide support and assistance. No one program or service can do what must be done alone, nor should it try. Each program must develop partnerships, working collaboratively to share information and resources and explore opportunities to establish and commit to common goals. Libraries are especially important partners because they are a highly visible and historically valued resource in the community; a resource that is easily accessible and available, which offers a nonjudgmental environment for people of all backgrounds.

This informative step-by-step guide gives librarians the information to develop successful, collaborative ventures with other organizations in an effort to provide comprehensive and integrated services for children and families. We welcome this resource to the growing body of information on successful strategies and mechanisms to support and strengthen families.

Gail Koser
Director, STATES Initiative
Family Resource Coalition

PREFACE

Serving Families and Children Through Partnerships: A How-To-Do-It Manual for Librarians provides a step-by-step approach to focusing public library services on the needs of families with young children. It will also teach you to create meaningful partnerships with other community services. Today's libraries, particularly in the field of children's services, are changing and reevaluating their priorities and goals. Services to children must include families as well as those adults who work with and for children. No longer can librarians isolate themselves behind "closed doors" or create services in a vacuum. To be effective, libraries must collaborate and align with agencies and organizations that focus on families and young children in an effort to design a family-centered community environment.

In an effort to create coalitions and partnerships, *Serving Families and Children Through Partnerships* provides practical and theoretical information for those librarians willing to take risks, and to seek new and innovative liaisons within the community. *Serving Families and Children Through Partnerships* is particularly targeted for children's services librarians or librarians interested in outreach, parent education, community information and referral, literacy, young adult, or any related family information and support services. It will also be useful to public library administrators who are actively developing grants or positioning the library as a Preschoolers Door to Learning, a Parent Information and Resource Service, and/or a Center of Community Activity.

Each chapter outlines steps to take in the creation of a family-centered library environment. The introduction offers a summary of main concepts; each chapter develops these concepts more fully; illustrations and examples are also included. The topics discussed are serving children within the family context, developing library-based family support services, changing libraries to meet the needs of changing families, providing parent education and support, exploring new partnerships to create new services, developing strategies for service, building resource collections for families, and providing more for families through the sharing of resources.

Chapter 1 tells how to get started. It looks inside the library at the available resources and current status of family services as well as outside at the community, examining both demographic and social challenges and the existing family support system. Suggestions for how to go about developing a mission statement and give guidelines for creating a family support service policy are included.

Chapter 2 explores the coalition-building process with a description and illustration of four models or levels of coalitions. It explains the importance of coalition building to the development of family support services in public libraries. A step-by-step outline on how to establish coalitions for the librarian who wishes to lead or partner in the development of a local coalition is included. Appendix H provides a list of National Agencies and Organizations for the purpose of identifying potential partners in family services.

Chapter 3 provides strategies for librarians to become involved in the coalition-building process. There are specific examples of model networks that have been developed with the involvement of librarians, which will help you design your own. Appendix A contains practical information such as meeting topics, a membership list, sample agendas, and recruitment letters that have been produced in the development of these coalitions.

Chapter 4 discusses the basic principles, philosophy, and core components that make up the foundation of the family support movement. Included is an outline of the essential elements of library-based early childhood services, which are integral to the development of the parent/child activities component of family support services.

Chapter 5 focuses on specific family support services in public libraries that have been developed through coordination, cooperation, and networking. It provides a sampling of library based programs and services with brief descriptions. Program flyers, publicity items, and sample brochures relative to these programs and services are available in Appendix D.

Chapter 6 outlines basic steps in developing a collaborative project and highlights several examples of collaborative programs and services between public libraries and other agencies. These examples will help you to develop your own collaborative programs.

Chapter 7 examines fund development and budgeting for family service projects. Topics covered include grant proposals, budgets, requests for money, and contracts. Both print and Internet resources on grants are provided within this chapter. Appendix B gives samples of letters of request, letters of support, project descriptions, workplans, and agreements.

Chapter 8 reviews the competencies and skills that you will need in order to develop family programs; as well it discusses several self-assessment tools and checklists that you can use to determine where your particular strengths and weaknesses lie. Appendix E—"Self Study for Children's Librarians"—is an excellent tool for librarians to use in assessing their own skills to build services for families and young children.

Chapter 9 teaches you how to teach others about the importance of family support services in libraries. It outlines topics and issues to be considered when educating other family resource professionals about library service and provides a course curricula on family support services in public libraries specially aimed at librarians.

Chapter 10 covers measurement, quality review, and assessment. Using guidelines developed by other early childhood and parent initiatives, your library can assess its own service strategies, programs, and policies to evaluate their effectiveness and appropriateness. Appendices F and G include a survey and a checklist for evaluating our family support services.

The major issues to be considered when building a collection, a list of selection sources, a look at marketing the materials for families and agencies, and identification of materials targeted to special populations are included in the extensive overview provided in Chapters 11 and 12.

Chapter 13 introduces Internet Listservs, discussion groups, and information resources as a "jumping off" point to expand information access on family issues and family support. As we all know, electronic resources are the key to all library services.

With *Serving Families and Children Through Partnerships*, expanding and developing public library services for families and children will be easier. We have attempted to cover every anticipated question with the knowledge of years of experience. We are confident that you, as a librarian dedicated to the future of public libraries and their relationship to children, families, and communitites, will find the information useful when creating your own program.

INTRODUCTION

The role of the public library in early childhood learning, parent education, and family support service empowers librarians to become gatekeepers of the family literacy movement and initiators of the lifelong learning process. "Reading Begins at Birth," "Born to Read," and the "Preschoolers Door to Learning" are a few of the common themes that run through the public library world and underlie the development of today's service to families and young children. The images of early childhood educator, parent resource and information specialist, and family support professional must be nurtured by the library profession. Public libraries must not only be recognized for the historical contribution that children's librarians, in partnership with parents, have played in "giving birth to readers," but beyond this, for a major role in developing language, thinking skills, and confidence in children. Library resources can help give context and perspective to young lives.

SERVING CHILDREN WITHIN THE FAMILY CONTEXT

One of the public library's significant contributions in the current family literacy, early childhood, and parent education movements is its involvement in teaching children to read and the recognition that learning to read is more than books. Through their families, children learn communication skills, cultural values, and personal beliefs. These things all affect childrens' attitudes towards learning. Making the public library an influential partner in the family resource movement and gaining the recognition that the library is the central institution for lifelong learning requires the involvement and participation of the family, beginning with the birth of a child, if not before.

CHANGING FAMILIES; CHANGING LIBRARIES

It has become increasingly important for children's librarians to build and take an active role in library-based family support services. Dramatic social, demographic, and economic changes during the past thirty years have transformed the American family. For many children and parents, the experiences of family life are different today than a generation ago. Families are smaller. More children live with only one parent, usually their mothers, and many lack consistent involvement and support of their fathers. Families are experiencing more stress than ever before; parents are spending less and less time with their children. Statistics show

"An essential mission of public libraries is to ensure that young children receive services and support that help to prepare them for success in school and to become lifelong learners. This mission is accomplished by adopting the role of "Preschoolers' Door to Learning" as a national priority in public libraries, centering children's services around the developmental needs of children and their families, and building coalitions and developing a shared vision with the early care and education community."

Achieving School Readiness: Public Libraries and National Education Goal No.1. Chicago, IL: American Library Association, 1995. p. 140.

that situations such as both parents working outside the home, divorce, the uncertainty of the work environment, the need for quality child care, teenage pregnancy, poverty, and child abuse and neglect are taking their toll on the security and healthy growth of children today.

The early childhood education community is the natural partner for public librarians concerned with the needs of families of young children. These partnerships focus primarily on family literacy and revolve around emergent literacy, language development, and the printed word. Parenting information may overlap here but, for the purposes of this book, partnerships with early childhood education programs will not be a primary focus.

The new partners to be cultivated by public librarians serving families are agencies, organizations, and services that focus on health care, literacy, prevention and early intervention of developmental disabilities, parent education, nutrition, child care, family violence, and child abuse. Serving parents and the professionals who work with families expands the constituency of children's librarians and shifts the focus from serving the child as an individual to serving the child as part of the family unit. It is crucial that public librarians, particularly children's librarians, recognize their strengths, share their resources, and participate as a full partner with those who are designing our future community structures for families.

PROVIDING MORE WITH LESS AND DOING IT BETTER

Service to families and children is political gold to the future of libraries. Not only does this population have the greatest need for information and educational resources but it offers the greatest future potential for maintaining public support. Libraries that are integrated into the community of family-centered services have the greatest opportunity for real growth as a community resource.

Resources are shrinking and all public entities are feeling the necessity to provide more with less. Partnerships, collaborations and sharing of energies are essential to this process. The identity of the public library as a family centered institution designed for the pursuit of lifelong learning must be deliberately nurtured and expressed in word and action before it will be recognized and accepted by others. Through relationships with other educational and social service and health agencies, the ability to meet the needs of children and their families is maximized, while duplication of services is minimized.

The challenge to communities to collaborate, create, and change the quality of family services is a challenge to public libraries. It is crucial that public librarians, particularly children's librarians, recognize their strengths, share their resources, and participate as a full partner with those who are designing our future community structures for families.

It also must be recognized that the term "parents and families" includes all those with primary responsibility for the care of children. Single parents, adolescent parents, grandparents, foster parents, caregivers, and friends are among the diverse group described as parents. Cultural diversity, sexual orientation, and lifestyle choice are all factors creating change in the definition of families. While the spectrum of today's parents and families is as varied as the fabric of American life, all families benefit from strong family resource and support programs. Recognizing the public library as a family support institution and offering family-centered services and programs, enhances the role of the public library in the community.

THE LIBRARY AS A FAMILY SUPPORT INSTITUTION

Beyond family literacy and early childhood education, the public library has a responsibility to provide the much needed opportunity for family information literacy. This environment, which includes resources and information that support the health and well-being of parents and children, can only be created within an extended community and must include an integrated approach to service delivery. Knowledge of and communication with local agencies, schools, and community organizations are essential ingredients to the future success of children's services in public libraries.

Parents and other adults concerned with children also have a great need for information on a variety of topics concerning child development, education, nutrition, health, social, intellectual and cultural needs of children. These information needs, greatly enhanced by current social trends, place an ever increasing responsibility on public librarians as well as other professionals to be both providers and problem solvers. The parent/professional/librarian alliance is an important collaboration in serving families and young children in the library. Librarians can function as key parent educators by sharing their expertise and knowledge on how to acquire, organize, and disseminate information within a family centered environment.

NEW PARTNERS: A NEW FOCUS

A proliferation of options and information is not enough to ensure that parents have the knowledge, skills, and abilities to do their best by their children. The entire community must do more to support families and young children. Through coalition-building and collaborative efforts, services and programs and provide seamless support, creating an integrated, family-centered environment, from the prenatal through the adult years. It is imperative that the public library be an acknowledged integral partner within this service delivery system.

The Carnegie Task Force on Meeting the Needs of Young Children reports the following statistics that show the harsh realities of childhood and family life in America:

In 1960, only 5% of all births in the U.S. were to unmarried mothers; by 1988, the proportion had risen to 26%.

About every minute, an American Adolescent has a baby.

Divorce rates are rising. In 1960, less than 1% of children endured their parents' divorce each year; and by 1993 almost half of all children could expect to experience a divorce.

Children are increasingly likely to live with just one parent, from 10% in 1960 to almost a quarter of all children in 1989.

One in four infants and toddlers under the age of three (nearly 3 million children) live in families with incomes below the federal poverty level.

In a mere five years, from 1987 to 1991, the number of children in foster care jumped by more than 50%—from 300,000 to 460,000.

Pressures on both parents to work mean that they have less time with their young children; more than half of mothers of infants now work outside the home.

More than 5 million children under the age of three are in the care of other adults while their parents work.

In the United States, nine out of every thousand infants die before age one and the mortality rate is higher for infants born in minority families, 50% higher in African American families.

One in three victims of physical abuse is a baby less than a year old.

The leading cause of death among children aged one to four is unintentional injury.

Starting Points: Meeting the Needs of Our Youngest Children (abridged version). New York: Carnegie Corporation of New York, 1994. p 3.

RESOURCES

Achieving School Readiness: Public Libraries and National Education Goal No.1. Chicago, IL: American Library Association, 1995.

Beyond Rhetoric—A New American Agenda for Children and Families: Final Report of the National Commission on Children. Washington, DC: National Commission on Children, 1991.

Bruner, Charles. "Building Bridges: Supporting Families Across Service Systems." *FRC Report* (Spring/Summer 1994): 5–8.

Elsmo, Nancy and Micki Nevett. "The Public Library; A Resource Center for Parents: A Drama in Three Acts." *Public Libraries* (Fall 1983): 96–98.

Family Support Programs and Comprehensive Collaborative Services. Chicago, IL: Family Resource Coalition, 1993.

Farrell, Diane G. "Library and Information Needs of Young Children." *Proceedings of the Conference on the Needs of Occupational, Ethnic and Other Groups in the United States.* Washington, DC: National Commission on Libraries and Information Science, (May 1973): 142–52.

The Health/Education Connection: Initiating Dialogue on Integrated Services to Children at Risk and Their Families. Symposium (Alexandria, Virginia, March 1990). ERIC Document #ED360278, 1990.

Human Needs in Onondaga County, 1991: A Status Report. Syracuse, NY: Coalition for Health and Welfare of Syracuse and Onondaga County, 1991.

Just the Facts. Albany, NY: State Communities Aid Association, 1992.

Leave No Children Behind: An Opinion Maker's Guide to Children in Election Year 1992. Washington, DC: Children's Defense Fund, 1991.

Naylor, Alice Phoebe. "Reaching All Children: A Public Library Dilemma." *Library Trends* 35 (Winter 1987): 369–392.

Richmond, Jayne, and Robert Shoop. *Prevention Through Coalitions: The Role of the Human Service Professional.* Paper presented at the Annual Convention of the American Psychological Association (92nd, Toronto, Canada, Aug. 24-28, 1984) ERIC Document #ED257029.

Starting Points: Meeting the Needs of Our Youngest Children (abridged version). New York: Carnegie Corporation of New York, 1994.

Supporting Young Children and Families: A Regents Policy Statement on Early Childhood. Albany, NY: New York State Education Department, 1993.

Weissbourd, Bernice. "Help for Busy Parents." *Parents* (June 1991): 141.

What Lies Ahead: A Decade of Decision. Syracuse, NY: United Way Strategic Institute, 1992.

1 GETTING STARTED

Introducing family services into a public library's overall plan of service, and assigning them a major role for the library in the community is critical. "Realizing the vision of service and support for young children and their families will require new organizational structures within individual libraries as well as in the broader library community. Changes will be required in library policies, in personnel deployment, in facilities design and utilization, in patterns of communication, and in education for librarianship." (*Achieving School Readiness* 1995, p. 143)

The process of thinking through and clearly articulating the role of the public library in family service will help you to evaluate the current status of the library, examine the level of service within the community, and develop a policy for public library service to families.

MISSION

Drafting a working mission statement will help to set the tone for family service. A sample mission may look like this:

> The mission of the _____ Public Library's family service role is to provide resources and information in a variety of formats and methods to support the health, well-being, and education of families with young children through direct service and in partnership with other agencies sharing this mission.

A small public library may need to adjust the mission statement by providing family service in stages. A sample statement may look like this:

> The mission of the _____ Public Library's family service role is to provide a print and nonprint collection that meets the information and education needs of families in _____ community.

While the library may currently perform components of the family service role, attaching a mission statement and packaging the various components will change the way staff and users look at the library's role in serving families. This process requires that the library examine its current staff, collection, physical environment, and programs in relationship to family service. In addition, since the library's plan of service does not exist in a vacuum, the library must also explore the community's involvement in family service.

What is the cost benefit of creating a family service role or program? If a public library identifies itself as a center of reference or information services, this may have little impact on the lives of children and families. As soon as the information services are focused and packaged to meet the needs of child-rearing adults and family service professionals, there is increased understanding and appreciation for the role of public libraries in serving families within the community. Improving the understanding of adult users on the importance of libraries to families increases the value of the public library in a community.

In ranking or prioritizing services, public libraries would be loath to cut services to children even in an austere budget. Service to children is essential and popular, as well as an emotionally charged issue. Family services have the same cost benefit as children's services. They are essential, popular, and emotionally or politically important services for all public or government institutions. Selecting family services as a role and strengthening children's services to include service to parents and agencies that serve parents increases the political worth of the public library.

Government, private, and corporate funding has increasingly rewarded communities with strong networks and coalitions in family support services. By embracing the family services ideology, the public library is positioned to participate in projects that should bring real dollars for library service.

FIRST THINGS FIRST

Putting goals and objectives into writing can make the difference between a clear reflection of the library's capacity for change and service, and the library plunging into the community donned in the "emperor's new clothes." To avoid a silly, naked, and vulnerable image, the library must not only look at itself and the community as a whole with regard to the family service environment—it must "do its homework" before laying claims or making promises.

There are many effective ways to examine the library's current status in serving families, but one of the best models may be an adaptation of the "Whole Services Worksheet" created by Lindsay Ruth of the Geneva Free Library in New York State. (Ruth and Feldman, 1994). The "Whole Services Worksheet: An Internal Review" (see Appendix C, Figure C-1) relies on observation, intuition, and common sense. It is a relaxed and informal approach to the planning process that can involve each staff member at his or her own level.

The following are four main areas that require close examination. Asking questions about internal operations and organizing the questions and responses will help to clarify the current status of family service.

STAFF

What are the staff resources?

How does the staff relate to children and parents using the library?

Are staff members providing information and referral to other agencies serving families?

Is the staff flexible about accepting new ideas and adaptable to change?

Are there staff barriers that must be overcome?

COLLECTION

What are the collection resources within the library?

How does the collection serve parents, caregivers, and other agencies involved with the families of young children?

What are the effects of displays or booklists that promote family information resources?

What percentage of questions is answered with materials that are relevant to family services?

Are there collection development barriers that must be overcome?

PHYSICAL SPACE

Is the library family friendly?

Is there space to organize a special collection?

Is there a meeting room or small group room available for programming or training?

Does the physical space of the library promote access to information, including community information?

Are there physical barriers that must be overcome?

SPECIAL ACTIVITIES/PROGRAMS

What kinds of programs are offered to families of young children?

What level of family involvement exists in children's programs?

Are the meeting rooms used by outside agencies to present programs to families of young children?

Does the library staff conduct outreach programs at sites within the community?

Are there barriers to effective programming?

After reviewing the answers to these questions it is time to involve other staff. At a small public library, a discussion with the director and/or a focus group of other staff members and volunteers will more clearly identify the strengths and weaknesses of the library's service to families. Depending on one's status in a medium or large library, weaving through a maze of bureaucracy may be necessary before being successfully heard. Sharing thoughts and beginning discussion with staff, other professionals, and patrons can strengthen the exploratory process to gain support of the library administration. An ideal scenario would give an initiator the autonomy to evolve a plan of family service in a free and creative environment.

The next step involves another review of the current status of service to families using the questions above—this time with staff involvement. Garnering information from library staff representing a wide variety of job titles will provide different images and opinions while formulating creative ideas for breaking down or contending with barriers.

For example, if the library does not have a space for a special family resource collection then staff may suggest tagging each item with a color or symbol, compiling bibliographies, or other solutions to the problem. Since any change may result in increased workload, particularly for support staff, involving key players early on is essential.

The internal review flows directly into the external review— examining the library's position within the community. There are many planning tools that can assist libraries in "looking around," and some of these are listed at the end of this chapter.

A long-range planning process, however, may dampen enthusiasm. It may be valuable to check with other agencies or organizations. Head Start, local schools, and other community groups are required to conduct community assessments. Many communities have private and government planning agencies. Libraries may find it most effective to piggyback on the existing work of groups that have the resources and professional expertise to prepare a comprehensive community analysis.

Public librarians often have instincts about their communities, but they may be founded on incomplete information. This intuition is usually based on who uses the library and who doesn't, so entire groups may be virtually invisible. Reading the local newspaper or summary publications from the local government can provide a good demographic picture without allotting time to prepare complicated worksheets. Each library needs to determine the level of effort in analyzing the community.

CUSTOMER PROFILE

The first question to ask is who the library's customers are. In developing family services there are two potential customers: parents/caregivers and adults who work with families and children. Most businesses create a profile of their "regular" customer. In a library, this might be your present users, which include children and maybe parents. Businesses also look at potential markets. These might be nonusers, families that use the library in very limited ways (such as only for videos), and other agencies or organizations that serve families in the community.

Simple demographics can develop the customer profile and compare families in the community with families in other parts of the country. Determine the level of family service already available in your community. Choose a community of similar size and get a copy of its yellow pages and/or human service directory. Compare the gross number of agencies and organizations between communities for a sense of customer need that may exist in the community. Need for family support services may determine the complexity of the library service proposed for the locality.

COMPETITION PROFILE

Other agencies and organizations that serve families with young children in the community now may be perceived or see themselves as the library's competition. Once the library's family service is under way these same agencies are likely to become community partners and collaborators. The phone book, human service directories, city directories, driving around, asking friends and family, and gathering input from staff and users can all provide information about the services in your community. Learn from these other agencies by focusing on the visibility of this type of family service in the community and the ability of each agency and organization to attract users to its service.

Use the "Whole Services Worksheet: An External Review" (Appendix C, Figure C-2) as a quick way to examine the staff, collection, physical space, and special activities of each agency or organization that holds a prominent role in family service in the community.

You will want to find out about the resources of other agencies and organizations serving families with young children. You will want to ask the following questions.

STAFF

What is the background or training for the staff from other agencies?

How is funding for staff at these agencies provided?

Is staff from a competitive agency available for library staff development or programs at the library?

COLLECTION

Are other agencies collecting print and nonprint materials?

Are there agencies that have the capacity for developing an electronic network?

Are there other agencies that loan materials to families? Each other?

Is there a catalog of local resources?

Do other agencies publish newsletters or local publications?

PHYSICAL SPACE

Are there agencies that have meeting rooms?

Are there agencies that have community-based outreach sites?

Are there agencies that have family friendly space?

SPECIAL ACTIVITIES/PROGRAMS

Are there agencies that provide programs for families and children?

Are there networks or coalitions for family service providers or parent educators?

Are there area conferences for family service providers or parent educators?

Getting to know agency personnel from other programs will be covered in the chapters on coalition building. There are many natural alliances for libraries and, more important, librarians will find a comfortable fit with individuals from other family service organizations. These warm and natural relationships are the essential ingredient for successful collaborations.

Once the customer/competition profiles and external review are completed and the internal strengths and weaknesses are examined, it is necessary to set goals, objectives, an action plan, statements of library policy, and a budget.

GOALS

Goals are broad statements that project an ideal level of service. They are achievable, but the success will be measured over a long period of time.

Sample:
Focusing on the family as a unit, the _____ library will significantly improve service to parents, caregivers, and the community agencies and organizations who serve them.

OBJECTIVES

Objectives get closer to how the goal will be accomplished. They are action-oriented, measurable, and provide meaning to the goal and steps toward achieving it.

Sample:

OBJECTIVE ONE
To increase the number of families with young children using library programs by __ percent over the next __ months.

OBJECTIVE TWO
To increase the number of available resources on topics of interest to parents and caregivers by __ percent over the next __ months.

OBJECTIVE THREE
To increase the staff's involvement in family service coalitions by developing closer working relationships with at least __ agencies over the next __ months.

ACTION PLAN

The action plan outlines the steps or tasks that ensure the successful achievement of each objective. Both the action plan and objectives should include the elements of evaluation. Libraries need to examine alternatives to each action step based on cost, available staff, the ability to evaluate the plan, and the appropriateness of the activity.

Some of the questions to consider regarding Objective One include:

> How will the library determine the baseline number of users of the library in order to measure growth in family programming and services?
>
> Is there staff available to provide outreach or increased programming?
>
> Are there incentives that could be offered that are cost-effective and would entice families to use the library?
>
> How can this objective be broken down into discreet pieces to be achieved over a period of time?

Sample:

OBJECTIVE ONE

To increase the number of families with young children using library programs by __ percent over the next __ months.

ACTION PLAN

> Conduct three additional toddler storytimes each week.
>
> Form a family reading club focused on families and young children.
>
> Contact the local child care coordinating council to offer joint programs to family home day-care providers.

The previous brief discussion of goals and objectives introduces the topic. Suggested readings on planning are included at the end of this chapter.

SERVICE POLICY

A statement of policy is needed to establish the level of service that families, caregivers, and agencies or organizations can expect. Policy ensures a level of consistency among staff and uniformity in the quality and quantity of service provided to patrons. Policy also enables the community and staff to understand the priority of family support services.

The policy can be developed by library staff with input and approval of trustees, collaborations between staff from the library and other agencies, and input from parents and children. The following elements are suggestions for what to include in a policy manual.

1. Begin with an introduction, which can be an elaboration of the mission statement.
2. Include the goals and current short-term and long-term objectives of the service.
3. Give a description of the types and level of library services that are included as part of family service—for example, a small library may define collection development as a priority but larger libraries may emphasize programming, staff development, coalition work, and parent-child workshops as components of the service.
4. Provide a description of the primary customer or user group for the service. The needs of this group may be highlighted as part of the policy.
5. Provide information on methods to access the service. Is there telephone service? Is there electronic access? Are all aspects of the service available only through the library or are there elements such as requests for information that can be made to any agency and then forwarded to the library?
6. A restatement of general library policies could be included. Statements of confidentiality, privacy, free access to information, copyright law, and code of staff conduct as well as policies that may be specific to the individual library would all be possible choices.

The planning components described in this chapter form the elements of an effective grant proposal. This will be discussed further in Chapter 7.

Many of the steps from planning to delivering family services do not fall in sequence. When a great opportunity to collaborate, get funding, or join a coalition comes the way of the library, "seize the day." Fill in the blanks afterwards, however, and take the time to create a quality, holistic service for families in the community.

BUDGET

The budget for any library program or service is an essential part of the planning process. A program budget allocates money to a major service within a library. A performance budget allocates money in the same way but details the service level and attaches performance measures or data to the budget. Each of these types of budgets:

> reflects the mission, goals, and objectives of the service;
> emphasizes what is being done, not what is being purchased;
> can be used to assess need and future planning;
> refocuses goals and objectives as needed and identifies costs for each alternative; and
> ranks alternatives for cost-effectiveness.

The program budget focuses on planning and effectiveness. The performance budget focuses on efficiency. Within the program or performance budget there will be at least two dominant line items. Staff is the key to the development and maintenance of the service, which is why salaries and benefits are the largest portion of any budget. Personnel costs are the most expensive part of providing service to the community.

Materials are the second dominant cost. The public wants to know why libraries buy books, videos, and magazines when they hear that everything is available in electronic format. There are actually two answers to this issue. First, the community continues to demand that the traditional formats of print, audio, and video be available in public libraries. Second, telecommunications and databases or networked CD-ROM products are resources that actually can be more expensive than their print predecessors. In any form, information costs money and will be reflected as a substantial portion of a budget.

A percentage of supplies, operations, travel, continuing education, and other miscellaneous items should also be part of the overall budget for family services. Although line item expenditures for staff and materials may cut across many departments and services, having a dollar amount affixed to family services provides the library with the best planning and management to meet the needs of the community.

RESOURCES FOR THE PLANNING PROCESS

Jacob, M.E.L. *Strategic Planning: A How-To-Do-It Manual for Librarians*. New York: Neal-Schuman, 1990.

McClure, Charles R. et al. *Planning and Role Setting for Public Libraries*. Chicago: American Library Association, 1987.

Robbins, Jane et al. "Information to Support Planning for Children's Services." *Evaluation Strategies and Techniques for Public Library Children's Services: A Sourcebook*. Madison, WI: University of Wisconsin, 1990.

Weingand, Darlene. *Marketing/Planning Library and Information Services*, Littleton. CO: Libraries Unlimited, 1987.

Wood, Elizabeth J. "Strategic Planning and the Marketing Process: Library Applications." *Journal of Academic Librarianship* (March 1983): 15–20.

REFERENCES

Achieving School Readiness: Public Libraries and National Education Goal No.1. Chicago, IL: American Library Association, 1995.

Ruth, Lindsay and Sari Feldman. "The Whole Service Approach." *School Library Journal* (May 1994): 28–31.

2 COALITION BUILDING: AN OVERVIEW

One of the public librarian's major roles is to provide information and referral on community services to patrons. This information is found not only through books and computer resources but, to be accurate and effective, must be augmented with personal knowledge of existing community resources. By communicating with professionals from the other "helping" professions in the fields of health and human services, librarians can be more effective in providing information and referral.

This communication is particularly important for those who work in the area of children's and parents' services. Children's librarians may be attracted to the field because they want to work with children, but they soon find out that one of the first requirements in working with children is to recognize the importance of working with the child's parents and primary caregivers as well as other professionals who work with families. "Library staff must embrace the belief that all children and their families are library customers of primary importance and that librarians share responsibility for ensuring that children succeed in school and become lifelong learners. Librarians must form partnerships with parents, early care and education providers, and other community-based agencies serving youth to provide appropriate services and support for young children and their families." (*Achieving School Readiness* 1995, p. 142)

Through the development of coalitions and networks, librarians can expand their horizons, become more informed professionals, and be alerted to trends in youth services, and early childhood and parent education. They can integrate the library's youth and parenting services with the greater community of services and increase the library's potential for reaching families. In addition to what the librarian will gain, parents and professionals will learn:

- to recognize the library's ability to organize and disseminate information to its community;
- to understand the role of the library in providing free access to information;
- to look towards the library as a primary community center for serving families and young children;
- to place the library and the children's librarian in a leadership role in advocating for youth and family services; and

- to appreciate the library's role in sharing community resources, building a democratic nation, and beginning the lifelong learning process.

This chapter will focus on coalition building as a tool that can expand the capability of the librarian to serve families and youth service professionals. It explores the concept of coalition building, outlines the underlying assumptions, describes the different types of coalitions and how a library might participate in the various types of networks, and provides a step-by-step approach to forming a coalition.

COALITION BUILDING: A WORKING DEFINITION

To start our exploration of coalition building, it is important for us to look at the type of characteristics common to people who form coalitions. One definition states that: "Coalition builders articulate the heartfelt concerns of all sides of an issue. They recognize, listen to and publicly communicate the legitimacy of different perspectives. They facilitate emotional healing and understanding by enabling the sharing of personal experiences. They reframe issues in a way that encourages the best thinking on all sides to come together to shape new policies and possibilities. They have the skills to avoid an adversarial stance when reconciliation and bridge building are the most appropriate and productive leadership behaviors." (Brown, 1993, p. 11)

A number of assumptions underlie the process of building cooperation between agencies in a community:

- Economically it is often unsound to duplicate existing facilities in a community.
- Cooperation is preferable to competition.
- It is more logical to serve one specific need well than to serve partially many needs.
- There is more need for service in any community than there are services available.
- Needs change within a community.
- Needs within a given community differ from person to person.
- There are many services that have logical relatedness.
- The people for whom the service is designed should be provided with the opportunity to participate in the decisions affecting the delivery system.

- Services should be provided at a location that is convenient to the people. (Shoop, 1976, p. 10)

FOUR MODELS OF COALITION BUILDING

Coalitions improve community-wide communication and foster the most effective problem-solving techniques. Coalition building includes four models of interaction: networking; coordination and cooperation; partnership; and collaboration. Each model has specific goals and requires different skills for effective implementation. The coalition building process often displays a combination or variation of the models and can be viewed as a continuous and creative process, defined by the agencies involved, the changing needs of the community, and the level of commitment necessary to accomplish a common goal.

Networking is the most appropriate model to use if the goal is to facilitate communication among individuals. It requires a minimal level of interaction among participants and generally allows for the exchange of information amongst agencies. At this level the library sticks to family literacy activities such as Mother Goose Nursery Rhyme programs, toddler storytimes, or the development of a parent's collection, while advertising these activities to outside agencies and organizations to increase visibility. The publication of a local listing of community services would be another example of a networking activity.

Coordination and Cooperation aim to combine the efforts of two or more agencies to eliminate duplication and needless competition. Little agency autonomy is lost and only a modest form of communication is required to coordinate a program. The joint sponsorship of a workshop on a topic of concern to the clients/patrons of two agencies is an example of coordination.

Cooperation is a higher level of commitment on the part of agencies. Conducting a joint needs assessment, followed by joint planning and the delineation of roles between two or more agencies is an example of cooperation. The library, in this model, could develop a parent support group in cooperation with professionals from other agencies. The Parent/Child Workshop (Chapter 5), a new mothers discussion group, or a Parents Anonymous group held in a library setting with input and involvement from library staff are specific examples of this type of cooperation.

COORDINATION & COOPERATION

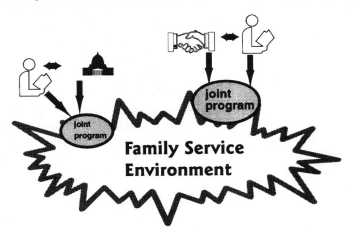

A Partnership involves a significant increase in agency commitment and considerable personal contact between staff members of the cooperating agencies. Partnerships occur when: each agency takes financial responsibility for part of a joint project, a more formal agreement is reached as to the roles of each agency, a common goal exists, and the staff time and energy expended show a visible commitment on the part of each agency. The partnership can be identified by the community at large as a function of each agency. When two or more agencies cosponsor a conference, each taking responsibility for the various tasks associated with organizing the conference, or when several agencies agree to cross-train amongst staff and utilize each other's expertise at no external expense, a partnership is in place.

PARTNERSHIP

Collaboration requires a formal relationship of shared activities and commitment to a common goal—a goal that may be unattainable by one agency. A high degree of contact and mutual trust is demanded, there is frequent face-to-face communication, and a great deal of energy and dedication to the collaborative process is visible. A truly collaborative process takes on a life of its own and may become a separate entity from the original collaboration. In spite of the risks of conflict, collaboration is the best model for introducing a new program into a community's human service delivery system.

COLLABORATION

In the first stage of the coalition-building process, a library may organize and actively participate in a local professional network that focuses on services to children and parents, a task force on the prevention of child abuse, or an early childhood professional development alliance. A second step in the process may involve the sponsorship of a major conference that focuses on sharing information on local resources, joint delivery of service to families, a new way of funding a service, or an integration of services to better serve families and children. Writing collaborative grants with other agencies or incorporating policies and legislative initiatives into library practice are examples of even more progressive stages of the coalition-building process. When another agency places a family intervention specialist or health educator in the public library, a higher form of commitment is involved. This type of arrangement requires a true collaboration.

Although the public library is only one of many service components that exists in a community, it does have a unique contribution to make to the processes of networking, coordination/cooperation, forming partnerships, and collaboration.

1. It is generally accepted that communities respect and appreciate the public library. The library lays claim to being the community's center for information, culture, intellectual development, educational enrichment, and recreation in today's world.

2. The public library is usually centrally located and reasonably accessible to a community. It could act as a mini-service center in the neighborhood, provide meeting space for services, and offer coalition support.
3. The library as a public facility already exists. Why build another building?
4. Children and families compose one of the largest population groups in a community. Many families already use the library and, with the help of coalition building, they could learn about other community resources or be provided extended services beyond the traditional library fare.
5. Educators and librarians talk of serving the whole child within the family. Using the library as a service delivery center or incorporating the library professional into a community coalition promotes the idea that education and lifelong learning are key parts of the total process in which "a village raises one child."

FORMING A COALITION

Coalitions and the process of forming them vary greatly from place to place. They can be formal or informal, temporary or permanent, meet regularly or not at all, deal with one issue or many. In some cases, they represent a broad-based community effort. In other situations, they seek to accomplish specific objectives or manage particular projects.

Coalitions, alliances, networks, or task forces in support of services to families and young children already exist in many communities. Before starting to form a new one, it is incumbent upon the librarian to search the community for existing coalitions, make contact with the leaders, attend meetings and conferences with the participants, and inform them about the library's services to families. Contacts include:

YMCA, Family Service League, or another not-for-profit agency
Cooperative Extension (Human Development Agent)
Child Care or Day Care Council
Youth bureau
Public health department, particularly the nursing division
United Way

Local agencies involved in services to victims of child abuse
A parent educator's network or parent resource center
School nurses or social workers
University and college departments of child development, education, psychology, nursing, social work
Churches
Organizations serving teen mothers/parents
Early Intervention specialists from the education and/or health departments

In some cases, the librarian will discover that no such coalition exists or that the issue that the existing coalition supports is limited. It may be that, through this community search, the librarian finds professionals in other agencies who are eager to form a general coalition that would focus on children and family issues, primary prevention, early intervention, or family support. The following guidelines provide steps to follow in initiating and organizing a coalition (Thomas, 1989, p. 272–279; Richmond, 1984, p. 4–5).

To initiate a coalition, it is important to gain commitment from various agencies to become involved in a collaborative effort. In a community, many diverse groups are in positions to assist in the development of family services. If a coalition is to be a constructive force in supporting this development, the groups involved must be able to work together to fulfill the goals of the coalition in addition to their own.

IDENTIFY POTENTIAL MEMBERS

To determine potential members, the coalition builder can compile a list in three categories:

1. all of the "natural" allies, groups, and types of people who may share the concern about families and support a similar position;
2. all of the types of persons, groups, and social structures likely to be affected by the issue or position taken; and
3. all potentially interested and civic-minded groups who might stand to gain indirectly by supporting the same issue or constituents.

Chapter 3 provides information on the Suffolk (NY) Coalition for Parents and Children. A glance through the current mailing list provides many ideas for potential coalition members (Appendix A, Figure A-8). Also appended is a list of National Agencies and Organizations involved in family support (Appendix H). Their local affiliates may provide a good place to start in the identification process. Inventory forms that can be used to gather initial information on potential members are also appended (Appendix A, Figures A-1 and A-2).

RECRUIT MEMBERS

Once potential members are identified, the next step is to develop a strategy for marketing the coalition. Coalition builders must clearly understand and be able to appeal to the potential members' self-interest, for the pursuit of self-interest is fundamental to effective political action. Identifying the mutual needs of each agency and being able to demonstrate how the members will benefit from participation is critical to the success of building a coalition. It is also important to understand the advantages of coalitions over working independently and to be able to express the advantages with conviction:

- Coalitions can conserve resources;
- Coalitions can reach more people within a community than a single organization;
- Coalitions can accomplish objectives beyond the scope of any single organization;
- Coalitions have greater credibility than individual organizations;
- Coalitions provide a forum for sharing information;
- Coalitions provide a range of advice and perspectives to participating agencies;
- Coalitions foster personal satisfaction and help members to understand their jobs in a broader perspective;
- Coalitions can foster cooperation among grassroots organizations, community members, and diverse sectors of a large organization (Cohen, 1994, p. 4).

When taking the "sales pitch" to the key persons in the targeted organizations, coalition organizers should not only ask for help in developing the coalition, but also actively welcome ideas. The goal is to enable all participants to feel a sense of ownership in the coalition's direction.

ORGANIZE A MEETING

Invite representatives from targeted organizations to an area-wide meeting to make decisions about whether to form a coalition, how the coalition should be structured, and what coalition strategies and activities to initiate. Using the library as a meeting place introduces the other participants to one of the library's greatest assets—meeting space. Sample invitation/confirmation letters are appended (Appendix A, Figures A-3 through A-7b).

SET GOALS AND OBJECTIVES

Coalitions and networks have different sets of goals and objectives. In some cases, coalitions can undertake efforts to improve services in general, such as all services in a particular geographic area that effect children. In other cases, coalitions seek to accomplish specific objectives such as the passage of a legislative bill or the management of a specific project. (Thomas, 1989, p. 272)

Goals should be mutually advantageous and broad enough to involve all of the participants in the coalition. Keep in mind the following fundamental elements to consider when the group begins to formulate goals.

- A statement of purpose broad enough to accommodate all parties, but specific enough to identify a target for action;
- A statement of long- and short-range goals focusing both on internal capacity-building and external efforts, including a process for identifying, recruiting, and developing leaders;
- A commitment to continually incorporate community input and societal influences into coalition goals and to interpret these goals to the community.

OPERATE THE COALITION

In order to effectively operate and sustain a coalition, some organizational structure needs to be instituted. A simple organizational structure should include:

- A group that is willing to take the responsibility for convening the relevant parties;
- A steering committee or governing board to assist in identifying the direction of the coalition;
- Committees to oversee the coalition's planned projects and draw up by-laws and rules of governance.

Critical elements of a successful coalition structure include an understanding of the coalition's life expectancy, meeting location, frequency and length of meetings, membership parameters, decision-making methods, meeting structure, and participation between meetings.

ANTICIPATE CONFLICT

Maintaining the coalition and communication amongst the members must be given high priority for coalitions to succeed. Some of the difficulties that coalitions usually face include turf and pecking order issues, diverting resources from an organization's own goals, cumbersome decision-making processes utilizing a consensus approach to solving problems, and a tendency to turn the coalition into a club or exclusive alliance. Even the coalition's meeting place can be a bone of contention. A neutral place is a necessity and, in many instances, the library provides this type of neutral meeting place.

COALITION BUILDING: THE LIBRARY'S ROLE

If the initiative to form a coalition is taken by the library, then the library will have a major role in shaping the coalition's mission. It must be prepared to allocate some resources (staff time, in-kind support, or some funds), both initially and as an ongoing commitment. Activities such as printing, duplicating, mailing, and preparing membership directories are among the activities that can cost money.

Librarians traditionally thought they could serve just as liaisons to other youth-serving agencies. While this activity points to team building and involvement, coalition building points to leadership and commitment. The librarian must be action-oriented and have a genuine concern for improving and developing services based on input from the coalition. In this active role, the librarian becomes the catalyst or change agent, providing new information to enhance group communication and an alternative way to serve families. Librarians as coalition builders must learn the skills of a political strategist who identifies potential allies for the library and its service to young children and families, recruits them to the cause, and helps the divergent groups overcome their differences as they work together.

Two common problems for a library when it first begins its involvement in coalition building are:

1. Some people within the library fear that cooperation will result in "outsiders" interfering with "their" program of library service. The process of developing trust must be ongoing within the library as well as with other agencies. The idea of "us and them" must be reduced as quickly as possible. This becomes part of the job of the coalition builder —the children's librarian.

2. The library administration feels that because it is providing financial backing (if it does) for the program it deserves "special treatment" in the process. In most cases, the library will gain recognition for its involvement in a coalition or network. Any financial participation either in the form of meeting space, paperwork, or staff participation will be returned to the library through increased visibility, increased activity in the library, and community good will. Administrators and funders will see the library as part of the solution to community problems instead of just a "frill."

Coalition building is visionary *and* productive. It can lead to better policies for children and families throughout society including libraries, schools, health and social service agencies, and a multitude of other organizations. It can reduce the amount of duplication of programs and services a community has to offer and effectively enhance the library's traditional role to share community resources.

REFERENCES

Achieving School Readiness: Public Libraries and National Education Goal No.1. Chicago, IL: American Library Association, 1995.

Brown, Cherie. "Leadership Training Institute Explores Community Leaders as Coalition Builders." *Nation's Cities Weekly* (Feb 22, 1993): 10 –11.

Cohen, Larry, Nancy Baer, and Pam Satterwhite. *Developing Effective Coalitions: An Eight-Step Guide*. Pleasant Hill, CA: Contra Costa County Health Services Prevention Program, Spring 1994.

Richmond, Jayne and Robert Shoop. *Prevention Through Coalitions: The Role of the Human Service Professional*. Paper presented at the Annual Convention of the American Psychological Association (92nd, Toronto, Ontario, Canada, August 24-28, 1984).

Shoop, Robert J. *Developing Interagency Cooperation*. Midland, MI: Pendell Pub, 1976.

Thomas, John and others. "Building Coalitions." *School Leadership: A Handbook for Excellence*. Washington, DC: Office of Educational Research and Improvement, 1989.

3 COALITION BUILDING: MODEL NETWORKS

There is no magic formula for building a coalition or network. "The important thing to remember is that librarians, especially those who work with significant numbers of young patrons (and their families), must make their voices heard and their library's services visible throughout the entire community" (Fairtile, 1985, p. 216). Community agencies may not be aware of the variety of services that the library offers and how librarians can contribute to youth advocacy and an enhancement of youth services. Stereotypes of elitism and complacency run deep. Most agency professionals do not think of the library as a community resource in their efforts to serve parents and children.

"Librarians who undertake preschool-parenting programs have an opportunity to extend library walls, and create community wide networks and exchanges. The parent population may be reached not only through schools, churches and hospitals, but through all the other childcare and advocacy agencies. . . . The library may be the chief coordinator and channel for all of these resources" (Rollock, 1988, p. 145).

For libraries, "the purposes for networking include:

> to educate other professionals about the value of incorporating library services with their services;
> to inform children about the existence and services of the public library by communicating through the myriad institutional structures, including the family, under which all children live;
> to extend the knowledge base of librarians by working in consort with other professionals who serve children; and
> to coordinate programs among all agencies serving children."
> (Naylor, 1987, p. 382)

PRACTICAL TIPS AND SUGGESTIONS

The following is a list of suggestions and activities, adapted from an article by Fairtile (Fairtile, 1985, p. 215–17), that enables a librarian to begin networking.

Contact local schools, churches, and hospitals and identify types of family support programs. Meet the individuals responsible for programs and services. Personal contact has the most impact.

Attend community and professional meetings that deal with youth issues, particularly those focused on early childhood and parenting. A librarian can bring a unique information provider's perspective to a group grappling with complicated social issues. Research topics for group discussion, utilizing traditional library skills, and become a catalyst for critical thinking.

Distribute literature about your library's services. Be available to schedule meetings and offer the library as a meeting place. These suggestions are basic to the library's role in the community.

Invite agency representatives to provide staff development programs for library professionals and support staff. Brainstorm with them about joint programs that might be of interest to families.

Meet with local agency representatives and learn about their services. Do a simple directory of services for your community if one does not exist. Keep a schedule of regular contact with agencies identified as priority resources for parents and children.

Offer your services as a speaker or presenter for parent support groups or other programs sponsored by community agencies. Use the opportunity to explain library collections, programs, and services.

Get involved with community-wide youth-related activities. If possible, serve on local boards.

Have agencies suggest topics and then prepare bibliographies aimed at parents and professionals on children's issues. Distribute these widely in the community.

Bring agencies, organizations and support groups together. Form a community network.

A few things that you should *not* do when establishing contacts:

1. DO NOT MAKE CONTACT BY PHONE ONLY. A much greater impression is made with a face-to-face meeting after the phone call followed up with a letter (Appendix A, Figures A-3 and A-4). A visit to the agency enhances the relationship. Coalitions, like politics, are people.

2. DO NOT DEVELOP PROGRAMS THAT MAY ALREADY EXIST. Duplication is costly and inefficient. It is better to seek ways of connecting to already existing

programs or expanding a library program to include the expertise of other professionals.

3. DO NOT FORGET TO FOLLOW UP ON CALLS, MAILINGS, AND VISITS. You have to communicate constantly. Agencies that are not familiar with libraries tend to forget about our role in the community. Don't let this happen.

SUFFOLK COALITION FOR PARENTS AND CHILDREN

In Suffolk County, New York, several coalitions have come about as the result of leadership on the part of children's librarians. These include the Suffolk Coalition for Parents and Children and the Parent Educator's Network. The New York State Task Force on Child Abuse and Neglect (1984–1994) also integrated the work of many children's librarians and served as an excellent example of how librarians enhance community networks. The following information provides a description of these networks, including an outline of their goals and objectives.

The Suffolk Coalition for Parents and Children, a loosely organized network of over 1,500 professionals and parents, has met bimonthly since 1981 at the Middle Country Public Library. Coordinated by the Suffolk Family Education Clearinghouse of the

Middle Country Public Library, the Suffolk County Youth Bureau, the Suffolk Cooperative Library System, and the Coalition's own membership, this network includes mental health and social service professionals, librarians, educators, public- and community-based agencies, youth serving professionals, parents, and interested citizens.

The Coalition began as an outgrowth of a library-based family support program entitled the Parent/Child Workshop. Started in 1979, the workshop is now conducted in twenty-one Suffolk County libraries. Because this workshop utilizes outside resource professionals from a variety of social and health service agencies and emphasizes the role of children's librarians in the provision of information and referral to parents, the need to learn more about community services emerged. Reluctant to rely solely on printed lists, the librarians reached out to the community for information. The Coalition emerged as a result of this outreach.

OBJECTIVES OF THE COALITION

The Coalition has the following objectives:

> To share information, ideas and resources;
> To plan cooperative programs and services;
> To advocate for children and parents;
> To educate professionals and the public about topics related to children and families; and
> To demonstrate the ways in which working together can make professionals more effective family support agents.

ACCOMPLISHMENTS

The Coalition has achieved the following goals:

- Held bimonthly information exchange meetings, focused on children and family issues, continuously since 1980. Appendix A provides a list of meeting topics (Figure A-9) and agendas (Figures A-10 through A-15);
- Recognized as the comprehensive planning committee on children and family issues for the Suffolk County Youth Bureau;
- Sponsored two countywide conferences, a resource fair, and a public hearing on issues related to families and children;
- Coordinated the initial development of an information and referral data base on health and human services;
- Backed the establishment of the Suffolk Family Education Clearinghouse, a countywide resource center that provides materials, technical assistance, and training for professionals and librarians who work with children and families;

- Established the Parent Educator's Network, a subcommittee that emphasizes the needs of professionals who work in the field of parent education.

PARENT EDUCATOR'S NETWORK

P.E.N. in Suffolk County was formed in early 1991 as an outgrowth of the Suffolk Coalition for Parents and Children. The Coalition's membership includes professionals from a wide variety of family support agencies and programs. Members of the Coalition working in the field of parent education expressed a need for a professional networking group with parent education as a specific focus, and P.E.N. was formed. This network currently has over 150 members.

The Parent Educator's Network has three main functions:

1. To serve as a professional "support group" for parent educators
2. To provide informal program support to each one through sharing of expertise, skills, training opportunities, and new resource materials
3. To enhance the coordination of parent education and support services in Suffolk County

Sharing practical and useful information is the goal of every meeting. Each meeting incorporates a time for networking and information sharing, a focused discussion on a specific issue related to parent education, and an opportunity to learn about new parenting resources. Topics have included outreach to parents (what works, what doesn't), evaluation methods, strategies for parent education programs, and "tricks of the trade," i.e., group activities, exercises, and ice breakers.

THE NEW YORK STATE TASK FORCE ON CHILD ABUSE AND NEGLECT

Cochaired by First Lady Matilda Cuomo and the State Department of Social Services Commissioner Cesar Perales, the New York State Task Force on Child Abuse and Neglect (1983–1994) was a statewide coalition of representatives from both the public and private sectors with a wide variety of expertise and backgrounds, including a children's librarian from the Middle Country Public Library. Its mission was twofold: To educate the public about the problem of child abuse and neglect and to promote parenting programs as the most effective prevention strategy.

The Citizens Task Force believed that parenting is a difficult job and that all parents can benefit from access to information and support in raising children. Therefore, the Task Force's agenda emphasized the development and support of educational materials and programs designed to enhance a family's abilities to cope with problems inherent in family living.

From 1984 to 1994, the Task Force conducted public education campaigns in April, which is Child Abuse Prevention Month, both in New York State and at the national level. Integral to these campaigns was the publication of a number of educational materials for parents and professionals.

THE FAMILY RESOURCE BOOK

Children's librarians in Suffolk County were involved in Task Force projects beginning in the fall of 1985. *The Family Resource Book*, compiled through the efforts of fifteen children's librarians in Suffolk County, provides an annotated bibliography of books, pamphlets, curricula, and audiovisual materials available on a wide range of contemporary family-life issues. Designed to meet the information needs of parents, children, community leaders, and professionals, *The Family Resource Book* included a special section on children's books and a listing of selected state and national organizations that can be of assistance to families. With more than 40,000 copies distributed throughout the fifty states, it reached a national audience and served as an outstanding example of what can be achieved when librarians join efforts with educators, psychologists, social workers, and community professionals on behalf of children and families.

WELCOME TO PARENTHOOD: RESOURCE LISTINGS FOR NEW PARENTS

The 1988 campaign "New York Loves Parents" was designed to promote public awareness of the idea that all parents need help and support to properly care for their children. As part of the campaign, the Task Force launched its new initiative, The Pre- and Postnatal Parent Education Hospital Program (PPPEHP). Called "PEP," this program was designed to promote hospital participation in the delivery of parent education and support services and encourage the creation of links between hospitals and community-based parenting programs.

PPPEHP has three components: 1) a survey of hospital-based parent education programs; 2) the publication and distribution of a book for parents of newborns; and 3) the compilation and publication of county listings of community-based parent education and support programs. Librarians across New York State were involved in the production and coordination of the community listings.

A crucial component of PPPEHP was the establishment of links between hospitals and community programs for parents. The Task Force recruited county coordinators from every county in New York State to establish a community resource listing for new parents. One third of these county coordinators were children's services consultants or children's librarians. In taking a community leadership role, these coordinators were responsible for convening committees to survey local service providers for information about parenting programs. In addition to compiling the list, the committee was responsible for locating a printing source. Many librarians and libraries throughout New York State provided the leadership and support to get these publications completed.

The Task Force projects provided opportune moments to make the library visible to other professionals working with children and families and those community resources needed by today's families. Librarians skilled at organizing information, conducting viable and positive programs for families, creating nonthreatening environments for children, and advocating library services to youth were an asset to the Task Force and the goals it wanted to accomplish. The projects were examples of how librarians can join with all people struggling to make a better world for our children. (Feinberg, 1988, p. 195–7)

REFERENCES

Fairtile, Ricki. "Libraries and Liaisons: An Introduction." *Top of the News*; Spring, 1985: pp 215–17.

Feinberg, Sandra. "The New York State Task Force on Child Abuse and Neglect: The Library Connection". *The Bookmark* (The New York State Library); Spring, 1988: pp 195–7.

Naylor, Alice Phoebe. "Reaching All Children: A Public Library Dilemma." *Library Trends*, 35, Winter 1987: pp 369–392.

Parent Educators Network (PEN). Fact Sheet. Riverhead, NY: Cornell Cooperative Extension.

Rollock, Barbara T. *Public Library Services for Children*. Hamden, CT: Library Professional Publications, 1988. p. 195.
Suffolk Coalition for Parents and Children. Fact Sheet. Centereach, NY: Middle Country Public Library.

4 BUILDING FAMILY SUPPORT SERVICES: GUIDELINES

WHAT IS A FAMILY SUPPORT PROGRAM?

According to the Family Resource Coalition in Chicago, Illinois, family resource and support programs serve parents, children, and families in diverse structures and settings, including schools, churches, hospitals, military bases, shelters, prisons, and libraries. The types of programs offered include parent education classes, parent/child activities, resource and referral information, support and discussion groups, home visiting services, warm lines, and stress management workshops. They fulfill the basic goals: "to optimize the development of parent skills; to optimize adult development as parents; and to strengthen families in ways that promote achieving the first two goals." (Haskins, 1981, p. 9)

Community-based family resource and support programs are responsive to local needs and can operate as free-standing entities or as parts of larger agencies, organizations, or institutions. Services vary in each community and setting, and the library can, depending on its level of commitment, design its own family support center or set of services.

CHARACTERISTICS AND PRINCIPLES

The principles and characteristics upon which the movement rests serve as underlying values and guideposts that can help the professional build a healthy, integrated level of service to families and children. They provide the foundation for developing library relationships with other community agencies, which can be viewed as part of a continuum ranging from networking to collaboration. Within this framework, the library can expand its program and service opportunities and become fully integrated into the fabric of community life. The following characteristics and principles provide the philosophical foundation for developing family support services. (Coyne, 1983, pp. 331–2; *Family Support Programs*, 1993, p. 1; Interagency Work Group, pp. 2–3; Haskins, 1981, pp. 12–13)

Focus on Prevention

These principles are designed to:

- provide a system of care that promotes family well-being, health, and stability;

- make services readily available to all parents at the earliest opportunity;
- seek to reduce risk for a whole population (a community concept); and
- provide intervention, in the form of information, prior to the manifestation of problems.

Build on Family Strengths

This aspect of a family services program:

- emphasizes family-identified strengths, skills, and abilities;
- assists parents in identifying and clarifying their own values;
- preserves families by helping them acquire the resources needed to care for their children;
- helps parents develop skills so they can use information and services effectively without the need for institutional support; and
- uses parent education as a strategy to make parents independent.

Treat Parents as Partners to Feel Empowered to Act on Their Own Behalf

This part of the program is designed to:

- empower families to solve their own problems or attain self-sufficiency;
- promote the development of cooperative and equal partnerships between parents and staff;
- provide support in a nonexpert and nonjudgmental manner; and
- strengthen parental skills necessary to advocate on behalf of the child and family's needs.

Respect the Integrity of the Family Unit and Serve It Holistically

By respecting individual families, the program

- offers a family-centered and family-driven approach to services;
- supports parent, child, and others involved in the care of the child; and
- recognizes that the family is the constant in the child's life while the service systems and personnel within those systems fluctuate.

Enhance Parents' Capabilities to Foster the Optimal Development of Their Children

This part of the program

- incorporates the developmental needs of infants, toddlers, preschoolers, and their families within programs and services; and
- informs parents about their children in an appropriate and supportive manner.

Be Sensitive to the Cultural, Ethnic, and Religious Characteristics, and the Physical and Mental Differences of the Community

An important characteristic of a family services program is that it:

- respects the diversity of families;
- recognizes family uniqueness and respect for different methods of coping;
- develops programs which employ staff from the local community that are culturally and linguistically sensitive to the populations served; and
- assures that programs and services are accessible to people with disabilities.

Establish Linkages With Community Support Systems

These partnerships are designed to:

- assure the design of comprehensive, coordinated, multidiscipline service delivery systems;
- offer a flexible array of services in a convenient and supportive community setting.

Provide Settings Where Parents Can Gather, Interact, Support, and Learn From Each Other

Having the appropriate setting enables the program to:

- recognize the interconnectedness of child, family, and community;
- work to strengthen parents' social networks, social support, and community ties;
- encourage and facilitate parent-to-parent support;
- develop programs that are voluntary and universally available to all interested families;
- include parents, extended family members, and others directly involved in the care of children in the planning, delivery, and evaluation of services;

- provide financial, service, and/or psychological assistance to parents in fulfilling their child-rearing function; and
- maintain a balanced focus on the needs of both parent and child.

EXPANDING THE LIBRARY'S ROLE TO INCLUDE PARENT EDUCATION

Parent education has taken hold within the circles of education, health, and human services. "How well or poorly mothers stimulate their children's minds daily at home becomes the key variable in explaining the children's later success or failure in school and work" (Haskins, 1981, p. 2). "Programs of parent education and support offer promising strategies for facilitating the education and development of young children. It is crucial for educators and policymakers to find ways to alter educational practices, early childhood programs, and schools (libraries) to promote the family's contributions to early education and development" (Powell, p. 2).

Parents have routinely sought the advice and help of relatives, friends, and professionals. The traditional sources of yesterday, such as the extended family, are less available, and parents have come to rely on educators and health and human service professionals for child-rearing information and family support. In addition, the concept of parent education has broadened considerably. Less didactic, parent education programs and services are becoming family centered and emotionally supportive. Facilitators are looking at adult learning techniques and self-help practices in their efforts to design services and programs.

Underlying the widespread interest in parent education, educators believe that:

- the preschool years are critical to subsequent development;
- missed opportunities for development because of inadequate stimulation during these years can never be recovered;
- the influence of families is pervasive;
- adequately designed parent programs can significantly change the attitudes, values, and child-rearing practices of parents;
- parents have both a right and responsibility to participate in their child's development;

- the parent is the child's primary teacher and agent of socialization (Haskins, 1981, p 2–3).

Local communities throughout the country have fostered the creation of a rapidly growing number of parent-oriented programs. These efforts range from drop-in center formats to peer self-help group methods. Libraries and librarians need to recognize parent education by undertaking the arduous tasks of forming parent/professional partnerships and integrating services for parents and adults who work with families and children into their overall plan of service. These goals can only effectively be accomplished in partnership with other agencies and professionals.

CORE COMPONENTS

While it is recognized that not every organization will have the resources or capacity to provide a complete array of programs and include every service component, the expectation is that the different programs and services provided by an organization will establish linkages with other community resources to assure access to all core components. Access is the goal of a community-based family-service environment—an environment in which the library has the potential to be a key player. The core components (Interagency Work Group, pp. 4–5), integral to parent education and family support services, include:

- parent education information/skills training;
- parent support;
- information and referral to other services;
- parental involvement and leadership activities;
- parents' self-esteem;
- developmental examinations and health screenings of infants and children;
- outreach to the community; and
- joint parent/child activities.

The balance of this chapter describes the core components as well as the essential elements of quality early childhood services in public libraries—a companion set of guidelines that must be considered when offering parent or joint parent/child activities. Chapter 5 provides a potpourri of programs and services that exemplify how libraries can expand or alter existing services based on these core components.

Parent Education Information/Skills Training

Though professionals have moved away from the old assumption that if one just gives parents information their behavior will change, it is recognized that information is essential as a precursor to attitude change. Increasing understanding of child development and discovering skills to deal with raising children is a primary program element of parent education.

Parents learn in different ways and within different environments. Information can be accessed through print and audiovisual materials, the Internet, one-on-one discussion, group presentation, electronic mail, and more. The library, in conjunction with other organizations, can provide information in a variety of formats. It offers limitless possibilities within a neutral, information-oriented community setting.

Some topics to be covered include: child and human development information, family communication skills, family literacy, basic values, effective discipline and problem-solving techniques, stimulation of infants and other children, sibling rivalry, self-esteem enhancement, family responsibilities, and basic infant and toddler care. The life-enhancing importance of positive mental and emotional experiences before five years of age will be vital and unexpected news to many parents. Providing simple ways of supplying the information to them will be welcomed.

Parent Support

Support groups are highly valuable because they reduce the parents' sense of isolation and help them form a community devoted to achieving common goals. Support groups afford parents an opportunity to discuss parenting concerns and develop informal relationships with their peers. Examples include: traditional support groups, respite, drop-in centers, child care, transportation assistance, home visits, mentoring and networking, partnerships with schools and other community organizations, and newsletters.

Information and Referral to Other Services

Parent education is most effective when it is offered in conjunction with other services that address a family's needs. Parenting skills should not be taught in isolation from consideration of other family needs such as housing, income supports, vocational or educational training, transportation, or dependent care. It is important that a parent education program have the ability to refer and/or help obtain necessary services to meet a family's basic needs.

Parental Involvement and Leadership Activities

Parents benefit most from programs when they are involved in program operations and control. Parent involvement should create a partnership in which parents benefit from exercising their

FORMING PARENT SUPPORT GROUPS

Support groups provide mothers and fathers with a healthy outlet for venting their frustrations and fears. Although many traditional ways of forming community have disappeared, parents from around the country are beginning to fight their sense of isolation by creating support groups in which they can vent their feelings and receive advice from other parents on a regular basis.

"Mothers' groups across the country are driven by these twin engines: the need for information and the desire for companionship. Building on a foundation of friendship and commitment, a mothers' group can become the core of a community: a handful of not-necessarily-geographic neighbors who care about each other's families, who are there for each other every day as well as in time of change or crises." (Winik, 1992, p120 - 122)

Most parent support groups do not spring up ad hoc but are associated with a school, church, library or neighborhood organization. Some topics are perennial such as sibling rivalry or biting. Other topics discussed reflect the particular pressures of the times such as the conflict of parents working. (Louv, 1993, p171 - 172)

TIPS AND SUGGESTIONS FOR FORMING A GROUP

•Keep the group relatively small. Ten to 15 parents is the optimum if there are only parents in attendance. A new parent support group usually can be successful with fewer parents and babies attend with them.

•Find a place. Many groups are associated with a neighborhood institution. The library is a great place - it's neutral, information based, local and accessible.

•It may be necessary to provide child care particularly if the children are young. This may be impossible in a library setting, however parents can be quite creative, i.e., parents may take turns in a caretaking role. The library could offer a children's program in conjunction with the meeting. For a new parent's group, made up of parents and babies, no child care is necessary.

•Keep sessions to around an hour and a half. A light snack is fun and can be provided by the parents themselves.

•Ask a psychologist or other professional to serve as a facilitator if it will be helpful. Many times a local YMCA, social service or mental health agency, or a school district professional would be more than willing to facilitate a group.

•Schedule meeting times and pick topics for discussion in advance. The library can provide an array of support materials including books, videos, and vertical file materials. Sometimes the librarian can find a local professional who has expertise in a particular topic and would be willing to attend a session.

•Emphasize diversity. It's a good idea to have both moms and dads present. Include stay-at-home parents as well as parents who work outside the home.

References
Louv, Richard. "Why Parents Need One Another." **Parents**; Jul 1993: pp 171 - 178
Winik, Marion. "A Little Help From Your Friends." **Parenting**; Dec-Jan, 1992: pp 116 - 122.

rights and maximizing control over their lives. Parents can become systematically involved in evaluating programs and monitoring their effectiveness.

These activities should focus on empowering parents to articulate their family's needs and to advocate for themselves and their families as well as provide for staff to develop skills and abilities to work cooperatively with family members. Examples include joint planning and decision making on library programs and services and empowering parents to work as equal partners with individuals and institutions providing services to families.

Parents' Self-Esteem

To enhance parents' abilities to love and nurture their own children, parents need to be provided with the kind of nurturing toward self-esteem and confidence they may not have received as children. Programs should be developed that address the emotional needs of both parent and child.

Developmental Examinations and Health Screenings of Infants and Children

Parent education and support programs offer an ideal opportunity to ensure that children have access to important health services. These activities include developmental examinations, health screenings, and immunizations. The library can provide an ideal setting for accessing these screenings through joint advertising and the use of library meeting space for health services.

Outreach to the Community

To meet the needs of parents in a particular community, a parent education program should draw extensively from the surrounding community for its staff and participants. Community involvement enhances sensitivity, builds trust, and strengthens the program's ability to attract and retain participants. Outreach efforts should incorporate active methods such as home visits and field visits to local agencies where parents meet or go to obtain services.

Joint Parent/Child Activities

Developmentally appropriate parent/child activities provide opportunities for experimenting with new parenting techniques, role modeling with staff and other parents, and quality time shared by parent and child in the home or in other appropriate settings. It is important that librarians keep in mind that working with young children requires special expertise and that when creating developmentally appropriate programs there is a set of essential elements to consider. Librarians designing programs for families and young children need to incorporate these essential elements in the design of library-based parent/child activities.

ESSENTIAL ELEMENTS OF QUALITY EARLY CHILDHOOD SERVICES IN PUBLIC LIBRARIES

The essential elements described in this section of the chapter have been developed by the authors (Feinberg and Feldman, *Early Childhood*).

Physical Environment

The environment for young children must be physically safe, socially enhancing, emotionally nurturing, and intellectually and aesthetically stimulating. Libraries provide a climate of acceptance and are responsive to individual children's interests, strengths, capabilities, values, culture, race, and gender. Parents and adults who work with young children and families are active participants in children's services. The environment fosters self-selection from a wide array of age-appropriate materials in a carefully designed setting. The environment invites children and families to engage in active learning. It offers opportunities for children to construct their own learning through interaction with adults, other children, and materials.

The library is physically and psychologically safe. Physical environment affects the behavior and development of children and adults. The quality of the physical space, equipment, and materials provided affects the level of involvement of the children and the quality of the interaction between adults and children. A program must constantly evaluate the amount, arrangement, and use of its available space. How these foster optimal physical, cognitive, and socioemotional development through opportunities for exploration and learning determine the quality of a program. The library supports the natural human desire for learning and for achieving a sense of positive self-esteem.

A quality early childhood program provides for a safe and healthy environment. It should be designed to prevent accidental injuries and the spread of illness, be prepared to deal with emergencies, and educate children concerning safe and healthy practices.

Social Environment

For children to develop an understanding of self and others, interaction with staff must provide opportunities for positive, supportive, one-to-one relationships with adults. Young children develop socially and intellectually in a supportive environment through interactions with peers, siblings, parents, and both familial and nonfamilial adults. Personal respect, recognition, and responsiveness to the individual uniqueness of a child and his/her family is essential. Interactions should foster understanding and respect for diverse cultural and ethnic backgrounds, as well as nurture each individual's ability to learn at her or his own rate and according to personal interests.

Well-organized staffing is an important variable in the quality of a program. Research strongly suggests that the higher the ratio of staff to children, the more positive the outcomes are, including less aggression and greater cooperation among children. A program must be sufficiently staffed to meet the needs of and promote the physical, social, emotional, and cognitive development of children. Adequate staff must be available at the children's reference desk and throughout the children's room/area in addition to the staff involved with specific programming.

The nature and needs of children demand constant and consistent care and attention. Library programming for young children should be individualized and age appropriate. Infants and toddlers need to attend programs with their parents/caregivers. Ideally there should be two adults available for each group, with a librarian or professional and a paraprofessional sharing responsibility. The younger the child, the smaller the group. The recommended group size for infants is six to eight; for toddlers, ten to twelve; for three- and four-year- olds, fifteen and eighteen; and for children between the ages of five and eight, eighteen to twenty-two.

Programs, Services, and Evaluation

Developing program content and design in the early childhood years emerges from knowledge of how children learn as well as what they need to know. Planning acknowledges that learning is playful, interactive, interdisciplinary, and cohesive. There is a balance between individual and group needs, between librarian directed and child selected activities and between active and quiet times. Assessment of children's understanding and involvement occurs within the context of everyday experience and is congruent with the content and design of the program/service. Based on the staff's regular observations and evaluations, assessment informs teaching practice for both the librarian and parent, supports children's strengths and abilities, and is respectful of the many ways children learn, as well as the diversity of their experience, language, and cultural backgrounds.

Implicit in every program, activity, or learning area is the understanding that the one-to-one relationship that exists most often between a parent and his/her young child is particularly well suited for fostering and stimulating learning. All programming is primarily a way to show parents/caregivers what materials can be used with young children and how they can be used.

Collections

Principles of collection development are combined with theories of developmentally appropriate practice to create effective and valuable collections that serve children and families. Materials reflect diversity of age and skill level, experience, language, and cultural backgrounds. Formats are wide ranging and include access to new technologies. Principles of family literacy dominate the collection development philosophy. Resources encompass collections for children, parents, and adults who work with children.

Parent Participation

Library programs cannot adequately meet the needs of children until they recognize the importance and validity of the child's family. Programs and services must develop strategies to work effectively with families. Communication between the library and parents needs to be based on the concept that the parents or primary caregivers are and should be the principle influence in children's lives. A quality program is one in which parents are well informed and are welcomed as contributors and observers.

Parents play a critical role in supporting the growth and development of their children. In early childhood and family support programs, parents are viewed as partners in the planning, implementation, and evaluation of services. Opportunities are available for parents to actively participate in their children's education and learning activities. They are invited to participate in the decision-making processes integral to the development of services to children and families.

Comprehensive Services

Comprehensive services, including information and referral and coalition building, are an integral part of effective early childhood and family support programs. These services are designed to build upon the strengths and respond to the needs of young children and their families. Access to programs and services starting at an early age can create a lifelong learner and public library user. Interagency and interdepartmental communication are necessities that encourage families to make full use of library and community services that support young children and families.

Working together to bring services to children and their families provides a number of tangible benefits. The most important of these is the increase in the range and choice of services available to meet the needs of children and families. Active and creative involvement among all agencies is necessary in order to begin to close the gaps in existing programs and provide a maximum of service to children and families.

Staff Qualifications and Development

The quality of the staff is an important determinant of the quality of early childhood programs. Research has found that staff training in child development and/or early childhood education is related to positive outcomes for children, including increased social interaction with adults, development of prosocial behaviors, and improved language and cognitive development.

Since early childhood and family support services are expanding and developing in the public library field, there is a need for staff to be continually trained and updated. The amount and kind of training will vary depending on previous training and the needs of the program. In addition, to maintain staff morale and enthusiasm, there must be adequate supportive feedback from supervisory personnel.

Administration

Those responsible for daily administration of early childhood and family support programs and services must have the authority that comes from knowledge of and experience with young children and families. They require autonomy in the decision-making process for budgets, staffing, staff development, and program accountability. The leader/supervisor articulates the philosophy of the program to parents and the community and serves as a support for staff and families by facilitating ongoing opportunities for learning and development.

Administrative commitment and support is essential in order to assure appropriate policy and professional development and the acquisition of necessary resources.

It is clear after reviewing the essential elements of early childhood programs that there is overlap between the early childhood elements and the core components of family support programs. It is also evident that the elements and components that are not duplicative complement and enhance the concept of service to families and young children. The combination of essential elements of early childhood programs and the core components of family resource programs provides a firm foundation for the development of family support services in public libraries.

REFERENCES

Coyne, Robert K. "Two Critical Issues in Primary Prevention: What It Is and How To Do It." *The Personnel and Guidance Journal* (Feb 1983): 331–334.

Feinberg, Sandra and Sari Feldman. *The Early Childhood Quality Review Initiative for Public Libraries*. Chicago: American Library Association Loletta D. Fyan Grant, forthcoming. Contact: Sandra Feinberg, Middle Country Public Library, Centereach, NY 11720.

Feinberg, Sandra. "Parents, Children and Libraries." *Family Resource Coalition Report* Vol. 5, No. 2 (1986).

Family Support Programs and Comprehensive Collaborative Services. Chicago, IL: The National Resource Center for Family Support Programs, 1993.

Haskins, Ron. *Parent Education and Public Policy: A Conference Report*. Summary of conference on "Parent Education and Public Policy" (Durham, NC, March 1980). Washington, DC: National Institute of Education, 1981.

Interagency Work Group on Parent Education and Support. *New York Parents: Guiding Principles and Core Service Components for Parent Education and Support Programs*. Albany, NY: Council of Children and Families, n.d.

Powell, Douglas R. "Parent Education and Support Programs." *ERIC Digests*. U.S. Department of Education, Office of Educational Research and Improvement, ERIC Digests, n.d.

5 MODEL LIBRARY-BASED FAMILY SUPPORT SERVICES

Most programs conducted by libraries rely solely on library resources and do not emphasize the philosophy of working with community partners. Traditional library programs, however, can be viewed as stepping stones to the development of the library's role in providing support for families in a library setting. Librarians need to integrate the concept of parent information and support into their traditional parent/child programs and remember that what the child experiences within the family context sets the stage for positive emotional and mental development as well as for learning. When viewed from the family support perspective, traditional children's programs:

- acknowledge the roles of parents as primary teachers and agents of socialization of their young children;
- emphasize the importance of language, listening, and preliteracy skills in reading;
- recognize the necessity for the public library to further its role in helping children get ready for school;
- realize the importance of reaching out to infants and toddlers and their caregivers through library-based programming.

It is important to recognize that taking the step beyond the traditional family literacy role to the family support role expands the librarian's concept of library service and responsibility. This expansion:

- stretches the cadre of services and programs to include parents and adults who work with families;
- recognizes the "whole child," not to be isolated from the family unit, in the development of library service;
- understands that educating the parent is fundamental to educating the child;
- integrates prevention and early intervention concepts in the design of children's programs and services;
- recognizes learning as interactive and integrated in the overall development of the individual child.

Focusing on the core components of parent education and support services and the essential elements of early childhood services described in Chapter 4, this chapter provides practical examples of quality public library services for families and young children. All of the services highlighted have been developed in coordination, cooperation, or partnership with other agencies. These models exemplify integrated family-centered services to enhance the role of the public library in the community.

PARENT EDUCATION INFORMATION/ SKILLS TRAINING

PIRL (PARENT INFORMATION RESOURCE LIBRARY)

PARENT INFORMATION RESOURCE LIBRARY

This one-stop source for information and referral for parents, prospective parents, caregivers and agency personnel, the PIRL was established through a task force of Onondaga County Public Library staff—representatives of county agencies who provide prevention, parenting, and family support services—and PIRL clients. Funded initially by the New York State Developmental Disabilities Planning Council, the PIRL was coordinated by a health educator under the direction of the library's youth services coordinator. The health educator met with parents, worked with library and agency personnel, helped to build the collection, and designed a referral database. During the second year of the project, financial support for the health educator's position was provided by the school district. Information on establishing a parent/professional collection can be found in Chapters 11 and 12. Materials describing PIRL is appended (Appendix D, Figure D-1a and D1b and Appendix B, Figure B-8).

STEP (SYSTEMATIC TRAINING FOR EFFECTIVE PARENTING)

STEP is a parent education program that focuses on learning principles of behavior and applying them to parent-child relationships. STEP is not merely open discussion, nor is it family therapy. The program is intensive and will teach the group members new ideas and skills that can improve their effectiveness as parents. The program is designed and offered in both early childhood and elementary age versions.

This multiweek (eight or nine sessions) educational program is offered evenings three or four times during the year. Taught by a trained STEP professional, this popular course provides information on child development, discipline, behavior, and other issues of parental concern. Parents are provided a certificate upon completion of the course.

PARENT LECTURE SERIES

A variety of topics relating to the physical and mental health of families are explored at single-session lecture programs offered throughout the year. Generally held as an evening program, topics covered include toilet training, anger control, discipline, bed wetting, self-esteem, and sibling rivalry. A trained psychologist or social worker from a local agency or the state university is hired to conduct the seminar.

TOT SAVER: CPR FOR INFANTS AND YOUNG CHILDREN

This two-session evening or Saturday course provides specific information to parents, caregivers, and other professionals who work with young children on cardiopulmonary resuscitation (CPR) and emergency procedures to combat choking in infants and young children. It is taught by a certified professional from the American Red Cross, the American Heart Association, or other health education organization trained to facilitate this program.

PARENT SUPPORT

NEW MOTHERS DISCUSSION GROUP

Aimed at first-time mothers and babies (from birth to eleven months of age) this five-week program is designed to increase new mothers' awareness of infant development and reduce their sense of isolation. It encourages an informal exchange of information and provides support during the first year of parenting. The group is facilitated by a registered nurse with a background in childbearing and Lamaze. A public health nurse, a Lamaze instructor, or a professional trained in the field are all excellent choices for this role. A librarian is also present.

The program is held in a carpeted room. Mothers bring babies and any necessary equipment including blankets, strollers, toys, bottles, etc. Since children vary in age, mothers observe the various stages of growth and development.

This program serves as an introduction to the library and its resources. It is, in many instances, the first experience for a new mother and baby in venturing out by themselves and the first time going to a program at the library. The group often develops into a support network for the new mothers. Some groups continue to meet weekly at each other's homes and may eventually establish play groups. A flyer is appended (Appendix D, Figure D-2).

PARENTIPS

Since 1985 the Middle Country Public Library has published *Parentips*, a two-page newsletter aimed at parents of young children. Written in collaboration with a child psychologist, a health professional from the University Medical Center, a human development specialist from Cornell Cooperative Extension, and other local professionals, each issue focuses on a different topic such as discipline, immunization, early intervention, speech and language, and nutrition. Published twice a year, the newsletter is distributed within the library and also purchased by other local libraries for distribution.

INFORMATION AND REFERRAL TO OTHER SERVICES

DEVELOPMENT OF THE COMPUTERIZED INFORMATION AND REFERRAL DATABASE OF HEALTH AND HUMAN SERVICES IN SUFFOLK COUNTY

This computerized information and referral database project has been in existence since 1989. It was initiated by a consortium of public and private community agencies in Suffolk County under the leadership of the Suffolk Coalition for Parents and Children and the Middle Country Public Library. See Chapter 6 for more information on this project.

FAMILY RESOURCE FAIR

In 1990, the Suffolk Coalition for Parents and Children in cooperation with the Suffolk Family Education Clearinghouse and the Suffolk County's Youth Bureau/Office for Children sponsored a Family Resource Fair held at the Middle Country Public Library. Representatives from approximately thirty organizations participated. Tables and display areas were set up throughout the library's community room, the children's department, and adult services area. The focus of the fair was information sharing and networking for professionals who work with families and parents in the surrounding communities. A flyer advertising the event, the cover letter requesting agency participation and a participation form are appended (Appendix A, Figures A-6a, A–6b, A–7a, and A–7b; Appendix D, Figure D-3).

PARENTAL INVOLVEMENT AND LEADERSHIP ACTIVITIES

PUBLIC HEARING: SEARCHING FOR SOLUTIONS

In 1991, the Suffolk Coalition for Parents and Children sponsored a public hearing addressing local legislators and policymakers on the state of children and families in Suffolk County. This hearing was cosponsored by a number of local organizations, including the Child Care Council, Family Service League, Suffolk County Youth Bureau, the Children's Librarians

Association of Suffolk County, and the Brookhaven Youth Bureau. The coordinating committee solicited formal support and participation from all major youth and family organizations. Funding support was solicited from local businesses. The hearing was held at the Middle Country Public Library. Request forms for sponsorship and request for corporate support forms are appended (Appendix A, Figures A-7a, A-7b, and A-8).

At the public hearing, more than forty health and human service providers, parents, educators, elected officials, and members of the business community provided testimony to a panel of legislators, the county executives, and policymakers. All of the major issues facing Suffolk's families were addressed, expanding awareness regarding the problems and their potential solutions. The funds provided by local businesses were used to publish a summary of the testimony. The document was subsequently used for grant proposals and research.

PARENT CONNECTIONS

Parent Connections—a unique support group for parents of children with special needs that originated at the Middle Country Public Library—combines elements of parent-to-parent support, positive reinforcement, skill building, and information/training activities. Parent Connections recognizes that to become effective advocates for their children, parents must first meet their own needs for support, information, and mentoring. Originally designed to address a central theme at each session (such as coping, stress management, grieving, and communication with professionals) the compelling need of the participants for specific support and information has resulted in a flexible program structure which is responsive to individual priorities.

The program coordinator, a family intervention specialist, is a parent of children with special needs and experienced in group facilitation and designing programs for parents. A children's librarian works with the Parent Connections coordinator and has been instrumental in obtaining informational materials requested by parents. In addition, by participating in a library setting, parents without the requisite skills have learned to use library services to effectively meet their information needs.

The program coordinator position is funded by New York State under the Early Intervention Program of the NYS Department of Health. This position has been jointly developed by state and local library personnel and has afforded the library an opportunity to reach out to children with special needs and their families. A copy of the registration flyer is appended (Appendix D, Figure D-4).

KIDS' ANSWER PLACE

Located at the Central Library of the Onondaga County Public Library System, the Kids' Answer Place, a multimedia resource center, is designed to help children, young adults, parents, caregivers and agency representatives find information to improve communication around both difficult and everyday family and community issues. Topics include chronic or terminal childhood illness, separation and loss, prejudice, cultural diversity, and conflict resolution. This project was an outgrowth of the PIRL (see above). A flyer is appended (Appendix D, Figure D-5)

PARENT'S SELF-ESTEEM

PARENTS ANONYMOUS

Parents Anonymous, primarily designed for parents at risk of child abuse, gives parents who are under stress support and help during weekly meetings. Parents discuss problems in an anonymous and confidential atmosphere. They also learn social skills, find out about child development and family functioning, explore better parenting techniques, and discover other resources in the community to help with economic, educational, and medical problems.

This professionally lead support group is facilitated by a social worker from the North Suffolk Mental Health Agency. The program participants are registered by the agency and strict confidentiality is required. This program is held in five local Suffolk County libraries. A flyer is appended (Appendix D, Figure D-6).

DEVELOPMENTAL EXAMINATIONS AND HEALTH SCREENING OF INFANTS AND CHILDREN

INFANT-TODDLER SCREENING

Developmental screenings, conducted by Just Kids Diagnostic and Treatment Center for children from birth through age two, are offered at the Mastics-Moriches-Shirley Community Library. Focused on infant and toddler development, the screenings are designed to detect children at risk of developmental delay. Some of the issues covered include learning to talk, learning to walk, eating or sleeping, playing and/or relating to others. Screenings are held annually for one full day, at the Mastics-Moriches-Shirley Community Library and are open to those who make an appointment. A press release advertising the screening is appended (Appendix D, Figure D-7).

OUTREACH TO THE COMMUNITY

NURSERY SCHOOL FAIR

This annual resource fair brings together teachers and staff from area nursery schools, day care centers, the Child Care Council, and the School District's own preschool program to provide specific information to parents about local early childhood programs and services. This popular one-stop shopping exercise is designed for parents interested in sending their children to a preschool program.

Organized by a children's librarian in cooperation with local early childhood programs, the fair is held in the community room of the library on a Saturday morning or afternoon. It is usually conducted during the winter months when parents are most interested in making decisions for the following year concerning the education of their preschool children. Many libraries in Suffolk County offer this popular service. A flyer is appended (Appendix D, Figure D-8).

READY TO READ

This special Onondaga County Library project, originally titled Ready, Set, Read: Family Literacy For Family Child Care Providers, introduced the resources of the library to family child care providers and facilitated the use of the library through a home-based education support program. Training materials that focused on the use of children's books and presenting story programs for children in the home were also developed. Originally funded by the Central New York Community Foundation, this project was expanded under a Library Services and Construction Act Title I grant. The expansion allowed for an increase in the number of home visits, the development of Parent Paks that could be left with the day care providers, and additional workshops for library staff and parents.

PROJECT LINK: THE LIBRARY, FAMILY DAY CARE, PARENT/CHILD CONNECTION

Aimed at reaching children and parents through family home day-care providers, this project, funded initially through a New York State Parent/Child Grant, is an ongoing service of the Middle Country Public Library. Forty-five storytime kits emphasizing fifteen themes were designed to enhance reading readiness activities in the family through the child's day care environment and at home. The kits included books, audiovisual materials, realia, puzzles, games, flannel board materials, and an activity folder.

Programs for the day-care home providers and parents were sponsored by the library and several family service agencies, including the Child Care Council and Cornell Cooperative Extension. Program topics focused on discipline and how children learn. Home visits to instruct the providers on the use of the kits were provided by library staff. The Child Care Council provided the direct link to the family home day-care provider community. Cooperative Extension provided input on the evaluation tool designed for the project. A flyer is appended (Appendix D, Figure D-9).

JOINT PARENT/CHILD ACTIVITIES

PARENT/CHILD WORKSHOP

A model library program, designed for parents and toddlers, the Parent/Child Workshop emphasizes the children's librarian's roles as information specialist, parent and early childhood educator, and community networking professional. The workshop serves as a recreational and social vehicle for families with very young children, offers enormous potential for prevention and early intervention, and is a mechanism for creating philosophical change in local library services to children and families.

The Parent/Child Workshop is designed to serve the family as a unit and to assist parents in their roles as primary educators of their young children. Unlike programs that are aimed at the children themselves, the Parent/Child Workshop focuses on the parent and child being together. It emphasizes the need for parental

Parent/Child Workshop

Middle Country Public Library

involvement in the child's earliest learning experiences, encourages parents to make use of library resources in their parenting role, and allows libraries to increase service to the very youngest members of their community in the form of new collections and programs.

The most interesting and unique aspect of the program is the coordination of expertise from social service and health agencies with library services. Each week of the program, an outside professional specially trained in child development, speech and language, nutrition, and physical movement meets with parents in a casual, low-key format in order to introduce themselves, their agencies, and their expertise. The parent discovers that there are many professionals available in the community to help them in their parenting role. Often, parents will get help immediately through the referral process or simply by an answer to a personal question or concern. Many times, the parent returns to the library asking not just for library materials but for names and numbers of community resources.

Created by the staff of the Middle Country Public Library in 1979, this program has been replicated in over thirty libraries in New York State. In addition, the program has been successfully adapted to serve parents and children with special needs, teen parents, and culturally diverse families. For further information, see *Running a Parent/Child Workshop: A How-To-Do-It-Manual* by Sandra Feinberg and Kathleen Deerr (New York: Neal-Schuman Publishers, 1995).

TEEN PARENT/CHILD WORKSHOP

The Mastics-Moriches-Shirley Community Library has sponsored Teen Parent/Child Workshops since 1984. Composed of pregnant and parenting teens and their children, the success of this program rests on the partnership that developed between the Teen Parent Program at the local youth center and the library. The agency provides the teen parents, the transportation to and from the library, and support through its professional staff. The library provides the materials, space, and its own staff to conduct the program.

Some changes to the traditional Parent/Child Workshop were required to make this program work. This particular workshop is held one evening per month at the library, not the usual five-week sequence. The librarian arranges for setting up and taking down the workshop as well as staffing an evening program. It is also important that the librarian realize the differences between the "typical" parent who comes to the library for the regular workshop and the "teenage" parent. Adaptations to the workshop were made to account for the developmental stages of the teens as well as their babies.

PARENT/CHILD WORKSHOP PLUS

The Orange County Department of Health and the Newburgh Free Library have modified and expanded the initial workshop and developed Parent/Child Workshop Plus—a six-week early intervention workshop aimed at environmentally at-risk children (birth through three years old) and families. This workshop targets adolescent parents, homeless families, and parents experiencing undue stress and at risk of committing child abuse and neglect. Many of these parents lack parenting skills.

The basic Parent/Child Workshop and the development of a parents' collection (originally developed from grants) are part of regular library service. The library, in partnership with the Department of Health, requested an expansion of the workshop with a special effort to attract at-risk families. This adaptation involved the incorporation of a screening process into the series of workshop programs, utilizing and training of health department staff as members of the resource team, and the development of a cooperative evaluation process. Funding for this project was successfully obtained through an early intervention model service program sponsored by the state.

Perceived as an ideal setting, the library became an integral part of the health and human services community. The library coordinator for the project, particularly attuned to community resources, has made considerable contact with agencies and organizations. The library foresees expanding its services to parents through this cooperative process and partnering with the professional community in its efforts to reach families. Three flyers from the Newburgh Library are appended (Appendix D, Figures D-10 through D-12). The original proposed workplan for the joint project can be found in Appendix B, Figure B-11.

CHILDREN WITH SPECIAL NEEDS

The Mastics-Moriches-Shirley Community Library received a grant in 1992 to establish an integrated Parent/Child Workshop for families and children with developmental disabilities. The library staff worked cooperatively with Just Kids Diagnostic and Treatment Center, a local day care facility that includes infants, toddlers, and preschoolers with special needs and aims to integrate their families into the basic Parent/Toddler Workshop at the library. Some modifications were made regarding registration procedures and attendance rules, but the basic tenets of the program remained intact, and the workshop was successful at getting these families to become regular library users.

CULTURALLY DIVERSE COMMUNITIES

From 1991 to 1994, the Rauch Foundation of Long Island funded the establishment of the workshop in two ethnically diverse communities in an attempt to increase the libraries' role with their minority populations. Both the Wyandanch Public Library (Suffolk County, New York) and the Freeport Public Library (Nassau County, New York) have established the workshop through this effort. The success of these workshops relied on the development of a community advisory committee made up of members from the various ethnic populations that were targeted, community representatives, and library professionals. This program replication has been refunded and is currently (1995–1997) being implemented in the Westbury Public Library, the Farmingdale Public Library, and the Peninusula Public Library (Nassau County, New York).

ADDITIONAL RESOURCES FOR THE DEVELOPMENT OF LIBRARY-BASED FAMILY SUPPORT PROGRAMS

Joint parent/child activities provide the greatest opportunity and most obvious connection point for the development of family support services in public libraries. It cannot be overemphasized that these programs should encompass the dual underpinnings: the essential elements of early childhood services and the core components of family support services. The following resources will help librarians develop a core set of public library services to families and children.

Baechtold, Marguerite, and Eleanor Ruth McKinney. *Library Service for Families.* Hamden, CT: Library Professional Publications, 1983.

Carlson, Ann D. *Early Childhood Literature Sharing Programs in Libraries.* Hamden, CT: Library Professional Publications, 1985.

Feinberg, Sandra, and Kathleen Deerr. *Running a Parent/Child Workshop: A How-To-Do-It Manual for Librarians.* New York: Neal-Schuman Publishers, 1995.

Giacoma, Pete, and Marilyn Getts. "Children's Services in a Developmental Key." *Top of the News,* (Spring 1985): 267–273.

Greene, Ellin. *Books, Babies, and Libraries: Serving Infants, Toddlers, their Parents, and Caregivers.* Chicago: American Library Association, 1991.

Guide to Developing Neighborhood Family Centers: Strategies for Service Integration and Community Building. Cleveland: Federation For Community Planning, 1992.

Jeffery, Debby Ann. *Literate Beginnings: Programs for Babies and Toddlers.* Chicago: American Library Association, 1995.

Levine, James A. *Getting Men Involved: Strategies for Early Childhood Programs.* New York: Scholastic, 1993.

Library-Based Parent Resource Centers: A Guide to Implementing Programs. Albany, NY: New York State Developmental Disabilities Planning Council, 1995.

Marino, Jane. *Mother Goose Time: Library Programs for Babies and Their Caregivers.* Bronx, NY: H. W. Wilson Co., 1992.

Markowsky, Juliet Kellogg. "Storytime for Toddlers". *School Library Journal* Volume 23, Number 9 (May 1977): 18–31.

Monsour, Margaret, and Carole Talan. *Library-Based Family Literacy Projects.* Chicago: American Library Association, 1993.

Musick, Judith Smith, and Bernice Weissbourd. *Guidelines for Establishing Family Resource Programs*. Chicago: National Committee for Prevention of Child Abuse, 1988.

Nespeca, Sue McCleaf. *Library Programming For Families With Young Children*. New York: Neal-Schuman Publishers, 1994.

Programs to Strengthen Families, Third edition. Chicago: Family Resource Coalition, 1992.

Rogers, Pat, and Barbara Herrin. "Parent-Child Learning Centers: An Alternative Approach to Library Programming for Preschoolers." *Top of the News*, (Summer 1986): 343–355.

Rollock, Barbara T. *Public Library Services for Children*. Hamden, CT: Library Professional Publications, 1988.

PUBLIC LIBRARY RESOURCES

Children's Services Department, Middle Country Public Library, Centereach NY 11720. 516–585–9393.

Children's and Parents' Services, Mastics-Moriches-Shirley Community Library, Shirley, NY. 516–399–1511.

Youth Services, Onondaga County Public Library, Syracuse, NY, 315–435–1800.

Children's Services Department, Newburgh Free Library, Newburgh, NY, 914–561–2401.

6 COLLABORATIONS: FORGING A NEW IDENTITY

"A collaboration is a formal and complex relationship that requires two or more groups, each of which retains its autonomy to share authority, resources, and vision in a process that leads to the creation of common goals, a new identity, and shared responsibility to the community. Collaboration brings groups together to achieve common goals that could not be effectively or efficiently achieved by an individual group acting independently." ("A Model. . . . 1993)

Libraries are essential partners in interagency collaborations that effect policies and services for families within communities. The library brings essential problem-solving resources, including the librarian's information-seeking skills that can advance the work of collaborating partners. The library's basic policies of mutual respect, confidentiality of clients, privacy of individuals, inclusiveness of all families and children, and nonaffiliation to any cause or political group enhance the collaborative process and minimize the possibility of conflict with other human or community service programs.

Collaborations may be difficult to achieve. Collaborations require creative attention and time to develop, but good ones are well worth the effort. Each agency entering into the process must realize that to be successful a piece of its personal identity may be sacrificed and that the collaboration may take on a life of its own. Collaborations usually occur when organizations have worked effectively together to establish community networks, coordinate family services, or cooperate in a joint project. Sometimes collaboration can be pure serendipity. For example, one agency representative has a great idea but realizes that the need for expertise is beyond the representative's own field. The agency representative calls around and catches the fire of another professional from a different agency. Agency two "clicks on" to the idea and, through a good collaborative process, they create a successful endeavor.

This chapter outlines the collaborative process, which includes initiating, planning, financing, taking "root," and maintainance and describes specific collaborative projects between libraries and other agencies.

READY, SET, READ

INITIATING

Great ideas abound in the family service community, but how do agencies share information? Existing networks are the perfect forum but the right people might not be at the table when a problem or creative solution is introduced. The stakeholder or key personnel must be involved right from the start. The target group must also have a voice even before planning begins.

"Ready, Set, Read," a successful collaborative project, began at the SUNY Health Science Center Outpatient Pediatric Clinic as the germ of an idea stimulated by ROAR (Reach Out and Read), a program begun at the Boston City Hospital. The pediatric social worker called around to various organizations looking for funding to start a similar family literacy and information program but found no takers. The social worker, a library user herself, eventually connected with a children's services coordinator at the Onondaga County Public Library. As soon as the coordinator heard the idea, she was "in" and "Ready, Set, Read" was born.

PLANNING

The idea or project exists in the minds of two or more individuals, but mapping the work on paper is a difficult task. Good planning, from needs assessment to an evaluation tool, must be incorporated into any collaboration.

"Ready, Set, Read" carefully considered the client group of educationally and economically disadvantaged families as the two agencies began the planning process. In addition, the library staff, the doctors, and other health care professionals brought their own areas of expertise to bear on the project. Each group respected the others' knowledge and experience and there were few territorial conflicts. The library was particularly enthusiastic about serving the "hard to reach" client group with information about library service and family literacy issues. The clinic was particularly concerned about adult literacy levels and reducing educational and health risk factors for children beginning at birth.

Three big factors impacted on the planning process. The library needed to change its library card registration policies to allow children to get library cards beginning at birth, and the library staff needed to commit to teaching clinic professionals about family literacy and the library's role in serving families. The clinic needed to commit the training time of medical students, resident physicians, and other health care professionals to the project and, once trained, they needed to ensure that the information would be imparted to clients. The clinic and the library each contributed real funds and in-kind services to begin the project, thus forging a true collaboration.

FINANCING

Often agencies write joint grant proposals to overcome any problems that may arise over funding. Without joint funding the project may be more effective as a cooperative venture with one party managing and the other voluntarily agreeing to participate. A Library Services and Construction Act grant and a grant from the SUNY Health Science Center Miracle Children's Network provided the initial funding for "Ready, Set, Read."

A formal contract or agreement may work best for collaboration. In particular, agencies should specifically identify financial and/or in-kind obligations, ongoing maintenance responsibilities, methods of communication, problem solving, and evaluation.

TAKING ROOT

Whether the collaboration results in an entirely new entity or advances the work of the partners, the community must identify with the collaboration and not the individual agencies. The public relations must not favor one agency over the other but should focus on the new service.

"Ready, Set, Read" involved three components. Teaching the clinic staff about family literacy and family library services was a primary responsibility of the library. A curriculum was written to ensure that the professional standards of the teaching hospital were maintained. See Chapter 9.

The clinic and library jointly contracted with a library assistant to present story programs at the clinic. The assistant recruited volunteer story readers for the clinic waiting room, promoted the program, and raised additional funds to maintain her salary and to purchase books necessary for the book giveaway program. The library staff trained the volunteer readers in story time techniques for children ranging from babies to school-age children. The staff also worked with the volunteers until they were knowledgeable about library service and could share this information with the mothers, fathers and care providers they met in the clinic.

The new baby program involved registering the babies for library cards, gathering information about the families, providing six developmentally appropriate books for the first year of a baby's life, and scripting information about libraries, reading aloud, and picture books for doctors to convey to the parent at each well child check-up.

The library staff did book selection and scripting, and created printed materials to share with all families. The library not only focused on family literacy but stressed the library's PIRL (Parent Information Resource Library) and other family services. The library collected data about families and developed evaluation tools.

MAINTAINING THE PROGRAM

A collaborative service or program can go in many directions:

1) If the collaboration takes on a life of its own then the collaboration may move outside the realm of any single agency.
2) The collaboration may dissolve if it has solved a problem or addressed a need that is not ongoing.
3) The collaboration may come to rely on one partner more than another or the interest of partners may wane.
4) The collaboration may end if funding or support becomes a serious problem.

"Ready, Set, Read" continues to operate with contract staff and volunteers. The library's responsibility has been minimized but the library maintains an active support and teaching role. The program is based in the clinic so the clinic staff continues to have a high level of involvement in daily operations of the project and fund raising.

WHAT MAKES A COLLABORATION WORK?

- A clear vision, goals, objectives, and plan
- Joint investment in vision, goals, objectives, and plan
- A shared financial responsibility
- A project that addresses a real need identified by each partner agency
- A written contract or agreement
- A family focus that can effect real change
- Strong communication between partners
- Minimal turf issues
- Publicity that focuses on the collaboration and not the partners

- A relevant project
- Early success for at least a piece of the collaboration
- Few barriers from parent agencies or government
- The ability of participants to make real decisions
- A willingness to give up the collaboration when it becomes an independent service.

Designing and defining collaborative services is a growing movement and one in which librarians need to get on board. Becoming knowledgeable about building collaborations is the key to success. The problems, pitfalls, and conflicts can be minimized if all partners understand the obligation to the collaborative process that exists at the onset. The remaining portion of this chapter outlines two other examples of collaborations. Additional resources are listed at the end of this chapter.

THE COMPUTERIZED INFORMATION AND REFERRAL DATABASE OF HEALTH AND HUMAN SERVICES FOR SUFFOLK COUNTY (NEW YORK)

INITIATING

In the fall of 1989, a core group of professionals from the Suffolk Coalition for Parents and Children and selected representatives from the eight major hotlines and helplines in the county began the process of developing a computerized information and referral database of health and human services. During the prior ten years, members of the Coalition and particularly the librarians had been involved in designing and publishing local resource directories. Most of these publications were aimed at specific target groups or centered on special issues such as child care, child abuse, or parenting. It seemed to be a never-ending task.

The professionals involved agreed it was time to eliminate this duplicative, time-consuming process. Computer technology provided the method; librarians provided the organizational ability. Health and human service professionals provided the guidance and expertise. All that was needed was funding and a willingness to work together to eliminate turf issues, break down barriers, and trust one another in the process of creating our database.

PLANNING

Three committees were formed, including the technology committee, the steering committee, and the fund development committee. The committees proceeded to identify major issues regarding the development of such a database. Who was to be the central manager? Why is it necessary to have a computerized database? What types of services and resources would the database encompass? What type of computerized system should be developed, i.e., online or disk distribution? How would the database be maintained?

The library was recognized from the onset as the best agency to serve as the central manager because it was the most technologically up-to-date and firmly committed to resource sharing, coalition building, and family-centered services. The library, information neutral and "agenda free" in the political arena, could easily take—without repercussions—a leadership role in the development of a comprehensive and accurate database.

FINANCING

The initial funding was provided through a special state legislative grant sponsored by five New York State senators. Subsequent funding has been provided through grants from the county's youth bureau, social services and health departments, and library. In 1994, the library invested in software as part of the library's online catalog, and today's funding is provided by the library and the county's executive department. The library has accepted responsibility for maintaining the current database, while other members of the steering committee and the health and human services community are constantly looking for funds to stabilize the budget.

In addition to grants, the library has been successful in gaining in-kind contributions such as agency staff and volunteers to collect and input data. Librarian interns and trainees, students, and senior volunteers have been utilized in the development of this project.

TAKING ROOT

The initial work focused on two major issues: technology and money. The technology committee selected a software program specially designed for information and referral programs. This program, known as the Community Services Locator, required a central manager and used a disk distribution system that operated on a PC. In addition, the committee determined that the database follow the *Info Line Taxonomy of Human Services* as a foundation for cataloging and organizing the information. This taxonomy has been accepted as the national standard by the Alliance of Information and Referral Systems (AIRS).

The second goal was to purchase the software, collect and input a basic cadre of services, and select several pilot sites for testing. This goal was pursued by the fund development committee: representatives from the library, United Way, health services, youth bureau, and social services. Original inquiries were aimed at New York State Senators who have access to legislative funds for local projects. Personal meetings were arranged with the five senators who represented Suffolk County. After many meetings, letters and phone calls, a legislative grant was provided to begin the project.

MAINTAINING THE DATABASE

During the five years of development, the steering committee, active members of the Coalition, and helpline professionals have given the guidance and support necessary for the successful implementation of the database.

The library has provided the financial stability to maintain the current database and provides leadership for its ongoing development. The steering committee has changed as the database takes on new dimensions and because of changes in agency personnel. Current goals are to make the database more comprehensive and accessible to a wider audience and to locate a steady stream of funding. Several documents related to the development and requests for support of the database are appended (Appendix B, Figures B–5a, B–5b, B-6, and B–10a, B–10b, B–10c).

Collaborations begin with one or two people who have good ideas, and then a whole community can invest in the project. Public libraries are often the catalyst for good ideas, solid information, and the awareness of community resources. The process keeps the public library staff active, involved, and aware of the future of family services.

THE LIBRARY/MUSEUM/HEAD START PARTNERSHIP PROJECT

The following describes a national project with local impact. This description was written by the project coordinator, Virginia H. Mathews.

INITIATING

An Interagency Agreement between the Center for the Book in the Library of Congress and the Head Start Bureau of the Department of Health and Human Services was signed and ready to be implemented in May 1992. It resulted from a proposal requested by Head Start following a symposium on the potential of partnerships between libraries and other agencies serving children and families held at the Library of Congress in November 1989. The program officers who had attended returned from the symposium with enthusiasm for the possible benefits to Head Start children, parents, and teachers of close collaboration with children's librarians.

PLANNING

A three-day planning meeting on the proposed project resulted in a set of guidelines for the production of a proposed video, the development of regional workshops, and written materials, including a resource book and training guide to be used with the video. Leaders from both Head Start and libraries were solidly behind the concept and its potential.

FINANCING

In the first year of funding, the Center for the Book director and project director, John Y. Cole; the project coordinator, Virginia H. Mathews; and the consultant for the Association for Library Service to Children (American Library Association), Susan Roman, initiated and developed the concepts, chose the location sites for the video production, and worked with Head Start staff on the video and guidebook. Three multistate workshops also took place between December 1993 and May 1994, reaching an equal number of Head Start leaders and children's librarians from almost every state and the District of Columbia.

TAKING ROOT

In the spring of 1994, the Center for the Book was asked to include members of the Association of Youth Museums in its training workshops so that museum directors or education coordinators could join with the team of Head Start and library personnel in each locality. A planning conference to discuss integration of museums into the ongoing project was held in Washington in September 1994. Museums were included in the next two workshops held in 1995. A news release on the Library/Head Start/Discovery Center Museum Partnership Project is appended (Appendix D, Figure D-13).

All of the regional and the state workshops held were organized under the auspices of the state Centers of the Book. To date, nearly 500 Head Start staff, librarians, and museum personnel have been exposed to the training and many have become involved in partnership projects, spin-off institutes, and related grant-funded projects.

MAINTAINING THE PARTNERSHIP

In the summer of 1995 an unprecedented additional year of funding had been granted to the Partnership Project. The focus of the funding is single state workshops. Four are planned for the 1995–1996 grant period.

The Partnership Project recognized that it had not invented a new relationship, that there had been interactions in the past between Head Start classrooms and librarians and between Head Start classrooms and museums. These relationships, however, had usually been haphazard and irregular. This project intends to strengthen existing relationships, raise them to a higher level, and make them part of the expectations of children, parents, teachers, librarians, and museum specialists.

It has been reported that these goals have indeed become a normal part of the routine, complete with memorandums of agreement between the partners (Appendix B, Figures B-13 and B-14). In no previous instances, as far as the partnership has been able to determine, have library resources and services integrated Head Start priorities such as family literacy, parent involvement in children's learning, parent training, and technological assistance to teachers and volunteers. As a national initiative, the Partnership Project provides an exemplary model of the collaborative process at work.

RESOURCES

Bruner, C. *Thinking Collaboratively: Ten Questions and Answers to Help Policy Makers Improve Children's Services.* Washington, DC: The Education and Human Service Consortium, 1991.

Melaville, A.I., and M.J. Blank. *What It Takes: Structuring Interagency Partnerships to Connect Children and Families With Comprehensive Services.* Washington, DC: The Education and Human Service Consortium, 1991.

Mathews, Virginia H. *Guide to the Use of The Library Head Start Partnership: Video for Programs and Workshops*, Washington, DC: The Center for the Book, Library of Congress, 1993.

Quezada, Shelley, and Ruth S. Nickse. *Community Collaborations for Family Literacy Handbook*. New York: Neal-Schuman, 1993.

REFERENCES

"A Model for Collaboration." *Success By Six*. Syracuse, New York: United Way, 1993.

7 FUNDING BASICS

Fund development and grant writing for family support services is an integral part of the total process. It takes skill, time, and energy as well as determination and a generous amount of creative thinking. Many librarians avoid responsibility for this part of the process, not through lack of ability or intelligence, but most likely through lack of experience, knowledge, information, or just plain courage. Our profession is new to this arena. Jumping into the process, for most professionals, is the only way to begin.

FUNDING ISSUES

Starting on the road to coalition building and the desire to develop collaborative projects will bring the funding issue to the forefront. Librarians can often learn skills and techniques from their networking partners, who may be more knowledgeable about fund raising and grant writing for a project. Many education, social services, and health professionals are involved constantly with fund raising and grant writing and, as part of the grant writing process, are more than willing to share their expertise.

Before embarking on the development of a grant proposal or a formal fund raising program, it is essential to consider the following steps:

- Outline and review the goals and objectives of the family service project.
- Conduct a needs assessment of the community with coalition members to determine the actual needs that exist.
- Assess the potential impact of a grant on the library and on the agencies that have established informal or formal relationships with the library.
- Analyze how outside funding will effect these relationships and the operating budgets of each agency or organization.
- Brainstorm potential problems or pitfalls for the library, other agencies, and that important community relationship.
- Conduct a literature search to see if recommended ideas have been tried. In preparing a grant proposal it is always good to be aware of other similar and/or successful programs.

- Determine the ongoing and maintenance structure of the program. A grant will provide seed money and sometimes a multiple-year contract, but it won't indefinitely continue to support a program. In fact, most grants cover operating expenses in the first year but not the following year.
- Ascertain the possible extent of in-kind contributions by both the library and participating agencies.

Targeting the best funding source is another consideration. Will it be government, local foundations, national foundations, or corporations? Choosing the wrong funding source can cause an unnecessary delay in funding your project. Keep a "wish" file of fairly well-developed large and small projects that would enhance family services at the library and in the community. Always be prepared for the donor who comes searching for interesting programs and services. Successful projects and providers are often approached by foundations and private donors.

A grant concept form is appended (Appendix B, figure B-1) as well as samples of grant proposal overviews, project descriptions, and workplans (Appendix B, Figures B-8 through B-11). Use the concept form to begin the process of finding outside funding for local projects to support family services or fill out the form for the idea file. A list of resources is provided at the end of this chapter.

SIMPLE AND DIRECT

LETTERS OF REQUEST

Sometimes a project can be stymied because there is a need for something large like appropriate space or something small like a diaper changing unit. These contributions can often come from within the community, and all a person has to do is ask. The art of asking can be as difficult as writing a full grant proposal or finding the funding for a library expansion project but it never hurts to ask. Requests for funding asking businesses to provide dollars, equipment, or space in order to eliminate economic barriers from projects are appended (Appendix B, Figures B-2 through B-5).

LETTERS OF SUPPORT

In many cases, when professionals are involved in coalitions or in designing a collaborative program or project, a lead agency will request that the library provide a letter of support. These letters confirm the library's involvement and support of the project as well as support for the lead agency applying for funds. Often, the lead agency will provide a sample letter that a library needs only to type on its own letterhead. In the case of the library being a lead agency, the grant writer should consider providing the participating agencies with this type of sample support letter. Examples of letters of support are located in the appendix (Appendix B, Figures B-6 and B-7).

BUDGETING

If the request for funds amounts to more than a simple item or one-time expenditure, the development of a budget will be required. These vary with each type of grant and the funding agency. Sometimes forms are provided with descriptions of items that can be purchased under each category and account code. With private foundations, there is often a less formal approach.

A budget summary that accompanies the budget is usually required by most funding agencies and foundations. This summary outlines the justification for each expenditure, i.e., staff positions and duty statements, what materials are to be purchased and the purpose of the materials, consultant fees and a description of how the consultant will be used, and travel and conference fees if they are necessary to accomplish the goals of the project.

Often there are limitations on specific items that can be reimbursed through grant funds. It is important to read the requirements and be aware of the restrictions that the funding agency has placed on expenditures.

In-kind contributions are another important segment of the budget and need to be itemized for the funding agency. Often there is a stipulation or percentage requirement for in-kind contributions. A common form of in-kind contribution is an employee's benefits, use of facilities and equipment, or administrative costs.

An additional consideration for grant writers regarding budgetary concerns for a grant proposal is the reporting mechanism required by the funding agency. These vary greatly from one funding source to another. Private foundations are usually less rigid in their accounting demands. Public agencies generally require a more rigorous method of accounting that demands copies of bills and invoices, check numbers, and payroll information. It is important that the responsible person formulate the budget procedures and requirements immediately upon receipt of the grant to avoid confusion and an inordinate amount of time locating paperwork.

COLLABORATION CONTRACTS

Many collaborations, joint projects, and partnerships require a formal agreement between agencies. This need usually arises as the coalition develops or after the project is funded and the lead agency requires that partner agencies sign a subcontract or general consensus agreement. Many coalitions ask that members sign an agreement that outlines their responsibilities in the coalition. A more formal contract or agreement is usually required if money is involved in the project. These contracts are prepared by the lead agency. Fundamental elements of an agreement or contract include:

Agency Names: Includes agencies directly involved in the project and/or steering committees.

Agency Representatives and Titles: Agency directors or department heads usually attach letters of agreement to the contract.

Project Title: Most projects or services have coined a phrase or special title. This is important for public relations and fund raising purposes.

Goals and Objectives: Restate the goals and objectives that the project will achieve.

Funding Source(s) and Financial Commitment: Attach the project budget with funding sources and in-kind contributions clearly defined or state the funding commitment or in-kind contribution of each agency.

Project Staff: Define the supervisory responsibility of each agency.

Decision Making and Maintenance of the Project: Define how decisions will be made and if there is any authority role between agencies. Daily work flow procedures must also be decided.

Communication and Problem Sovling: How will agencies exchange information and keep abreast of the collaborative project? This can be particularly difficult if agencies do not provide direct service to the project or if the collaboration is off-site from all partners.

Public Relations Plan: Agencies should come to prior agreement on wording for any news releases generated by the project.

Time Line: Attach time line and responsibilities for each agency.

Evaluation: Prior agreement on evaluation and benchmarks for project success. This requires clear, mutually agreed-upon goals.

Project's Future: Decisions about the future of the project should be jointly agreed upon. Some sample agreements are appended (Appendix B, Figures B-13 and B-14)

RESOURCES FOR RAISING MONEY

Coalitions encourage librarians to expand their skill base and broaden their personal competencies. A first step for many librarians begins with using published materials.

BOOKS

There are many books on grant and proposal writing. The following are a few choice titles that can help libraries and agencies get started in the grant-seeking process.

Barber, Peggy, and Linda D. Crowe. *Getting Your Grant: A How-to-do-it Manual for Librarians.* New York: Neal-Schuman, 1992.

Corry, Emmett. *Grants for Libraries,* Second Edition. Littleton, CO: Libraries Unlimited, 1986.

Gilpatrick, Eleanor G. *Grants for Nonprofit Organizations: A Guide to Funding and Grant Writing.* New York: Praeger, 1989.

Miner, Lynn E., and Jerry Griffith. *Proposal Planning and Writing.* Phoenix, AZ: Oryx, 1993.

Read, Patricia E. *Foundation Fundamentals: A Guide for Grantseekers.* Third Edition. New York: The Foundation Center, 1986.

Many materials are published by The Grantsmanship Center in Los Angeles, California, in particular a 48-page reprint entitled "Program Planning & Proposal Writing" (expanded version, 1980) by Norton J. Kiritz.

INTERNET RESOURCES

Many resources for funding and grant proposals are now available on the Internet. The following is a list prepared, as of July 1995, by Beth Vella (MLS, Syracuse University, 1995).

Resources Accessible through Gopher

American Library Association

gopher.uic.edu
- The Library
- American Library Association (ALA)
- ALA's Divisions
- Library Administration and Management Association (LAMA)
- Fund raising and Financial Development Clearinghouse Information

Lists materials available through interlibrary loan from LAMA.

Carnegie Corporation of New York

gopher.carnegie.org 3000
- Carnegie Corporation of New York

Instructions on applying for a grant from the Carnegie Corporation.

Department of Health and Human Services

gopher.os.dhhs.gov
- DHHS Resources by Topic
- GrantsNet — An Info Hub for Federal Grant Resources

Information about HHS and other federal grant programs.

Gopher Jewels

cwis.usc.edu
- Other Gophers and Information Resources
- Gopher-Jewels
- Research, Technology Transfer, and Grants Opportunities
- Grants

Listing of gophers that specialize in grant-related information.

MultiMedia Schools

online.Lib.uic.edu
- MultiMedia Schools Magazine
- Feature Articles (selected full text)
- Using Your Modem to Find Grants (Cheely, 5/95)

An article about using DIALOG and the Internet.

National Institutes of Health (NIH)

gopher.nih.gov
- Grants and Research Information

Includes the NIH Guide for grants, contracts, and other information.

Rice University

riceinfo.rice.edu
- Research Interests and Opportunities
- Miscellaneous grant and scholarship information from around the Internet

Access to several sites with grant information. Much of the information is from the NIH or National Science Foundation.

University of Idaho

gopher.uidaho.edu
- Science, Research, & Grant Information
- Grant Information

Includes the helpful document "A Grant Getter's Guide to the Internet," plus the Catalog of Federal Domestic Assistance and links to many other sites.

University of Michigan

una.hh.lib.umich.edu
- genref
- Grant, Foundation & Scholarship Information

Includes advice on proposal writing and links to other sites, including the Foundation Center.

University of North Carolina

gibbs.oit.unc.edu
- Research
- GrantSource(R)

Most of the information is from the National Institute of Health.

University of Wisconsin at Milwaukee

alphal.csd.uwm.edu
- UWM Information
- Grants Opportunities

Covers federal and nonfederal grant sources and gives information about writing grants.

U.S. Department of Education

gopher.ed.gov
- Announcements, Bulletins, and Press Releases
- Current Funding Opportunities

also
- U.S. Dept. of Education Programs—General Information
- Grant-Related Information—Publications and Notices

Information about Education Department grants.

Resources Accessible through the World Wide Web

Eisenhower National Clearinghouse

http.//www.enc.org/other_grant.html

Galaxy

http://www.einet.net/galaxy/Reference-and-Interdisciplinary-Information/Grants.html

or

http://www.einet.net/
- Reference and Interdisciplinary Information
- Grants

GrantsWeb

http://infoserv.rttonet.psu.edu/gweb.htm2

3 COMPETENCIES: REDEFINING OUR SKILLS

Can public libraries redefine themselves to become service and information centers for families? Can public libraries ensure that services are family-centered and include parent involvement at all levels? What professional skills define family service? What can librarians teach other agencies about how libraries serve families? Family services present new and exciting models for public libraries, but librarians in the field may need skills to plan, teach, collaborate, and evaluate family services.

ROLES OF THE FAMILY RESOURCE PROFESSIONAL

According to some of the leading experts in parent education and family support, all professionals who work with families need special training and education. Seven basic recommendations evolved from a conference on Parent Education and Public Policy:

1. All human service professionals—as well as professionals (such as police) who have contact with families on a regular basis—should be trained in working with parents. More specifically, they should have training in human growth and development and in understanding the responsibilities of professionals to promote family development and integrity. In addition, professionals should be trained to understand and accept their responsibility to help parents deal with the institutions that influence child and family development.
2. Professionals should be responsive and sensitive—but not aggressive—about offering their advice and information to parents. In order to accomplish this goal, professionals should receive both preservice and inservice training which includes the following elements:
   a. how to avoid cultural bias;
   b. how to increase sensitivity to the needs of parents and their children—including the special needs of nontraditional family types such as single-parent families; and

    c. how to enhance parents' understanding of the operation of institutions and how to improve the relationship between institutions, professionals, and parents.

3. In addition to enhancing the roles of professionals in parent education, policy should encourage development of community support systems. Researchers should try to become 'family advocates' by identifying actual needs of parents and communities and by trying to identify and delineate what support systems are already available.

4. The media should be used as vehicles for providing information on subjects of concern to parents e.g. health, nutrition, education, and so on. Development and distribution of public service announcements and exploration of the potential of cable television should be undertaken.

5. The role of schools (and libraries) in providing parent education should be expanded. Such education should include:
    a. information about child and family development in the elementary school (and birth through age 5);
    b. technical information about family life and the values underlying family responsibility at the junior and senior high levels.

6. Evaluation and reporting requirements should be built into all programs providing for parent education so that the strengths and weaknesses of various models are consciously addressed and documented.

7. The development of new roles and jobs for professionals working with families, as well as the creation of new models of parent involvement in public and private programs, should be undertaken. (Haskins, 1981, pp. 13-14)

In May of 1994 a powerful five-day institute, "Achieving School Readiness: Public Libraries and the First of the National Education Goals," was held at the University of Texas at Austin. The institute participants, state library consultants, early childhood educators, children's librarians, and others from the field met with three purposes in mind:

1. to broaden understanding of the five critical dimensions of school readiness
2. to examine the services provided to preschool children in the nation's public libraries in light of that understanding

3. to develop and disseminate a prototype of library service to preschool children to assist in achievement of Goal 1. (*Achieving School Readiness*, 1995, p. xiii)

At the institute, Alice Sterling Honig, professor of child and family studies at the College of Human Development at Syracuse University, lectured on "Children's Socioemotional Development: Implications for School Readiness." In her section on the library's role she states, "The library is a splendid, sometimes underutilized community resource for boosting effective parenting and thus children's positive socioemotional development. Libraries serve as resource centers for parent education groups and parenting materials...Informational and collaborative networks of librarians and other professionals who serve preschoolers in child care can promote secure emotional growth so that a child grows up deeply confident that he or she is lovable and loved...*Proactive* library programs whereby librarians *reach-out as well as teach-in with families* can help parents become positively involved with infant and toddler growth toward literacy within a loving, responsive parenting context." (*Achieving School Readiness*, 1995, pp. 46-48)

This chapter focuses on specific skills and training needed in order for librarians to pursue the development of family services in public libraries. It emphasizes the need for librarians to become involved in a self-assessment process and describes how to expand library services to reach the family service community and work with parents as adult learners. Let's begin the process by reviewing family centered principles (p. 82) as outlined by the Division of Maternal and Child Health, U.S. Public Health Service.

ATTITUDE IS EVERYTHING: A SELF-ASSESSMENT TOOL ON FAMILY-CENTERED SERVICE

The first step toward developing training and skill building should be a self-assessment to determine each staff member's own attitude about providing a family-centered model of service. A self-assessment tool, developed by the Waisman Center UAP at the University of Wisconsin-Madison, "Self-Assessment and the Change Process: Applications in Early Intervention," has been

Principles Underlying the Family-Centered Approach

Recognition that the family is the constant in the child's life while the service systems and personnel within those systems fluctuate.

Facilitation of parent/professional collaboration.

Sharing of unbiased and complete information with parents about their children on an ongoing basis in an appropriate and supportive manner.

Implementation of appropriate policies and programs that are comprehensive and provide emotional and financial support to meet the needs of families.

Understanding and incorporating the developmental needs of infants, toddlers, preschoolers, and their families into service delivery systems.

Encouragement and facilitation of parent-to- parent support.

Recognition of family strengths and individuality and respect for different methods of coping.

Assurance that the design of comprehensive, coordinated, multi-discipline service delivery systems is flexible, accessible, and responsive to family identified needs.

Adapted from Association for the Care of Children's Health, with support from the Division of Maternal and Child Health, U.S. Public Health Service, 1987.

adapted as one example of a questionnaire that examines attitude and areas of concern for librarians (Appendix C, Figure C-3). By substituting the words "family service" for "early intervention service" the open-ended, self-assessment questionnaire promotes a guided reflection and consideration from a consumer or customer point of view.

The second part of the "Self-Assessment and the Change Process: Applications in Early Intervention" features a quality indicator and a measurement of current status, ranking items from "strength" to "not a priority," and importance from "very important" to "not important" (Appendix C, Figure C-4). The quality indicators that are most relevant to public libraries serving families are included. Consider if these are personal strengths and how important these are to working with families and with agencies that work with families.

By matching items of importance to your current status, the self-assessment should identify areas of concern in ensuring that family service develops or continues as a family-centered program, with strong parent involvement and interagency coordination. Attitude toward serving families is the first step in reaching the goal.

A CHECKLIST OF KNOWLEDGE-BASED AND SKILL-BASED COMPETENCIES FOR FAMILY SERVICES

Beyond attitude there is a necessary set of skills for professional librarians serving families with young children. Children's librarians may need to increase their knowledge of adult learning; adult services librarians may want to focus their training on child development, and both specialists may need continuing education that develops reflective listening skills. The Self Study for Children's Librarian in Appendix E provides a tool to help individual librarians identify their strengths and weaknesses.

The following list of competencies is the basis of training and continuing education for librarians who wish to focus their services on families and young children. It would be beneficial to evaluate these skills and competencies on the basis of whether an individual is competent, needs training, or could train others in the skill.

Demonstrates knowledge of:
- child development
- family support systems
- family cultural systems
- the family and community resources
- adult learning
- family literacy
- child abuse and neglect laws
- parenting a child with special needs
- parenting and parent training

Demonstrates skill of:
- communication
- communication facilitation
- problem solving
- advocacy and assisting people in getting services
- networking, coordination, and collaboration
- presentation and instruction
- facilitating parent/child activities
- facilitating parent support groups
- program planning
- program evaluation
- grant writing
- collection management
- Internet and online searching
- reader's, listener's, and viewer's advisories
- written communication including policy, procedure, and program plans
- outreach
- working with volunteers
- education consultant
- public relations
- material development, including curriculum, bibliographies, videotapes, etc.
- reference and question negotiation

The prototype developed at the Achieving School Readiness Institute provides another powerful training matrix for public libraries seeking to expand programs to young children by including services for parents, caregivers, and community agencies.

> Throughout the prototype document, much attention is given to cooperation and collaboration between librarians and members of the early care and education community. In regard to young children, care and education take place continuously and simultaneously. When librarians work with toddlers and preschoolers, they join with parents, teachers, child care workers, health care providers, and a host of other individuals who are concerned with the care and education of young children. The prototype encourages children's librarians to become more actively involved with members of the early care and education community, and as a consequence, to become more knowledgeable and empathetic toward members of that community (*Achieving School Readiness*, 1995, p. 137).

REFERENCE, QUESTION NEGOTIATION, AND ADULT LEARNING: IT'S NOT THE SAME OLD SKILL

ADULT LEARNERS

Parents of new babies and young children are adult learners with special needs and concerns. If the crying baby kept them up all night, the need to get information to solve that problem is very immediate and strong, but listening skills and the ability to concentrate is minimal to say the least. "Many times we provide information but feel the patron may ignore it" (Zweizig, 1979, p. 241).

Sensitivity, empathy, flexibility, and good question negotiation skills are at the heart of this basic information service. In general, adult learners:

> learn at their own paces;
> learn in their own styles;
> desire flexible activity and exercise their right to change the way they learn;
> desire immediate learning gratification;
> have a lack of time or interest in formal class structure;
> generally dislike a classroom setting;
> lack the money or prefer not to pay for adult education;
> lack transportation, child care, and other conveniences so that adult education opportunities need to be convenient;
> prefer facilitated learning that takes advantage of their own knowledge;
> prefer a facilitated exchange of ideas rather than an instructor who dominates learning (Tough, 1979, p. 18; Penland, 1978, pp. 6–7).

Reference, readers' advisory, and library-based information programs offer parents many of the desired features of adult learning. For example, if a parent is concerned about a lack of child rearing knowledge, he/she might come to the library for a parent education program one week but find it impossible to attend the whole series planned by the library staff. The librarian might select articles or videos held in the collection to meet the parent's learning needs. The librarian might also seek permission from the program presenter to videotape the library parenting programs, initiate the exchange of telephone numbers between new parents, or set up an electronic parent discussion group. (See Chapter 5 for more ideas on family support services.) All of these techniques may provide the information needed by the parent.

Parents may need information on very specific or specialized concerns, not just the general parenting information that comes easily packaged in a book or video. Getting at the knowledge needed can be difficult because individuals may not be able to articulate their needs, may not have confidence in the library's ability to meet their needs, and may not be able to use the information once it is obtained. In addition, "patrons are impatient when they are seeking information because to seek information is a detour from the main task." (Zweizig, 1979, p.243)

QUESTION NEGOTIATION

It starts with the eyes. That first point of face-to-face contact can make all the difference in a successful reference interview. A relaxed body posture; a warm, open facial expression; maintaining eye contact; and few controlled gestures of interest or concern can offer the parent an opportunity to discuss his/her information need.

Listening is as important as talking. Some good listening tips include: Never interrupt or cut off the speaker; empathize but don't project; don't jump to conclusions or make assumptions; listen for what is not being said; and find a quiet place to talk if there are too many distractions. Use a combination of open questions (who, what, when, where, why), closed questions (yes or no), and neutral questions (a subset of open questions with more structure—user oriented) to narrow the focus as you come to a resolution. Start with neutral questions that allow a person to focus on the reason for coming to the library; in effect, state the problem. Through the use of all types of questioning the librarian and the parent can close the gap between information seeking and information using (Dervin and Dewdney, 1986, pp. 506–512).

The questioning should become a kind of dialogue that isolates the real question, translates the question into something that can be answered, and is followed by a search for the answer that may result in retrieving answers, documents, a referral, or a combination of these. Make sure the response is in a format of information that is useful for the parent, not just a convenient package for the library. See the example below.

An obviously distressed parent comes up to the librarian and asks, "Do you have anything on toilet training?"

    1.   Do you want a book? (closed question)

2. What kind of information do you want? (open question)
3. If you tell me what sort of problem you are working on, I may be able to help you better. (neutral question)

Patron response:

To 1. Yes. (After all, isn't that what libraries are all about?)

To 2. I don't know. (After all, that's the librarians' arena. The patron came to the library to find out what kind of information was available.)

To 3. The distraught parent pours out the story of a child who had toilet trained herself at 1 1/2! The mother is concerned that there would be permanent psychological damage. The toilet training book provided in response to number 1 would not have addressed this need at all.

Neutral questioning and the whole question negotiation process is just one of the many things librarians can offer the greater community of parent service.

DESIGNING FAMILY SERVICES: A PERSONAL JOURNEY

The librarian who embarks on the journey of transforming the public library into a family support center or a community center for families and young children personally grapples with professional roles and responsibilities. It is sometimes a lonely journey and one that provides challenges beyond the traditional librarian role. The next section outlines some of the personal growth and development a children's librarian may experience while exploring new avenues of service to families. The journey is based on the Maslow Hierachy of Self-Actualization.

PHYSIOLOGICAL NEEDS

There is a basic need for the family—the parent-child unit—to be accepted and welcomed in the community. The librarian identifies this need through parent questions, the density of parent population, library literature, and the desire on the library's part to increase circulation and maintain its role as a community resource. Existing library users affirm the need.

Through an examination of available staff and resources, the

SELF-ACTUALIZATION:
The librarian becomes comfortable with the fundamental role of the library in the community. The library is recognized for its unique contributions to family support; is invited to collaborate and participate in program and policy development.

PSYCHOLOGICAL NEEDS:
The library becomes a vital community partner with parents and the professionals who work with families; library services will come to be recognized as integral to community; circulation begins to climb. The director and board realize the "power" of parent services.

LOVE AND BELONGING NEEDS:
The success of connecting with the parenting community becomes natural and the library is viewed as a player with other institutions who provide family support services; the librarian expands his/her professional network to include other youth serving professionals; the librarian markets all library services to families through this network.

SAFETY AND SECURITY NEEDS:
Partnership is formed between you and the librarians already in the field of parent education; parents affirm your first efforts, become your partner; a more proactive parent information and programming service evolves.

PHYSIOLOGICAL NEEDS:
Basic need for the family - the parent-child unit - to be accepted and welcomed in the community; librarian identifies this need; expansion of programming and services to include parents and the development of a parents collection.

The Librarian's Professional Development

librarian decides on the best way to reach out to parents. See Chapter 2 for more information about the environmental scan of the community. Selection of the most comfortable approach will be the first step. This may include:

> an expansion of programming to include parents
> the development of a parents' collection
> separating out parenting books
> establishing a parents' collection vertical file
> hanging posters

SAFETY AND SECURITY NEEDS

Outreach to fellow librarians and a simple look at library literature focusing on programs for families will probably occur next. A partnership is formed between you and the librarians already in the field of parent education who provide a safety net of good practical advice and sure methods for success. Parents affirm your first efforts, become your allies and express enthusiasm for the program. They begin to form a partnership with you and the library.

At this level, a more proactive information service or parent education program may evolve. Parent information and education becomes a specialized reference service. A look at how to market this service becomes a priority. Flyers, posters, bibliographies, kits, and other traditional forms of marketing begin to focus on family support services in the library. A *new* way to market the parent programs and collections also becomes a goal. It requires exploring literature on ways to market this new service— an entrepreneurial approach.

LOVE AND BELONGING NEEDS

The success of connecting with the parenting community becomes natural, and the library is viewed as a player with other institutions that provide family-centered support services.

The librarian who has success with family services and considers deepening the level of commitment reaches out to other organizations for support and finds a receptive community of professionals who relish the connection to the library. Many professionals are examining the family-centered concept in their approaches to serving children and families. Family support, primary prevention and early intervention are the buzz words of the day, and the library can play a key role in these movements. The librarian can expand his/her professional network to include other youth-serving professionals and is sure to find the interaction with them stimulating and empowering.

PSYCHOLOGICAL NEEDS

Realization of the library's potential and the librarian's role in providing family support services is the recognition that points to success. Agencies contact the library, and projects and services grow geometrically. The library becomes a vital community partner with parents and the professionals who work with them. Coalition building takes on a life of its own. The library is asked to participate in the development of family services throughout the community.

Other library services are recognized through these connections. The librarian's ability to access information, organize and develop information and referral files, humanize the information industry and make it comfortable for the non-technological public becomes noticeable. The neutral and non-threatening environment of the library are recognized as major pluses in public service.

Internally, circulation begins to climb. The director and board realize the "power" of parent services. Parents vote, can influence politicians, and can advocate for library services. As allies, they form a true partnership with the library community.

SELF-ACTUALIZATION

The librarian becomes comfortable with the fundamental role of the public library in the community. Families love the library and provide verbal and written support to the librarian. Other agencies invite the library's participation in the development of their services. New grant opportunities include a library component. Librarians are asked to be on advisory and policy development councils. These connections help to broaden the perspective of library services. The library is recognized for its unique contribution to the community.

REFERENCES

Achieving School Readiness: Public Libraries and National Education Goal No.1. Chicago, IL: American Library Association, 1995. p. xiii

Dervin, Brenda, and Patricia Dewdney. "Neutral Questioning: A New Approach to the Reference Interview," *RQ* (Summer 1986): 506–512.

Gaetz, Joan et al. *To Be the Best That We Can Be: A Self-Study Guide for Early Childhood Special Education Programs and Staff.* Poulsbo, WA: Educational Services District 114, Marine Science Center and Oak Harbor School District, 1987.

Haskins, Ron. *Parent Education and Public Policy: A Conference Report.* Summary of conference on "Parent Education and Public Policy" (Quail Roost Conference Center, Durham, NC, March 1980). Washington, DC: National Institute of Education, 1981. 13–14

Penland, Patrick. "Adult Self-Planned Learning." Public Libraries, (Summer 1978): 6–7.

Tough, Allen. "The Adult's Learning Projects: A Fresh Approach to Theory and Practice" in *Adult Learning*, Second Edition. Austin, TX: Austin Learning Concepts, 1979. 18

Van Fleet, Connie. "Lifelong Learning Theory and the Provision of Adult Services," in *Adult Services: An Enduring Focus for Public Libraries*. Chicago, IL: American Library Association, 1990.

Zweizig, Douglas. "The Informing Function of Adult Services in Public Libraries." *RQ* (Spring 1979): 240–244.

COMPETENCIES: EDUCATING OURSELVES AND OTHERS

Whether collaboration partners are professionals from family court, the department of health, the department of mental health, clinics, immunization programs, or the department of social services; whether they are pediatricians, day-care providers, early intervention personnel, parents, or teachers, they need libraries and libraries need them. Educating others about libraries and the library profession takes center stage as the professional librarian becomes involved in interagency cooperation. Explaining what a librarian does and what a library has to offer is essential. The scope of what librarians do and its relevance to other programs and services is not clear to most of those professionals, who are the library's natural partners.

It is also apparent that librarians need to educate themselves. Library schools traditionally do not teach librarians about interagency cooperation, family services, and parent education. The competencies outlined in the previous chapter and the Self-Study for Children's Librarian (Appendix E) exemplify the skills that are needed by the profession in order to provide quality family support services.

This chapter will examine practical examples of how the library profession can teach other professionals as well as itself the skills needed to build library service for families and children. In most cases, it takes energy on the part of librarians to create the curriculum, make themselves available, and be willing to teach themselves and others about the library's potential.

TEACHING OTHERS

GENERAL GUIDELINES
The first part of any workshop or in-service training for providers and groups working with parents should focus on the common elements between libraries and all other family services:

- Working with parents, particularly mothers, right from the start of a child's life and during the early development period

- Creating a long-term relationship and contact with families and children
- Ensuring a confidential and professional relationship
- Providing opinions and information that is respected and used by parents
- Participating in a process that helps young children get a good start in life
- Changing models of service to working with whole families and not just one member of the unit
- Realizing that it is impossible to reach all the families that need services and that collaboration and cooperation are essential
- Depending on the community of service providers for information exchange, referral, and outreach

PRESENTATION IDEAS

The curriculum should cover specific services available for families at libraries. Maintain a low-key approach since many of the agency representatives may not be library users or may find it difficult to imagine their clients using libraries. Use anecdotes in fleshing out descriptions. Show clips of videos or read passages of books as illustrative examples of the collection.

Topics may include:

Parent support and education
Teen parent programs
Adult education and training
Family literacy, including storytimes, Mother Goose, parent-child workshops
Youth at risk
Services for parents of the disabled

Collections, reference service, programs, resource advisory, and electronic information directed at agency clients should be built into the presentation on family service programs rather than featured as separate services. Agency representatives are more likely to remember these elements of library service through an understanding of how they impact on their clients.

Services aimed at agency staff should also be part of the presentation. These topics may include:

Information and technical assistance
Research
Professional publications
Grant and foundation information
Special collections

Networking
Electronic resources
Meeting space

Don't leave questions until the end. Be sure to have give and take throughout your presentation, but facilitate and control the flow of discussion. Leave time for a brainstorming activity. Pick a discussion starter. An example that brings up many issues surrounding information and referral is a brainstorm that starts: If I heard it once, I've heard it a million times from parents _____. The result of this facilitated brainstorm is a list of services that should be available in the community but are not, or an acknowledgement of how difficult it is for parents to find information on much needed services. Tie the results of the brainstorming back into the highlights of your presentation rather than summarizing for the group. The brainstorm will also bring the group together with a common focus and may result in a future partnership or collaboration.

EVALUATION OF IN-SERVICE TRAINING

Teaching others about library service is fun. Not many people know about the many services offered in public libraries. Most of their knowledge is based on their childhood experiences or, at best, their own personal use of the library. In most cases, this is a very narrow vision of what the library has to offer. In teaching others about the library it is important that the audience begin to understand all of the roles a library plays in the community and its influence on the personal lives of individual patrons.

Productive teaching requires an evaluative process. In order to be really effective, the teacher needs to survey students regularly about the content of the course. In this context, the librarians who begin to teach must evaluate their efforts. They must also look for allies in the helping professions. This evaluative process gives them the opportunity to do just that.

An in-service evaluation form provided in the appendix (Appendix C, Figure C-8) will help to refine workshops and training sessions. The evaluation may be anonymous or, in some cases, if the participants are willing to sign, it may be used for follow-up on specific agency needs or as a trigger to contact agencies that show interest in family service collaborations.

READY, SET, READ: A SAMPLE IN-SERVICE CURRICULUM FOR HEALTH PROFESSIONALS

"Ready, Set, Read" was a program of the Onondaga County Public Library in Syracuse, New York, funded by Federal Library Services and Construction Act Title I funds granted by the State

Library of New York (see pages 62–64). This project included the opportunity for the children's services coordinator to regularly "teach" doctors, nurses, medical students, and other health care professionals about library service and the potential of partnerships between libraries and the health care community. The in-service took place at the SUNY Health Science Center at one session of the weekly morning meetings for the pediatric department. The project had a strong focus on family literacy but the curriculum, prepared by the children's services coordinator and the literacy coordinator at the library, is an excellent example of an in-service for professionals from other fields.

Opening discussion:
Reminiscence about being read to as a child.

Lecture:
　　The definitions and state of literacy in the United States and
　　　　Onondaga County.
　　The public library's role in literacy.
　　The parents' role in emerging literacy.

Read aloud:
A selection of picture books was read to the group to provide information about the effects of reading to children beginning at birth and the language development that comes from reading aloud and book sharing. The books were passed around, and brief discussion followed the reading and information presented by the children's services coordinator.

Video:
Prepared by the SUNY Health Science Center media department, the video explains the impetus and the activities of the joint project between the outpatient pediatric department and the public library.

Discussion:
The last topic covered the question of why librarians and health care professionals need to work together. While this was a group discussion, the children's services coordinator made sure that certain points were highlighted and used this as an opportunity to inform the staff about other parent and child services offered by the library.

The in-service concluded with a quick evaluation of the presentation. There was no formal question-and-answer period because the group freely asked questions throughout the presentation.

Other components of the "Ready, Set, Read" project included (1) the children's services coordinator's regular appearance in the clinic, which allowed for information to be reinforced to the doctors, nurses, and other staff, and (2) the distribution of handouts, fact sheets, and brochures.

TEACHING OURSELVES: LIBRARY-BASED FAMILY SUPPORT SERVICES

In addition to reaching out to other professionals who work with families, it is important that librarians teach each other and work to expand library education to include advanced courses and continuing education seminars in the area of early childhood education and family services. The Palmer School of Library and Information Science at the C.W. Post Campus of Long Island University has offered such a course since 1994. An outline is provided here as an example of how and what can be provided by the library community in our efforts to educate the contemporary librarian who works in public libraries now and will do so in the future.

COURSE TITLE:FAMILY SUPPORT SERVICES IN PUBLIC LIBRARIES

Course Description:

Participants will be exposed to intensive education and training in early childhood development and intervention, parent education, collection development, information and referral, community networking, and parent/professional partnerships. The curriculum will focus on the development of library programs, collections, and services for young children and their families. Adaptations and the integration of these services for special needs children and at-risk families will be highlighted throughout the Institute.

Using a variety of resource specialists, slide and video presentations, and handouts and bibliographies, this Institute will provide a dynamic introduction to the public library as a community resource for families. Specific topics include:

- Early childhood development and programming in public libraries
- The need for parent education and family support in today's society

- The parent/child workshop as a model library program
- Parenting collections in public libraries
- Special parents, special children: the adolescent parent, the parent of a special needs child
- The importance of community networking
- Information and referral: the librarian's role
- Active listening skills and sensitivity training

Specific Course objectives:

1. Articulate the mission of the public library and the children's services professional in serving families and young children.
2. Demonstrate an understanding of the role of the children's services librarian in providing library services to parents, caregivers, and professionals who work with families.
3. Identify services and programs specifically designed for diverse families, including parents of infants and young children, teen parents, parents of special needs children, and multiethnic families.
4. Demonstrate effective interpersonal communication skills that focus on parents and other youth serving professionals.
5. Introduce models of coalition building and collaborative efforts to expand and broaden library services within the community.

Course Outline:

I. INTRODUCTION

A. Participant and Instructor Introductions
B. Course Overview
C. Issues and Trends in Children's Services

An examination of current trends in public library service to children and families will focus on early childhood services, parenting education, youth advocacy, and information and referral service.

II. EARLY CHILDHOOD AND PARENT EDUCATION

A. Early Childhood Development

A lecture on the developmental stages of early childhood will be presented with a focus on the professional's role in designing materials and services that are appropriate for that age level. Special attention will be given to language and speech development, the infant and toddler's perception of the world outside the family, and the need for sensitivity and awareness of child development when designing library services.

B.   Parenting and Parent Education
A lecture on parent development, parenting, and parent education will explore such issues as parent esteem, the developmental stages of new parents, and parent empowerment and the role of the parents as primary educators of their young children. This discussion will also examine the role of the professional in relation to parents and the ways in which children's librarians can support parents through library programs and collections.

III. THE PARENT/CHILD WORKSHOP

A.   An In-Depth Presentation of the Parent/Child Workshop
This model library parent and early childhood education program emphasizes the children's librarian's roles as information specialist, parent and early childhood educator, and community networking professional and provides the mechanism for creating philosophical change in local library services to children and families. It also serves as a recreational and social vehicle for families with very young children and offers enormous potential for the prevention and early intervention of developmental disabilities.

B.   Replication through the Rauch Foundation
The Rauch Foundation, a local Long Island foundation, has funded the replication of the Parent/Child Workshop in low income and ethnically diverse community libraries. These models, funded in Wyandanch and Freeport, will be showcased and some of the unique strategies used to get the program up and running will be examined.

IV. A POTPOURRI OF PARENT PROGRAMS FOR LIBRARIES
An overview of other parent support programs will be provided, including Parents Anonymous, STEP Parenting Program, and Reach Out.

V. INFORMATION AND REFERRAL SERVICES

A.   The Role of the Librarian in Information and Referral
Students will view the movie "Tell Me Where to Turn," which portrays the role of the professional in providing information and referral to families. The librarian as a provider of information and referral services will be examined.

B.   Communication Skills and Techniques
In order to provide information and referral to parents, interact with other professionals and networks, and communicate the needs of children within one's library, the librarian must develop communication and active listening skills. A training workshop will focus on the development of specific skills and techniques.

VI. MIDDLE COUNTRY PUBLIC LIBRARY AS A FAMILY RE-SOURCE CENTER

A.   Tour of MCPL

The Middle Country Public Library's development as a model family center will be discussed as students receive a tour of the library's main building, which includes the Early Childhood Peninsula, the Suffolk Family Education Clearinghouse and Parents Collection, and the Museum Corner. A tour of MCPL's Cultural Center will include a discussion of services that are provided to children and parents through the Early Childhood Room and the Computer Place.

B.   Materials and Resources for Parents

This hands-on review will highlight a variety of materials for parents, including books, magazines, ephemeral materials, audio-visuals and databases. Core parent collection materials as well as special items of interest to professionals who specialize in work with families of young children will be examined. The Infant Kit and the Free Handout Collection will also be reviewed.

C.   Databases for Professionals Working With Families

Students will be introduced to MCPL's information and referral database, the SATURN database, and Internet resources.

D.   Essential Elements of Early Childhood Services

Eight essential elements for designing appropriate services for families and young children will be reviewed. Elements include the physical and social environment, programs and services, collections, professional development, parent participation, comprehensive services, and administration.

F.   Early Childhood Materials and Programs

Students will receive a hands-on introduction to materials and resources for babies, toddlers, and preschoolers. Collections include special books, toys, software, reading readiness activity kits, puzzles, and audiovisual materials. A discussion and slide presentation will focus on model library-based early childhood programs including the Mother Goose Program; Toddler Storytime; and Off to a Good Start, MCPL's reading readiness program for preschoolers and their parents.

VII.   SERVING PARENTS OF SPECIAL NEEDS CHILDREN

A.   Early Childhood Intervention

This presentation will focus on the need for early intervention through pre- and postnatal education and parent education as a primary prevention tool when working with families. Educating parents on high-risk factors that lead to developmental delays and disabilities, reaching potential parents to educate them concerning these factors, and making information and resources available for parents are some of the issues to be discussed.

B.   Working with Families of Special Needs Children
The importance of providing support to families of children with special needs will be explored. Training exercises in communication, language sensitivity, and family relationships will be conducted to introduce the student to the underlying emotional problems of raising a child with special needs. This presentation will emphasize the need to develop parent/professional partnerships within a community to provide support to these families.

C.   Inclusion in a Community Setting
Portions of a special film produced by the Ohio Project will be viewed as an example of an inclusive environment. Specific examples of how special needs children can be included in the public library setting will be provided.

VIII. THE ADOLESCENT PARENT
This discussion will focus on the needs of teen parents. The class will view the movie "A Day in the Life of a Teen Parent," which follows an adolescent parent through a day with her child, parents, and friends. A librarian's experience with teen parents through the Teen Parent/Child Workshop at the Mastics-Moriches-Shirley Community Library will explore issues and problems when designing services and programs for teen parents.

IX. COMMUNITY NETWORKING

A.   Coalition Building
An in-depth presentation of coalition building, including a step-by-step guide to building a professional network, will be provided. Topics covered include a description of four coalition models, how to form coalitions, identifying and recruiting members, organizing and operating a coalition, and anticipating conflict issues.

B.   The Role of the Librarian in Coalition Building
A discussion will focus on why the library should be involved in the broader community network of professionals who work with families and children. The role of the librarian in these networks will be examined, including information and resource sharing, program coordination at the community level, and public education on family and children's issues.

C.   Specific Examples of Coalitions
Some of Suffolk County's networks will be highlighted with a

look at the role the librarian plays in each network. Examples include the Suffolk Coalition for Parents and Children, The Librarians' Alliance for Parents and Children, the Parent Educator's Network, and the Child Care Council of Suffolk County.

D. Family Resource and Support Movement
The family resource movement will be examined with a look at why and how libraries are natural players in this movement. Some of New York State's parent education initiatives and policies will be highlighted, including the New York Parents Initiative, the core elements of parent education programs as outlined by the Family Resource Coalition, the Council on Children and Families, and the Pre- and Postnatal Parent Education Program.

E. An Examination of Model Programs and Collaborations
Model programs, including the Head Start Partnership, the Suffolk County Inclusion Grant, and the Community Information and Referral Data Base Project will be highlighted as excellent examples of collaborative efforts that include children's services librarians.

10 EVALUATING: LETTING QUALITY SERVICE SPEAK FOR ITSELF

Evaluation is the part of the planning process that often gets left behind. Librarians think of evaluation as coming at the end of the process so it is easy to put off and neglect. But the planning process is cyclical. Evaluation streamlines all activities of the library, completes the planning process for any one activity, and provides the tool for change and growth in public library service. It is essential to remember, however, that without the identification of goals and objectives at the beginning of the process, there can be no meaningful evaluation at the end.

Evaluation can be an opportunity for the "customer" to have his or her say. Creating an evaluation tool and using the information generated by surveys, patron focus groups, qualitative and quantitative analysis, and longitudinal studies can build the case for ongoing programming, additional funding, or increased staff. Evaluation can be the most professional activity of the librarian.

WHY DON'T LIBRARIANS LIKE TO EVALUATE?

Evaluation can be threatening; it is a force for change. Instinct is different from evaluation. Statistics or user input may result in unwelcome evidence or outcomes. Viewed in a positive way, evaluation information can assist the library staff in revamping a program or successfully reorganizing service delivery. Without evaluation, libraries may never know where they went wrong, how they went wrong, or, on the other hand, what is was specifically that made a project successful.

Like it or not, librarians, like all contemporary educators, live in the age of an evaluation imperative. Outcomes of programs and services are subject to unprecedented scrutiny by legislators, funding agencies, and sundry taxpayers. Controversial flags of accountability and cost analysis wave briskly, if not menacingly, in the social-political tradewinds.

Yet the meaning and importance of program evaluation in educational settings can hardly be overemphasized. Evaluation can help us to understand what we are doing (or have failed to do), examine the results of these actions and determine how worthwhile are these results. Systematic evaluation should enable more informed and deliberate decision-making about program installation, improvement, continuation, or termination—since it will often answer key, interrelated questions about standards of quality, program components that are linked variously to program outcomes, and the progress of individual participants, including children, parents, and staff (Evans, 1982, p. 1).

In a document entitled *Program Evaluation in Early Childhood/ Special Education: A Self-Help Guide for Practitioners* by Ellis Evans, seven basic questions are outlined for the first-time evaluator to consider:

What is the purpose of the evaluation?
What information is needed, and from what sources can it be obtained?
When and under what conditions will information be gathered?
By what means can information be obtained?
How will the information be analyzed?
How will the evaluation plan be accomplished, and what are the constraints on the plan?
How and to whom will the evaluation results be reported?

The first question—What is the purpose of the evaluation?—is most important for librarians to consider when deciding on an evaluation strategy. Five purposes may be considered.

To make decisions about program installation
To make decisions about program development and modification
To make decisions about continuation, expansion, certification, or termination of a program
To marshall evidence for support of or opposition to a program
To advance the understanding of basic psychological, educational, social, and other processes

There are many books to help librarians get started. Some resources are listed at the conclusion of this chapter. Taking a workshop or a course may also be necessary to develop measurement tools and understand management information systems. However librarians prepare for the process, the process must ensure effective and efficient delivery of service through ongoing oversight and assessment.

QUANTITATIVE MEASURES

Evaluation takes many different shapes. At first glance, looking at the library analytically may provide an understanding of services and resource allocation. State or local standards for libraries may hold one measure of comparison. Comparisons against past and current statistics gathered by a single library and comparisons between two libraries in like communities may also be of value. These statistical comparisons can be used when trying to equalize per capita contributions between communities, upgrade holdings per capita, or make the case for a larger building. These comparison statistics don't, however, have much meaning to the individual user, nor do they define quality library service. These statistics offer little understanding of the library's value to a particular community.

Output measures are a significant improvement in the area of evaluation. Output measures look at performance of a service in terms of the population served. In its most simplistic sense the outputs are measures that "count" something, like the comparison of standards, but the count has more meaning for the individual library because the count is compared to the count of potential users in a community. Examples of quantitative output measures are:

> circulation per capita
> in-house use of library materials per capita
> number of visits to the library per capita
> program attendance per capita
> number of reference transactions per capita
> library card holders per capita
> turnover rate of materials

This listing of output measures can be used to statistically define all aspects of library service and can effectively be put to use by librarians in their efforts to evaluate their programs, collections and services to families.

Cost effectiveness can also be determined by the output measures. For example: Cost out the inputs for a library program such as a series on parenting the two-year-old. Costs may be staff time + honorarium for the speaker(s) + materials for users attending the program + coffee = total cost for the program. Divide the total cost for the program by the number of people attending the program. Now there is a baseline figure.

An objective for the next set of programs could be to reduce the cost per program attendee. The reduction can be accomplished by not having an outside speaker, reducing the cost of the outside speaker by having only one program instead of a series, finding an agency volunteer to provide the service at no cost, or increasing the number of people attending the program.

The problems with these measures are two-fold. What is "per capita"? For the purpose of family services, per capita may be counted as all parents in the census tract with children under eight years of age. Demographic statistics may inflate your output measures because they do not take into account grandparents or child care providers who may use the service. Determining the target audience or the "market segment" is the real challenge of using output measures. Secondly, output measures do not really get at patron satisfaction or quality of service. How will libraries know when the programs are cost effective without sacrificing quality? Can the same subject matter be presented in one workshop when the first series took three? Can the program have the same impact on a group of fifty parents as it had on a group of twenty parents?

QUALITATIVE MEASURES

Output measures work best when they are juxtaposed against measures of impact and quality review. Ask not only whether family services doing the job they promised to do but *how well* the job is being done. Choosing process evaluation, which uses a variety of methods from surveys to focus groups, pre- and post-tests, and output measures and standards comparisons, is the most effective measure of library service.

SURVEYS AND QUESTIONNAIRES

Surveys may be structured to provide consistent, closed answers that are easy to code and quantify. Surveys may also be open-ended and probe for a deeper level of feeling on the part of the user. Open-ended surveys can evolve into in-depth interviews in which a limited number of survey subjects has a tremendous impact on a service. Surveys can be administered through the mail, over the telephone, or face-to-face with the researcher.

Many libraries approach universities, public relations agencies, or research groups to create surveys, administer the instrument, and code the responses. A large-scale survey is usually not conducted on an ongoing basis. This process may be reserved for long-range planning, the conclusion of an important project, or to set service and monetary priorities for a library.

Survey questionnaires, however, may be administered at the conclusion of an individual program, as part of the question negotiation process, or at the conclusion of a multifaceted interaction in which the librarian wants feedback from the patron or "customer." If interviews are the technique of choice, volunteers or paid outside consultants may administer the open-ended or in-depth interview. Administering a paper and pencil survey can also be used to attain this information. This type of survey requires little personal involvement and, generally, takes less time and money to implement. All survey processes should ensure anonymity, which is important for gathering patron input.

Questionnaires can be inserted into books and media packages, attached to articles, and handed to users after the completion of a reference process or particular program. The questionnaire is usually short, focusing on the question of patron satisfaction concerning a particular information need or program/service provided.

SURVEY #1

	Excellent	Good	OK	Unacceptable
How would you describe the assistance you received today?				
How would you describe the selection of resources you received?				

Would you return to the library if
you had other questions of this nature?   ___Yes ___No

Comments _____

Libraries may also want to know how patrons prefer to receive the service. Questionnaires or interviews may look at basic elements such as the time at which programs are offered or at the actual type of service delivery.

SURVEY #2

As a parent, I prefer to receive information and
services from the library in the following ways:

	Most Valued	Valued	Little Value	No Value
One-on-one reference service				
Lecture style programs				
Group discussion				
Parent support groups				
Programs for children that involve parents				
Videotapes				
Books				
Magazines				
CD-ROM information				
Electronic discussion groups				
E-mail				
Internet access				

PARENT SATISFACTION: MEASURING QUALITY OF PROGRAMS AND SERVICES FOR FAMILIES AND YOUNG CHILDREN

In family services, parent satisfaction is a key indicator that the library is meeting objectives. It indicates that the library is having an impact on the ability of individual parents to use library service to efficiently and effectively apply information in their parenting roles. A good example of a user satisfaction tool, targeted to interpret the service needs of families, is the *Program Evaluation Using the Project Dakota Parent Satisfaction Survey: A Manual for Administration and Interpretation of Findings Using a Validated Instrument* by JoAnne Kovach and Robert Jacks. Though the survey was not originally designed for public libraries, an adaptation (Appendix F) could be valuable to librarians in their efforts to evaluate their services, particularly parent satisfaction as it relates to the library's programs and services.

In Goal I, the questions and responses can reveal how parents feel when their young children participate in library programs such as the Parent/Child Workshop, Mother Goose Time, and toddler or preschool storytimes. Goal II measures the parents' reaction to the impact on their program participation. Programs may be geared for parents such as parent support groups in libraries, parenting skills workshops, or family literacy classes. Programs also include children's programs that require parent involvement. Goal III can be used to assess the impact of referral service on meeting the needs of the parent. Goal IV can be used to convey the value of the library program for families.

Results of this parent satisfaction survey are tabulated to show "parent's expectations of the programs" or "parent's satisfaction with the program." A four-point scale, such as the one used by Project Dakota, helps to avoid an evaluation or user survey in which all answers end up "in the middle."

PROGRAM RESPONSE QUESTIONNAIRES

Some forms are designed to elicit feedback from parents regarding a specific program or service. Two sample program evaluation forms are: the *Toddler Story Hour Parent's Evaluation*, courtesy of the Upper Merion Township Library in Pennsylvania, and the *Parent/Child Workshop Evaluation Form*, courtesy of the Middle Country Public Library. Another form, the *Program Registration Survey*, elicits information from parents regarding the library's registration procedures for programs. These forms are appended (Appendix C, Figures C-5 through C-7).

FOCUS GROUPS

Focus groups may help libraries gain insight and understanding without resorting to in-depth interviews. The structured discussion that takes place between a group of people with common characteristics may provide an analysis that, when combined with the closed questionnaire, demonstrates the effectiveness of the family service program or recommends essential changes in the family service program.

The focus group is usually comprised of approximately ten to fourteen individuals. Several focus groups are organized around either library services in general or a specific service or department. In this case, a library could organize focus groups around parenting services or early childhood programs and services.

Sessions should be scheduled for no more than ninety minutes. They are best conducted by an outside facilitator or moderator providing a sense of neutrality. The facilitator must be highly skilled and experienced, and usually he/she meets with the library staff prior to the sessions to discuss the focus group's purpose. Together they work at designing a set of questions and issues germane to family resources. The facilitator is responsible for providing verbal, summary, and detailed reports about the information gathered from the focus group sessions.

Recruiting participants for focus groups is the most important part of the process. Should participants be users? Nonusers? A blend? If a particular service is being evaluated, should only users of that service participate in the group? Will the recruitment be "over the counter" or through personal contact based on staff members' recommendations? In all cases, after the participants have been identified, a staff person must contact each individual, organize the meeting dates and times, send confirmation letters, and, after the meeting, send thank you notes. The library will also need staff to greet the "customers" the day of each session.

A series of questions and issues are targeted and, through facilitated probing and interaction, a high volume of information is gleaned from the group. Usually the beginning questions focus on general usage and then move onto more salient issues specific, in this case, to children's and parents' services. The goals of the focus session are to get the patrons to talk, to provide perceptions of the library or a specific service, to learn about library and information needs of patrons, and to elicit criticisms or concerns they may have about the library.

In designing a focus group around the issue of service to families and young children, several target groups could be organized: parents, community professionals who work with families and young children, and teachers/child care workers. The following questions could be considered.

Library Use

How do you use the library and how often? Do you use the library for your own needs? For your children's needs? For your professional needs?

Programs

Do you attend children's programs with your child? What do you think about the programming for children? Do you think there is too little, too much, or just the right amount of programming? What is your favorite program? Your child's favorite?

Do you attend parent programs? Do you use any other local service to satisfy parent program needs? Would you like more parent programs? Can you make suggestions?

Services

On a scale of one to ten, how would you rate the library in reference to your information needs as a parent? Would you ask the librarian for information about a local school or camp? About a childhood illness? About traveling with children? When you think of gathering information concerning your child/children, would you consider calling the library?

Collections

What collections do you make use of? Are you aware that there is a parents' collection in the children's department? Have you ever used material from this collection? Do you know that there are special databases that focus on parents? Would you be interested in more information about the resources that the library has for parents?

Staff

Are you familiar with the staff? Do you know the children's librarian? How would you rate the quality of the staff? How do you feel about coming to the library?

There can be problems with focus groups. The facilitator may not be able to shift the thinking of the group when misinformation is brought into the discussion without compromising his/her neutrality. In addition, the information generated by the focus group may be difficult to analyze. Finally, the focus group may become distracted and unable to return to the topic at hand.

Ultimately the focus group can provide good supplementary information but cannot usually stand alone as an interpretation of user needs, user satisfaction, or an understanding of the impact of services on users. Observing a focus group discussion or having access to a verbal summary or written impression of comments from a focus group can have an important impact on staff attitude. Hearing what users have to say about services and accessibility can be surprising. Information culled from focus groups may form the basis of a questionnaire designed to gather a wider and more objective response on use of and satisfaction with services and programs.

REVIEW AND SELF-ASSESSMENT

Quality review is another method to examine or evaluate current library service. The quality review is designed to assess the quality of library programs and to determine if teaching and learning occurs during the interaction between librarians and users. Chapter 9 of this book focuses on the role that public libraries play in the teaching and learning of parents as well as other community agency personnel. The quality review process can add validity to this role. Library staff who are open to the process can work on their own or invite outside reviewers to participate. The outside reviewers could include parents, caregivers, agency representatives, librarians from other settings, early childhood educators, pediatricians, and other participants who can add expertise to the process.

The strategies used to conduct a quality review may include, but are not limited to, the following.

Direct Observation

Environment for family services: How does the environment work as a center of learning for parents, children, and other community services?

Group size; Adult-Staff Ratio; Parent/Child-Staff Ratio: Are programs/services individualized; do staff work appropriately; are staff comfortable in the role of teachers?

Program Content: Can the observer determine the theoretical basis of what is being taught/learned? Is the program design promoting interaction and active learning? Does the librarian understand the adult learner? The young child?

Collections: Are materials multicultural and diverse in experience, language, family representation, and format? Are materials available to address the information needs of parents? Are materials appropriate for early childhood learning and development?

Parent Participation: Are parents involved in direct programming with and without their children? Are programs and services designed with input from parents? Is there a parents' advisory board or focus group?

Comprehensive Service: Is the children's librarian a member of a community or agency board? Do librarians regularly attend or participate in training and activities with other professionals who work with families? Do they provide access to a community information and referral file to help parents?

Administration: Is the librarian well versed in policies that affect children and parents, such as circulation policies, an unattended children policy, library card registration? Are child care givers and grandparents allowed to participate in programs in lieu of parents? Does the budget reflect separate funds for parent programs and collections?

Direct Examination

Analysis of documentation including written policies

Examination of other measurements such as surveys, output measures, focus group analysis, interviews, etc.

Examination of program or reference service products, such as homemade toys, family child care plan, set of questions prepared for a pediatrician or bibliography on child development

Attendance at programs

Analysis of funding

Credentials of staff

Collaborations with other agencies/groups/services

The quality review will lead you to develop a program of "better practice" in serving families through the public library. Better practice:

- is individualized, varied;
- uses a rich array of resources and learning opportunities;
- reflects the strengths, interests, diversity, and needs of families;
- fosters continuous individual development, creativity, critical thinking, cooperation, problem-solving skills, and parenting skills;
- implements appropriate policies, programs, and services;
- strengthens families and involves partnerships with parents and other like groups and agencies; and
- is flexible, accessible, and responsive to families (Feinberg and Feldman, work in progress).

A Parent Education and Support Checklist, designed by an Interagency Group on Parent Education and Support in New York State, is provided in Appendix G. This checklist provides professionals with recommended basic elements of a parent education and support program. It is intended to help providers infuse high quality parenting services into their program settings and can be used as a self-assessment tool for providers currently delivering services. It is an excellent review checklist for librarians who are offering parent support services and provides simple guidelines for improving and expanding services to families.

Goals, objectives, and action plans should all have evaluation as their planning partner. What method of evaluation, staff involvement in evaluation, time, audience, ultimate objectives and goals, and tools to use when conducting an evaluation are all part of the decision making process that looks at the question, "What Do I Need to Know?"

SAMPLE EVALUATION PROCESS

A small public library wants to evaluate a parent-to-parent electronic discussion group that the library supports and monitors on the community's freenet. The group serves parents of young children, from birth to age eight. The group has been in effect for one year, and the children's librarian, who regularly monitors the group and adds names to the listserv, questions the value of the information provided by other parents. She has recommended that the discussion group be changed to an electronic reference service.

Before making a decision, the library director decides to evaluate the existing service. The objectives of this evaluation are to determine the reasons people participate in the electronic discussion group and to determine the impact of participation on parent information. The library director does a review of the evaluation literature to decide on the evaluation activities that would support these two objectives.

The library director determines the number of parents of young children in the service area. About 15 percent of these families are currently signed onto the listserv. The library director posts a series of closed questions to the listserv. The library director also posts a series of closed questions to a control group using a babysitting exchange service on the community's freenet.

The library director follows up the survey with in-depth interviews with fifteen families participating in the discussion group. Students from a local college volunteer to conduct the interviews. Six interviews are conducted electronically and nine are face-to-face interviews. At the conclusion of the interviews the electronic discussion takes up the subject of why parents participate in the group.

As a result of the evaluation the library director determines that the electronic discussion group serves an invaluable purpose in the library's community. Through the evaluation, she can summarize some of the findings:

1. Isolated parents find it a great relief to post questions and respond to the questions of others whenever time allows. Parents enjoy reading the comments of others and view the discussion as a valuable source of information.
2. Many parents refer other parents to appropriate agencies or resources held by the library or others. They also encourage others to seek the help of a professional such as a pediatrician.

3. Many members of the control group were not aware of the parent-to-parent discussion group and signed on as a result of the closed questionnaire.

It was determined that the children's librarian needed to take a more active role in the promotion and monitoring of the discussion. The library also involved other agencies in the process to share the responsibility. One hundred percent of the families participating in the discussion group had become or continued to be library users. Of the fifteen families participating in the in-depth interview, fourteen were now involved in other parent education or involvement activities, read more about parenting, or had located parenting resources on the Internet.

The evaluation proved this was an important service. It might have shown that the children's librarian's instincts were right and the library needed a straight electronic reference service for parents. The library director selected the appropriate evaluation tool, used expertise (in this case the director's own expertise) to implement the evaluation, and completed the evaluation with a minimum of cost by using the freenet and volunteers. The director did not fall into the trap of gathering unnecessary information that can complicate or slow down the evaluation process. The objectives of the evaluation were met. Ultimately the service was improved.

RESOURCES

Chelton, Mary K. "Evaluation of Children's Service." *Library Trends* (Winter 1987): 463–484.

Hernon, Peter, and Charles R. McClure. *Evaluation and Library Decision Making.* Ablex, 1990.

Programming for Very Young Children. Chicago: American Library Association, Association for Library Service to Children, 1980.

Robbins, Jane, et al. *Evaluation Strategies and Techniques for Public Library Children's Services; A Sourcebook.* Madison, WI: School of Library and Information Studies, University of Wisconsin, 1990.

Van House, Nancy A., et al. *Output Measures for Public Libraries,* Second Edition. Chicago: American Library Association, 1987.

Walter, Virginia A. *Output Measures for Public Library Service to Children.* Chicago: American Library Association, 1992.

Young, Diana. "Evaluating Children's Services." *Public Libraries* (Spring, 1984): 20–22.

REFERENCES

Evans, Ellis. *Program Evaluation in Early Childhood/Special Education: A Self-Help Guide for Practitioners*. WESTAR Series Paper #13. Monmouth, OR: Western States Technical Assistance Resource, 1982.

Feinberg, Sandra, and Sari Feldman. *The Early Childhood Review Initiative for Public Libraries*. Chicago: American Library Association Loletta D. Fyan Grant, work in progress. Contact: Sandra Feinberg, Middle County Public Library, Centereach, NY 11720.

11 BUILDING A FAMILY SUPPORT COLLECTION: GUIDELINES

This chapter was coauthored by Barbara Jordan, Head of the Suffolk Family Education Clearinghouse, Middle Country Public Library, Centereach, New York.

When children's services departments shift their patron focus to include work with parents and professionals who serve families, it quickly becomes apparent that parenting and family support materials need to be made accessible within the children's department or in close proximity. One study (1985) conducted by the children's services department of Urbana (Illinois) Free Library found that 29 percent of their reference and readers' advisory questions were asked by adults (Harrington, 1985, p. 65). This study found that adults tended to ask complex readers' advisory questions, reference questions, and questions concerning library policies and practices. With the development of collections and services for this clientele—parents and adults who work with children—the children's department will see this percentage increase. Queries on child rearing and childhood problems, community resources, language development, discipline, developmentally appropriate activities, and specific health and disability issues will soon become the norm.

This expanded service necessitates that children's librarians accept responsibility for ordering and organizing books, videos, periodicals, Internet resources, and ephemeral materials aimed at parents and professionals. A community information resource file either on computer or in paper becomes a necessity. A new philosophy of children's services that blends service to young children and families with the traditional role of children's librarian will evolve with time, training, and resource development. The children's librarian may also work in partnership with an adult services librarian who shares a common philosophy and vision of family services.

This new philosophy of family services is entirely consistent with the emergence of the family support movement in the United States. Three of the family support movement's basic assumptions are that

1. the capacity of parents to raise their children effectively is influenced by their own development;
2. information about child development enhances parents' capacity to respond appropriately to children; and

117

3. families that receive support become empowered to advocate on their own behalf.

Bernice Weissbourd states that "In every instance, the family resource and support perspective underscores the importance of the fact that a child's sense of self is inextricably tied to that of his or her parent and that the quality of the parent's life is affected by the resources and environment of the community in which the family lives." (Kagan and Weissbourd, 1994, pp. 32–33). In tracing the national movement toward integrating services for children and families, Sharon Lynn Kagan looks at the growth of family support programs which "are committed to serving the entire family, to preventing social problems and intervening before problems escalate, and to broad-based community engagement." (Kagan, 1993, pp. 61–62)

Public libraries are in a wonderful position to participate in the family support movement by providing what is most empowering to parents: information. Providing access to information that will assist individuals to become more successful parents and better advocates for their children exemplifies public library service at its best. This chapter provides guidelines for building a family support collection, practical strategies for collection development, criteria for developing a family support collection policy, and a listing of professional tools that can help in this endeavor.

GUIDELINES TO BUILDING A FAMILY SUPPORT COLLECTION

OBJECTIVES

Description of clientele to be served

Will the collection serve parents only? Will it be limited to parents of young children or include materials on issues related to the parenting of school-age children and/or adolescents, as well as the expectant parent (i.e., pregnancy and childbirth)? Will it be targeting a diverse multicultural/multilingual population? Will materials for professionals who work with families be included? What types of professionals will the collection be aimed at—early childhood educators, day care providers, social service and health professionals, academics in related fields, or recreation specialists?

Purpose of the collection

This will require examining questions and issues concerning why the library and, more particularly, the children's department is going to provide this collection. Why should this collection be supported as a special collection by the library? How is this collection related to the library's goals and mission? Is the library committed to a philosophy of community responsibility for family support such as "It takes a whole village to raise a child"? Is there a general awareness that one can't assume that a new parent knows even the most basic information about infant care, or that the parent of an adolescent knows about communication skills? Is it recognized that not even the most well-informed parent has at hand the specific knowledge needed to parent a medically-challenged or handicapped child? Is the children's librarian the most logical and natural information specialist for parents in their parenting roles due to the trust and rapport already established? Is the decision influenced by good marketing strategy that targets a specific audience and places the collection where the audience is most likely to use it? Is there a third choice, neither children's or adult, that is the logical department of the library?

Definition of family support materials

Will the collection focus on general family and parenting issues or will it attempt to cover special needs such as parenting children with disabilities and chronic health problems, home schooling, teenage pregnancy and parenting, and child abuse and family dysfunction? Will it embrace the full range of modern family configurations—divorced, single-parent and stepparent families, adoptive and foster families, and homosexual parents? Though it may be of interest to other professionals who serve families, will the collection be geared primarily for the lay person or will it also contain research materials and educational and professional journals?

Description of the family support collection

In what formats will information be made available through this collection, i.e., books, videos, pamphlets, periodicals, audiocassettes, kits, electronic resources? Will it contain reference materials? Will a special vertical file be maintained?

SCOPE

1. Which general subject areas will be the main focus of the collection; e.g., child development, reading and language activities, discipline and parenting skills, play and

school issues? What other areas will be minimally collected, e.g., childhood illness, physical fitness, music education, family travel, self-esteem, communication, death and bereavement, sexuality education, divorce, single- and stepparenting issues?

2. Will any form of needs assessment or consumer survey be conducted to solicit input? Will professionals from other disciplines be utilized to suggest or assess materials for collection?

3. Will only popular titles be included? To what level will the collection be developed: beginning, research, comprehensive? Will these levels vary by the specific subject? Is there a long range plan for the development of this collection?

4. What professional materials will be available to support family focused library services, including children's programming, childhood environments, collection development, interagency cooperation, and parent education?

5. In addition to the library professionals, are there any special facilities or early childhood services within the library locale that dictate the development of a particular special collection?

6. Will school professionals be using the collection? Will consideration be given to school curriculum and teaching materials for these professionals?

7. Will a reference collection be provided that focuses on parent and professional issues? Will access to specialized databases be provided as part of this service? What about Internet access to resources that focus on family support?

8. What limits will be placed on the family support collection with regard to physical formats, purchasing multiple copies of titles, foreign language materials, and imprint dates? Will any items or topics be restricted or specifically not collected?

9. Will items that are written specifically for children but are most effective when introduced to the child by a parent be included within the parents' collection?

SIZE

1. What room is available to house the collection? What is the maximum capacity? Space may dictate the breadth of the collection.

2. Are collection guidelines clearly defined between the adult and children's departments? When a family support collection is first being developed, philosophical

    problems may occur around turf issues. Decisions about which department is responsible for making the materials available and to what extent need to be clearly stated.

3. Does a library with centralized audiovisual collections preclude the inclusion of video and audio materials in the family support collection?

4. What is the children's department's relationship to the adult department, other agencies, and other libraries with regard to resource sharing? These relationships may influence the size of the collection.

LOCATION AND ORGANIZATION

1. Where will the collection be housed—in the children's department or the adult department? Have parents' patterns of use been considered in locating the collection within the library? Will the collection be located where parents can keep an eye on young children? Will toys be available to occupy children while parents browse?

2. Which department will oversee the development of the collection? Will this include selection and acquisition of materials, procedure development, staff training, marketing and promotion, and evaluation? If the library has a central library and branches, how is the collection organized for the best accessibility? Which building will house the family support collection? Will branches have a separate collection or access to the main collection?

3. If in the children's department, will the collection duplicate materials already in the adult department? If so, how will this be coordinated? Will a certain amount of collection overlap be tolerated? Who provides database searching for parent inquiries? Can the children's department access sophisticated electronic resources for these inquiries?

4. Assuming interdepartmental issues are resolved, what mechanisms will be in place to identify the existence and location of the collection wherever the adult's point of entry such as a clear location field in the computerized catalog?

5. Will an advisory committee be utilized? Will this include library staff from other departments and representative users of the collection such as parents and professionals? What will their role be on the advisory group? Will they recommend and review materials, advise on policies and procedures, assist in promotion and marketing of collection, and/or participate in fundraising?

SELECTION AND RETENTION OF MATERIALS

Selection considerations

- Who is responsible for selecting materials?
- Is there a separate budget for parenting and family resource materials?
- Can patrons request and reserve items of interest?
- What guidelines will be used for deciding what titles will be ordered?
- What items are too specialized for the collection and which, if any, will be ordered in multiples?

Selection criteria

- Quality/clarity/accuracy of the material
- Demonstrated or anticipated demand for subject matter
- Strengths and weaknesses in present collection
- Usefulness of item within context of present collection
- Favorable reviews (a variety of specialized review media must be considered) or inclusion of title in bibliographies
- Author's reputation/credentials
- Currency of topic
- Reputation of publisher or distributor
- Format of item under consideration
- Date and price of publication

Retention considerations

- How long are materials housed in the collection and what criteria is used to consider retaining older materials?
- When new editions are published, will they automatically replace older editions?
- Are more stringent standards placed on medical/health information for currency and suitability for retention?
- Who weeds the collection?

Weeding criteria

- Imprint date of publication
- Historical significance of publication
- Availability of subject material in more recent works
- Physical condition of publication
- Content relative to new research findings, modern social standards
- Availability of material in other formats

WRITING A FAMILY SUPPORT COLLECTION POLICY

After deciding about the various issues outlined above, it may be helpful to write a family support collection policy. Essential elements of a policy could include:

Objectives
Subject Scope
Size of Collection
Types of Materials in Collection
Target audience
Who is Responsible for Collection
Location
Circulation criteria

SAMPLE POLICIES

Sample #1
The Family Resource Collection of the _____ Library, located in the Children's Services Department, is designed to promote the health and stability of families by providing access to current resource materials of interest to parents/caregivers and family service professionals. The collection consists of reference materials; a large and comprehensive circulating collection of books, videocassettes, audiocassettes, magazines, and newsletters; a pamphlet file; and a display rack of free handout materials. A computerized information and referral database of community resources is available at the library or by dial-up access via modem from home or agency. Maintained by the Children's Department, the collection is available to _____ Library District residents. Print materials circulate for twenty-one days, audiovisual materials for seven days. Online database searches are conducted at the discretion of the librarian as time permits.

Sample #2

SUFFOLK • FAMILY • EDUCATION
CLEARINGHOUSE

Middle Country Public Library

The Suffolk Family Education Clearinghouse is a countywide resource center for professionals working with children, youth, and families in Suffolk County, New York. Housed and administered by the Children's Services Department of the Middle Country Public Library, the Clearinghouse provides access to print and audiovisual material in the form of books, video and audio cassettes, general interest and research periodicals, multimedia kits, curricula, posters, and therapeutic games. It is designed to support families by assisting the professionals working directly with families in school and community settings. Reference and program planning assistance is provided by prior telephone request and appointment only. A current public library card from any Suffolk County library is required to borrow materials. Print items circulate for twenty-one days, nonprint items for seven days. Online and other specialized database searches are conducted at the discretion of the librarian as time permits. ERIC and Periodical Abstracts may be searched by the Clearinghouse user independently.

Sample #3

The PIRL (Parent Information Resource Library) is a comprehensive one-stop information source for parents, caregivers, and agency personnel located in the Hazard Branch of the Onondaga County Public Library in Syracuse, New York. The intent of the PIRL is to promote information and library resources as tools to help prevent the occurrence of developmental disabilities, to assist in early intervention, to provide parenting information for all families, and to empower families with children having developmental delays and disabilities. The services include a multimedia, multicultural collection for adults of all reading and learning levels. Library staff hold regular consultation sessions with parents and professionals at the PIRL and access the Internet to increase access to current information on parenting and related topics. Print items circulate for twenty-one days, nonprint items circulate for seven days.

THE PARENTS' COLLECTION

Circulating collections for parents may target the following subject areas and include titles on:

child development (mental, physical, and emotional)
common childhood illnesses
discipline and parenting skills
infant care and child rearing
language and reading activities
nutrition and physical fitness
speech and language development
children's fears
toilet training
home schooling
sleep problems
emotional disorders of childhood
children and the media
death and bereavement
home and school issues
working parents
developmentally appropriate activities for children

divorce, single parent, gay family, and stepfamily issues
communication and family relationships
family travel and recreation
safety and health
parenting children with special needs
sibling relationships
pregnancy and prenatal care
stress and depression in children
sexuality education
children's parties
children's toys, furniture, rooms, and equipment
adolescent issues
child abuse and family dysfunction
adoption and foster care
alcohol and substance abuse
specific health and disability topics

THE PROFESSIONAL COLLECTION

Basic collections for professionals who work with families and young children may include:

developmentally appropriate environments and activities
parent/teacher communications
early childhood curriculum materials
art and recreational activities
creative movement and music activities
parent education programs and curriculums
resource guides to children's books and related activities
classroom management and discipline techniques
working with pregnant and parenting teens
family-centered care
conflict resolution and multicultural education
model family support programs and services
child care management and training
working with culturally diverse audiences
working with diverse family structures
child abuse, neglect, and family dysfunction

RESOURCES

This list of suggested topics must be viewed within the context of the questions raised earlier in the chapter on the collection's targeted audience, size and scope. For collections focused on parents of young children and early childhood caregivers, the following titles are excellent books that provide resource lists and suggestions for building a family support collection.

Bredekamp, Sue. *Developmentally Appropriate Practice in Early Childhood Programs Serving Children From Birth Through Age 8*. Washington, DC: National Association for the Education of Young Children, 1987.
Books on child development, developmentally appropriate practices for early childhood, teaching strategies, and parent involvement. See pp.14–16, 32–33, 58–59, 79–84.

Carpenter, Kathryn H. *Sourcebook on Parenting and Child Care*. Phoenix, AZ: Oryx Press, 1995.
Thoroughly annotated, comprehensive, and selected collection development guide to parenting and family life resources from infancy through the teen years. Divided into popular and professional titles, the guide includes books, magazines and journals, important agencies and organizations, electronic resources on parenting and child care, and limited information on audiovisuals.

Cohen, Bonnie P., and Linda S. Simkin. *Library-Based Parent Resource Centers: A Guide to Implementing Programs*. New York: New York Developmental Disabilities Planning Council and the New York Library Association, 1994.
This replication guide was based on the experiences of eleven parent resource centers developed in public libraries in New York State through funding from the New York State Developmental Disabilities Planning Council. It provides a practical tool for starting such a center, including philosophy, staffing, collection development, community networking, programming for families, evaluation, and relevant forms and reading lists.

DeFrancis, Beth. *The Parents' Resource Almanac*. Holbrook, MA: Bob Adams, Inc., 1994.
Comprehensive resource guide, organized by subject, with annotated listings of books and magazines for parents and children as well as information on products, equipment, recreational facilities, mail order companies, helplines, and organizations.

Feinberg, Sandra, and Kathleen Deerr. *Running a Parent/Child Workshop: A How-To-Do-It Manual for Librarians*. New York: Neal-Schuman Publishers, 1995.
This practical manual for program development includes excellent suggested resource listings of books, magazines, pamphlets, and other material that focus on parenting and child development in the early childhood years. See pp. 11–16, 85–132, 150–159.

Feinberg, Sandra, Barbara Jordan, and Michele Lauer-Bader. *Parenting: An Annotated Bibliography, 1965-1987*. Metuchen, NJ: Scarecrow Press, 1995.
Comprehensive bibliography of nearly 3,000 parenting titles, including the classics of the genre, many of which are still in print and should be available in family support collections.

Greene, Ellin. *Books, Babies, and Libraries: Serving Infants, Toddlers, Their Parents and Caregivers*. Chicago: American Library Association, 1991.
One section of this very readable book is devoted to suggested resources for parent collections, selection guidelines, etc. See pp. 54–69.

Jordan, Barbara, and Noreen Stackpole. *Audiovisual Resources for Family Programming*. New York: Neal-Schuman Publishers, 1994.
Includes an annotated description and source information on more than 1,700 videos for parents and family-serving professionals on hundreds of different subjects. Search by title, subject, or series. An excellent resource for hard-to-locate information on nonprint items for family support collections.

Nuba, Hannah, Michael Searson and Deborah Lovitky Sheiman, editors. *Resources for Early Childhood: A Handbook*. New York: Garland Publishers, 1994.
Excellent resource lists of books for parents, teachers, children and early childhood professionals are cited under each chapter. The book includes chapters on all aspects of early childhood growth and development, nutrition, family issues, child abuse, child care, and early education. A wonderful source of parent and professional materials, especially for those concentrating family support collections on the early childhood years.

Steele, Barbara, and Carolyn Willard. *Guidelines for Establishing a Family Resource Library*, Second Edition. Washington, DC: Association for the Care of Children's Health, 1989.
Although written primarily for hospital-based or agency-based

family resource centers with a special focus on health and illness issues, this is a well-researched guide with useful information for anyone setting up such a library. A segment on sensitive listening skills with families is helpful, as is appendix material, including user surveys, a tool to aid in evaluating health education materials, and sample protocols for providing medical information to families.

Thurling, Jan. *Serving Families With Limited Resources: Selected Resources for Providers of Parent Education.* Canandaigua, NY: Cornell Cooperative Extension of Ontario County, 1994.
Booklet on low literacy, multicultural resources in print and video format. Although some of the items cited are from commercial sources, many are produced by Extension System, land grant university faculty. These are usually excellent, relatively inexpensive, and hard-to-locate resources.

The importance of a family support collection, easily accessible and available to all, is clear. Families and those who work with families need a great deal of support from all segments of the community, and one of the best supports is provided through information and resources. This is a fundamental service of every public library.

REFERENCES

Harrington, Janice N. "Reference Service in the Children's Department: A Case Study." *Public Library Quarterly* 6(3) (Fall 1985): 65

Kagan, Sharon Lynn. *Integrating Services for Children and Families.* New Haven, CT: Yale University Press, 1993.

Kagan, Sharon L., and Bernice Weissbourd, editors. *Putting Families First: America's Family Support Movement and the Challenge of Change.* San Francisco: Jossey-Bass, 1994.

12 BUILDING A FAMILY SUPPORT COLLECTION: PRINT AND NONPRINT RESOURCES

This chapter was written by Barbara Jordan, Head of the Suffolk Family Education Clearinghouse, and Parents' References Services at Middle Country Public Library in Centereach, New York.

A *Publishers Weekly* article that examined the explosion of parenting titles on the market today (Siegel, 1991, pp. 18–24) concluded that the baby boomer generation of parents relies heavily on advice from the experts to guide them. Parents' buying trends reveal their concern for education—books that can help them augment their child's education with stimulating home activities and particularly books that empower them to deal better with the school system. They want to parent better, or at least differently, than their parents, and so books on parenting skills, child development and discipline, particularly those that reflect new thinking and new research on the topic, are popular. Parents to be and new parents represent a strong segment of the market. Predictably, best sellers for this audience include topics on pregnancy, baby names, basic child care and feeding, toilet training, age-appropriate skills, and child behavior—with practical rather than theoretical approaches the preferred. Books on divorce, stepchildren, and single parenting remain strong, and new trends show more books looking at the moral education of children and more aimed at fathers. "These books sell because there is an increasing awareness that it is not automatic and natural to be a parent." (Siegel, 1991, p. 21).

Since the information now available for parents has exploded in recent years, perhaps the best way to stay abreast of newly available material is to regularly review subject specific ordering sources that publish for parents and family service professionals. This, and other suggestions for ordering and selection, are discussed in this chapter.

BASIC REFERENCE MATERIALS FOR PARENTS

There are certain questions that propel parents into the library looking for specific answers. Whether the collection has a specially designated reference section or not, anticipating these questions by having appropriate titles readily available in the collection will equip the children's librarian to dispatch these questions quickly and successfully. The following sections offer topics and possible reference selections for a comprehensive library collection.

READY REFERENCE

Sources such as Franck and Brownstone's *The Parent's Desk Reference* (Englewood Cliffs, NJ: Prentice Hall, 1991); Starer's *Who To Call: The Parent's Sourcebook* (New York: William Morrow, 1992); and DeFrancis' *Parents' Resource Almanac* (Holbrook, MA: Bob Adams, Inc., 1994) are compendiums of information that can often make further search unnecessary.

CHILDREN'S LITERATURE GUIDES

Whether utilized by the parent or the librarian, *A to Zoo: Subject Access to Children's Picture Books* (New Providence, RI: R.R.Bowker, 1993); *The Bookfinder: A Guide to Children's Literature About the Needs and Problems of Youth Aged 2–15* (Circle Pines, MN: American Guidance Service, 1994); and Rudman et al.'s *Books to Help Children Cope With Separation and Loss* (New Providence, RI: R.R.Bowker, 1993) can help find just the right book for that special time.

DIRECTORIES OF YOUTH SERVING ORGANIZATIONS

Erickson's *Directory of American Youth Organizations* (Minneapolis: Free Spirit Publishing, 1994).

ENCYCLOPEDIA, TEXTBOOK AND/OR DICTIONARY ON CHILD DEVELOPMENT

Medical Encyclopedia/References on Childhood Illness

There are many, including the *Marshall Cavendish Encyclopedia of Family Health* (New York: Marshall Cavendish, 1993); *Mayo Clinic Family Health Book* (New York: William Morrow, 1990) and *The Columbia University College of Physicians and Surgeons*

Complete Home Medical Guide (New York: Crown Publishers, 1989). For more extensive collections: *Jolly's Diseases of Children* (Boston: Blackwell Scientific, 1991); the *Encyclopedia of Genetic Disorders and Birth Defects* (New York: Facts on File, 1991); *Diseases of the Nervous System in Childhood* (New York: Cambridge University Press, 1992); *Infectious Diseases of Children* (Baltimore: Mosby Year Book, 1992) and *Schaffer and Avery's Diseases of the Newborn* (Philadelphia: W.B. Saunders, 1991)

TESTING RESOURCES

McCollough's *Testing and Your Child: What You Should Know About 150 of the Most Common Medical, Educational, and Psychological Tests* (New York: Plume, 1992) or the more esoteric *Tests: A Comprehensive Reference for Assessments in Psychology, Education and Business*, edited by Sweetland and Keyser (Austin, TX: Pro-Ed, 1986).

CONSUMER GUIDES FOR PARENTS

Guides to the best toys, videos, software, equipment, etc. There are many but the key is currency.

GUIDES TO SCHOOLS, FACILITIES, AND EQUIPMENT FOR CHILDREN WITH SPECIAL NEEDS

Caring for Kids With Special Needs: Residential Programs for Children and Adolescents (Princeton, NJ: Peterson's Guides, 1994); the Grey House Publishing series of guides including *Complete Directory for People With Chronic Illness* (Lakeville, CT: Grey House Publishing, 1994) and *Complete Directory for People With Disabilities* (Lakeville, CT: Grey House Publishing, 1991); the *BOSC Directory: Facilities for People With Learning Disabilities* (Congers, NY: BOSC Publishers, 1994); and the *Directory for Exceptional Children: A Listing of Educational and Training Facilities* (Boston: Porter Sargent, 1994).

CHILDREN'S MEDICATIONS

PDR Family Guide to Prescription Drugs (Montvale, NJ: Medical Economics Data, 1994); Coppola's *The Children's Medicine Chest* (New York: Doubleday, 1993); or Webber's *Children's Medications Guide Book* (Englewood Cliffs, NJ: Prentice Hall, 1993).

LEGAL ISSUES FOR PARENTS

Sources on homeschooling laws, custody, adoption and education law include *Educational Rights of Children With Disabilities: A Guide to Federal Law* (Horsham, PA: LRP Publications, 1991).

LOCALLY PUBLISHED GUIDES TO CAMPS, RECREATION FACILITIES, FAMILY ACTIVITIES, ETC. IN YOUR GEOGRAPHIC AREA.

GRANT AND FUNDING SOURCES

COMMUNITY INFORMATION AND REFERRAL FILE FOR REFERRALS TO LOCAL AGENCIES AND SERVICES

This file would include the "people" resources that are available in the community to provide that next level of support to families.

GOVERNMENT PUBLICATIONS

Particularly those available from sources like state education, social service, and health departments that provide information on statewide curriculum guidelines, comparative educational statistics from district to district, local health regulations, and entitlement program benefit information. This and other information for families published by these sources is valuable for parents and often very difficult for the average citizen to locate. These state-level agencies usually have publication departments that can provide lists of available documents, reports, etc. that can be ordered free of charge.

STANDARD SOURCES FOR PARENTING BOOKS

In order to have the broadest appeal, information should be available in a variety of formats. Each has its own strengths and may serve the needs of different members of the community. Usually considered the backbone of the collection, it is generally assumed that the book collection will be organized using the same classification and subject heading system as the rest of the library. A specially designed spine label can help to reinforce the identity of the family support collection for the user and make sorting and shelving easier for the staff. Thematic book displays can enhance user interest.

Standard reviewing sources that are traditionally utilized for general library ordering are a good place to start. *Booklist, Library Journal*, and *Publishers Weekly* all include reviews of popular trade book titles on parenting, child development, family life, and health issues that are aimed at or of interest to parents and professionals. Look for them primarily under the "Psychology," "Education," "Home Economics," "Health and Medicine," and "Social Sciences" adult nonfiction reviews. The newest titles by well-known authors and the hottest topics most likely to be featured on the talk shows and parent columns in the newspaper will be reviewed in these standard library reviewing sources. Because they are most likely to get the most media attention, these may also be the most requested titles by parents. So be forewarned and consider these seriously for purchase within the parameters of the other criteria mentioned in Chapter 11.

Regular perusals of the parenting or family issues section at a good bookstore can also be helpful. The most current and, it is assumed, the publishers' most marketable titles can be given a hands-on review. Remember, if you saw them at the bookstore, invariably so have many of your patrons. Again, be prepared for requests for many of these titles.

If the library—indeed, if your family support collection—subscribes to magazines and newsletters aimed at parents or on subjects of interest to parents and family service professionals, these are excellent sources of new material in book, pamphlet, audio, and video format. Many regularly include bibliographies or recommended reading sections, reviews of new resources, or references to important new titles in the context of their feature articles. Have someone on staff assigned to review specific periodicals on a regular basis, noting new and recommended titles for purchase. A listing of recommended basic newsletters and periodicals appears later in this chapter.

SPECIAL CATALOGS FOR PARENT AND PROFESSIONAL MATERIALS

Often the best way of learning about new resources for a family support collection is to regularly review catalogs of subject-specific ordering sources that publish for parents and family-serving professionals. If room can be found, it's a good idea to organize these catalogs alphabetically in file drawers. They can be invaluable to have on hand when searching for materials on a specific subject. The following are some of the best family and parent ordering sources by subject.

ADOPTION

Tapestry Books, P.O. Box 359, Ringoes, NJ 08551–0359; 800–765–2367

ADVOCACY FOR CHILDREN AND FAMILIES

Child Welfare League of America, 440 First Street, NW, Washington, DC 20001–2085; 202–638–2952

Children's Defense Fund 25 E Street, NW, Washington, DC 20001; 202–628–8787

Family Resource Center, 200 S. Michigan Avenue, Chicago, IL 60604; 312–341–0900

National Black Child Development Institute, 1023 15th Street NW, Washington, DC 20005; 202–387–1281

BOOKS AND READING

American Library Association, 50 East Huron Street, Chicago, IL 60611; 800–545–2433

International Reading Association, P.O. Box 8139, Newark, DE 19714–8139; 302–731–1600

Family Literacy Center, Indiana University, 2805 East 10th Street, Bloomington, IN 47408–2698; 812–855–5847

Reading is Fundamental (RIF) 600 Maryland Avenue SW, Washington, DC 20024–2520; 202–287–3220

CHILD ABUSE

Kidsrights, 10100 Park Cedar Drive, Charlotte, NC 28210; 800–892–KIDS

National Committee for the Prevention of Child Abuse (NCPCA), 200 State Road, South Deerfield, MA 01373–0200; 800–835–2671

Pueblo Distribution Center, 649 Main Street, Groveport, OH 43125; 800–858–5222

CHILD CARE AND EARLY CHILDHOOD EDUCATION

Building Blocks, 38W567 Brindlewood, Elgin, IL 60123; 800–233–2448

ERIC Clearinghouse on Elementary and Early Childhood Education, University of Illinois, 805 West Pennsylvania Avenue, Urbana, IL 61801; 217–333–1386

Gryphon House, P.O. Box 207, Beltsville, MD 20704; 800–638–0928

High/Scope Press, 600 North River Street, Ypsilanti, MI 48198–2898; 313–485–2000

National Association for the Education of Young Children (NAEYC), 1509 16th Street NW, Washington, DC 20036–1426; 800–424–2460

Redleaf Press, 450 North Syndicate, Suite 5, St. Paul, MN 55104–4125

Warren Publishing House, P.O. Box 2250, Everett, WA 98203; 800–773–7240

DEATH AND BEREAVEMENT

Centering Corporation, 1531 North Saddle Creek Road, Omaha, NE 68104–5064; 402–553–1200

Compassionate Friends, P.O. Box 3696, Oak Brook, IL 60522–3696; 708–990–0010

DISABILITY AND HEALTH ISSUES

American Foundation for the Blind, 11 Penn Plaza, New York, NY 10001; 212–502–7600

American Printing House for the Blind, P.O. Box 6085, Louisville, KY 40206–0085; 800–223–1839

Alexander Graham Bell Association for the Deaf, 3417 Volta Place NW, Washington, DC 20007–2778; 202–337–5220

American Academy of Pediatrics, P.O. Box 927, Elk Grove Village, IL 60009–0927; 800–433–9016

Association for the Care of Children's Health (ACCH), 7910 Woodmont Avenue, Bethesda, MD 20814–3015; 301–654–6549 or 800–808–ACCH

Autism Society of North Carolina, 3300 Woman's Club Drive, Raleigh, NC 27612–4811; 919–571–8555

Barnes & Noble Special Needs Collection, 122 Fifth Avenue, New York, NY 10010; 212–633–3458

Blind Children's Center, 4120 Marathon Street, Los Angeles, CA 90029; 800–222–3566 or 213–664–2153

Books on Special Children (BOSC), P.O. Box 305, Congers, NY 10920–0305; 914–638–1236

Charles C. Thomas, 2600 South First Street, Springfield, IL 62794–9265; 800–258–8980

Communication/Therapy Skill Builders, P.O. Box 42050–TS5, Tucson, AZ 85733; 800–866–4446

Epilepsy Foundation of America, 4351 Garden City Drive, Landover, MD 20785; 301–577–0100

Health Education Associates, 8 Jan Sebastian Way, Sandwich, MA 02563; 508–888–8044

National Association for Parents of the Visually Impaired, P.O. Box 317, Watertown, MA 02272; 800–562–6265

National Association of the Deaf, 814 Thayer Avenue, Silver Spring, MD 20910; 301–587–1788

National Down Syndrome Society, 666 Broadway, New York, NY 10012; 800–221–4602

National Information Center for Children and Youth With Disabilities (NICHCY), P.O. Box 1492, Washington, DC 20013–1492; 800–695–0285

National Maternal and Child Health Clearinghouse, 8201 Greensboro Drive, McLean, VA 22102–3810; 703–821–8955

National Organization for Rare Disorders (NORD), P.O. Box 8923, New Fairfield, CT 06812–8923; 203–746–6518

Paul H. Brookes, P.O. Box 10624, Baltimore, MD 21285–0624; 800–638–3775

TASH: The Association for Persons With Severe Handicaps, 29 West Susquehanna Avenue, Baltimore, MD 21204; 410–828–8274

Tourette Syndrome Association, 42–40 Bell Boulevard, Bayside, NY 11361; 718–224–2999

Visually Impaired Preschool Services, 1229 Garvin Place, Louisville, KY 40203; 502–636–3207

VORT Corporation, P.O. Box 60880, Palo Alto, CA 94306; 415–322–8282

Woodbine House, 6510 Bells Mill Road, Bethesda, MD 20817; 800–843–7323

Young Adult Institute, 460 West 34th Street, New York, NY 10001; 212–563–7474

EDUCATION

Association for Childhood Education International, 111501 Georgia Avenue, Wheaton, MD 20902; 800–423–3563

Council for Exceptional Children, 1920 Association Drive, Reston, VA 22091–1589; 703–620–3660

National Education Association, P.O. Box 509, West Haven, CT 06516; 203–934–2669

National PTA, 330 North Wabash Avenue, Chicago, IL 60611–3690; 312–670–6782

HOME-SCHOOLING

Holt Associates, 2269 Massachusetts Avenue, Cambridge, MA 02140; 617–864–3100

Home Education Press, P.O. Box 1083, Tonasket, WA 98855; 509–486–1351

LANGUAGE DEVELOPMENT

American Speech-Language-Hearing Association, 10801 Rockville Pike, Rockville, MD 20852; 301–897–5700

Communication/Therapy Skill Builders, P.O. Box 42050–TS5; Tucson, AZ 85733; 800–866–4446

LEARNING DISABILITIES

A.D.D. Warehouse, 300 Northwest 70th Avenue, Plantation, FL 33317; 305–792–8944

Learning Disabilities Association of America, 4156 Library Road, Pittsburgh, PA 15234; 412–341–1515

MENTAL HEALTH

American Academy of Child and Adolescent Psychiatry, 3615 Wisconsin Avenue, NW, Washington, DC 20016; 202–966–7300

Brunner-Mazel, 19 Union Square West, New York, NY 10003; 212–924–3344

Guilford Publications, 72 Spring Street, New York, NY 10012; 212–431–9800

Haworth Press, 10 Alice Street, Binghamton, NY 13904–1580; 800–342–9678

PARENT EDUCATION

Active Parenting, 810 Franklin Court, Marietta, GA 30067; 800–825–0060

American Guidance Service, P.O. Box 99, Circle Pines, MN 55014–1796; 800–328–2560

Boys Town, 13603 Flanagan Boulevard, Boys Town, NE 68010; 402–498–1111

Cambridge Parenting and Family Life, P.O. Box 2153, Charlestown, WV 25328–2153; 800–468–4227

Center for the Improvement of Child Caring, 11331 Ventura Boulevard, Studio City, CA 91604–3147; 800–325–CICC

Family Communications, 4802 Fifth Avenue, Pittsburgh, PA 15213; 412–687–2990

Family Development Resources, 3160 Pinebrook Road, Park City, UT 84060; 800–688–5822

Home Economics School Service, P.O. Box 802, Culver City, CA 90232–0802; 310–839–2436

La Leche League International, 1400 Meacham Road, Schaumburg, IL 60173; 708–519–7730

Parenting Press, P.O. Box 75267, Seattle, WA 98125; 800–992–6657

Research Press, P.O. Box 9177, Champaign, IL 61826; 217–352–3273

PREGNANCY AND CHILDBIRTH

Imprints Birth & Life Bookstore, 141 Commercial Street NE, Salem, OR 97301; 503–371–4445

Injoy Productions, 3970 Broadway, Boulder, CO 80304; 303–447–2082

International Childbirth Education Association (ICEA), P.O. Box 20048; Minneapolis, MN 55420; 800–624–4934

March of Dimes Birth Defects Foundation, 1275 Mamaroneck Avenue, White Plains, NY 10605; 914–428–7100

SAFETY

KidSafety of America, 4750 Chino Avenue, Chino, CA 91710; 800–524–1156

National Safe Kids Campaign, P.O. Box 4779, Monticello, MN 55365; 612–295–4135

SEXUALITY EDUCATION

ETR Associates, P.O. Box 1830, Santa Cruz, CA 95061–1830; 800–321–4407

STEPFAMILIES

Stepfamily Association of America, 215 South Centennial Mall, Lincoln, NE 68508; 402–477–STEP

SUBSTANCE ABUSE

Hazelden, P.O. Box 176, Center City, MN 55012–0176; 800–328–9000

Johnson Institute, 7205 Ohms Lane, Minneapolis, MN 55439–2159; 612–944–0511

OSAP Office for Substance Abuse Prevention, National Clearinghouse for Alcohol and Drug Information, P.O. Box 2345, Rockville, MD 20847–2345; 800–729–6686

Wisconsin Clearinghouse, P.O. Box 1468, Madison, WI 53701–1468; 800–322–1468

TEEN PREGNANCY AND PARENTING

Morning Glory Press, 6595–B San Haroldo Way, Buena Park, CA 90620–3748; 714–828–1998

Vida Health Communications, 6 Bigelow Street, Cambridge, MA 02139; 864–4334

SPECIALIZED CATALOGS FOR THE PROFESSIONAL COLLECTION

While many of the listed catalogs provide access to materials of interest to professionals who work with families as well as parents, there are many excellent sources directly aimed at professionals. Among the best are:

American Guidance Service, P.O. Box 99, Circle Pines, MN 55014–1796; 800–328–2560

Brunner-Mazel, 19 Union Square West, New York, NY 10003; 212–924–3344

Bureau for At-Risk Youth, 645 New York Avenue, Huntington, NY 11743; 800–999–6884

Center for the Improvement of Child Caring, 11331 Ventura Boulevard, Suite 102, Studio City, CA 91604–3147; 800–325–CICC

Family Resource Coalition, 200 South Michigan Avenue, Chicago, IL 60604; 312–341–0900

Guilford Publications, 72 Spring Street, New York, NY 10012; 212–431–9800

Haworth Press, 10 Alice Street, Binghamton, NY 13904–1580; 800–342–9678

Home Economics School Service, P.O. Box 802, Culver City, CA 90232–0802; 310–839–2436

Human Sciences Press, 233 Spring Street, New York, NY 10013–1578; 212–620–8000

Kidsrights, 10100 Park Cedar Drive, Charlotte, NC 28210; 800–892–KIDS

Paul H. Brookes, P.O. Box 10624, Baltimore, MD 21285–0624; 800–638–3775

Pro-Ed, 8700 Shoal Creek Boulevard, Austin, TX 78757–6897; 512–451–3246

Research Press, P.O. Box 9177, Champaign, IL 61826; 217–352–3273

Sage Publications, P.O. Box 5084, Newbury Park, CA 91359–9924; 805–499–0721

PERIODICALS

Magazines and newsletters written specifically for parents abound and, if extended to include titles of interest to professionals, can become a significant segment of the collection. Articles in popular journals are current and concise—a real attraction for the harried mom or dad short on time! Their eye-catching covers attract the browser and are easy reading for the less than avid reader. Titles are targeted to very specific audiences—from working moms to stay-at-home moms, parents of adopted children and parents of twins, Christian parents and home-schooling parents, single parents and stepparents, as well as parents of children with very specific disabilities and health problems. Some are focused on individual subjects like family travel or family recreation.

It would be wise to start a collection with a general parenting magazine such as *Parents Magazine* and perhaps *Exceptional Parent*, the most comprehensive titles for parents of children with special needs. *Sesame Street Parents* comes as a bonus with the children's magazine *Sesame Street Magazine* and is targeted at the parent with young children, and *PTA Today* is an excellent resource for the parents of school-age children. A title or two for the early childhood caregiver, like *Totline, Building Blocks*, or *First Teacher* will appeal to parents of young children looking for creative activities as well. The *Well-Centered Child* offers the special attraction of being presented as a camera-ready master which can be duplicated for free distribution to parents. As the collection expands, additional titles for parents and/or professionals can be considered. Again, all formats in the collection should reflect the needs of the community and the overall goals for the collection: target audience, scope, and size of collection.

The following list is included to give you an idea of the possibilities. An asterisk (*) denotes a magazine, newsletter, or journal that would be of particular interest to professionals working with families of young children, i.e., those with a more academic, policy, research, or practitioner orientation.

ACCH Advocate, Association for the Care of Children's Health, 7910 Woodmont Avenue, Bethesda, MD 20814; 301–654–6549

ADHD Report, Guilford Press, 72 Spring Street, New York, NY 10012; 800–365–7006

Adopted Child, P.O. Box 9362; Moscow, Idaho 83843; 208–882–1794

Adoptive Families, Adoptive Families of America, 3333 Highway 100 North, Minneapolis, MN 55422; 800–372–3300

American Baby, P.O. Box 53093, Boulder, CO 80322–3093; 303–604–1464

Attention!, C.H.A.D.D. (Children and Adults with Attention Deficit Disorders), 499 NW 70th Avenue, Plantation, Florida 33317; 305–587–3700

Baby Talk, 25 West 43rd Street, New York, NY 10036; 212–840–4200

Brown University Child and Adolescent Behavior Letter, 208 Governor Street, Providence, RI 02906; 800–333–7771

Building Blocks, 38W567 Brindlewood, Elgin, IL 60123; 800–233–2448

CDF Reports, Children's Defense Fund, 25 E Street NW, Washington, DC 20001; 202–628–8787

Child, P.O. Box 3176, Harlan, IA 51537; 800–777–0222

Child and Adolescent Social Work Journal, Human Sciences Press, 233 Spring Street, New York, NY 10013–1578; 212–620–8468

Child Care Information Exchange, 17916 NE 103rd Court, Redmond, WA 98052–3243; 800–221–2864

Child Development, University of Chicago Press, Journals Division, P.O. Box 37005; Chicago, IL 60637

Child Health Alert, P.O. Box 338, Newton Highlands, MA 02161; 800–238–6658

Child Health Talk, National Black Child Development Institute, 1023 15th Street, NW, Washington, DC 20005; 202–387–1281

Child Welfare, Child Welfare League of America, 440 First Street NW, Washington, DC 20001–2085; 202–638–2952

Childhood Education, Association for Childhood Education International, 11501 Georgia Avenue, Wheaton, MD 20902; 800–423–3563

Children Today, Administration for Children and Families, U.S. Department of Health and Human Services, 370 L'Enfant Promenade, SW, Washington DC 20447; 202–401–1312

Children's Voice, Child Welfare League of America, 440 First Street, NW, Suite 310, Washington, DC 20001–2085; 202–638–2952

Christian Parenting Today, P.O. Box 545, Mt. Morris, IL 60154; 800–238–2221

Copycat, P.O. Box 081546, Racine, WI 53408–1546; 414–634–0146

Daycare & Early Education, Human Sciences Press, 233 Spring Street, New York, NY 10013–1578; 212–620–8468

Early Childhood Research Quarterly, Ablex Publishing, 355 Chestnut Street, Norwood, NJ 07648; 201–767–8450

Early Childhood Today, Scholastic, Inc., P.O. Box 54814, Boulder, CO 80322–4814; 800–544–2917

Elementary School Journal, University of Chicago Press, Journals Division, P.O. Box 37005, Chicago, IL 60637

Elementary School Guidance and Counseling, 5999 Stevenson Avenue, Alexandria, VA 22304–3300; 800-633-4931

The Endeavor, American Society for Deaf Children, 2848 Arden Way, Suite 210, Sacramento, CA 95825; 800–942–ASDC

Eric Review, 1600 Research Boulevard, Rockville, MD 20850; 800–LET-ERIC

Exceptional Children, 1920 Association Drive, Reston, VA 22091–1589; 703–264–9467

Exceptional Parent, P.O. Box 3000, Denville, NJ 07834; 800–562–1973

Families and Disability Newsletter, University of Kansas, Beach Center on Families and Disability, c/o Institute for Life Span Studies, 3111 Haworth Hall, Lawrence, KS 66045–7516; 913–864–7600

Family Day Care Bulletin, The Children's Foundation, 725 15th Street, NW, Suite 505, Washington, DC 20005–2109; 202–347–3300

Family Fun, P.O. Box 10161; Des Moines, Iowa 50340; 800–289–4849

Family Life, Straight Arrow Publishers, 1290 Avenue of the Americas, New York, NY 10104; 212–484–1616

Family Relations: Journal of Applied Family and Child Studies, National Council on Family Relations, 3989 Central Avenue NE, Minneapolis, MN 55421; 612–781–9331

Family Resource Coalition Report, 200 South Michigan Avenue, Chicago, IL 60604; 312–341–0900

Family Safety and Health, National Safety Council, 1121 Spring Lakes Drive, Itasca, IL 60143; 800–621–7615

Family Travel Times, 45 West 18th Street, 7th Floor Tower, New York, NY 10011; 212–206–0688

First Teacher, P.O. Box 6781; Syracuse, NY 13217; 800–825–0061

Future Reflections, National Federation of the Blind, 1800 Johnson Street, Baltimore, MD 21230; 410–659–9314

Gifted Child Today Magazine, P.O. Box 8813, Waco, TX 76714–8813; 800–998–2208

Growing Child/Growing Parent and *Growing Child Research Review*, Dunn & Hargitt, Inc., 22 North 2nd Street, Lafayette, IN 47902; 800–927–7289

Growing Without Schooling, Holt Associates, 2269 Massachusetts Avenue, Cambridge, MA 02140; 617–864–3100

High/Scope Resource, High/Scope Press, 600 North River Street, Ypsilanti, MI 48198–2898; 313–485–2000

Home Education, P.O. Box 1083, Tonasket, WA 98855; 509–486–1351

Journal of Child and Family Studies, Human Sciences Press, 233 Spring Street, New York, NY 10013–1578; 212–620–8468

Journal of Family Issues, Sage Publications, 2455 Teller Road, Thousand Oaks, CA 91320; 805–499–0721

LDA Newsbriefs, Learning Disabilities Association, 4156 Library Road, Pittsburgh, PA 15234; 412–341–1515

Lollipops, P.O. Box 57175, Boulder, CO 80322–7175; 800-264-9873

M A Report, Mothers of Asthmatics, Inc., 3554 Chain Bridge Road, Suite 200, Fairfax, VA 22030–2709; 800–878–4403

Mailbox: The Idea Magazine for Teachers, P.O. Box 9753, Greensboro, NC 27429–0753; 800-334-0298

Mothering, P.O. Box 1690, Santa Fe, NM 87504; 800–984–8116

Mothers Resource Guide, P.O. Box 38, South Milwaukee, WI 53172; 414–762–8303

NICHCY News Digest, P.O. Box 1492, Washington, DC 20013–1492; 800–695–0285

Parent and Preschooler Newsletter, Preschool Publications, Inc., P.O. Box 1167, Cutchogue, NY 11935–0888; 800–726–1708

Parenting Magazine, P.O. Box 52424, Boulder, CO 80321–2424; 800–234–0847

Parents Magazine, P.O. Box 3055, Harlan, IA 51593–2119; 800–727–3682

Parents Choice, Parents Choice Foundation, P.O. Box 185, Newton, MA 02168; 617–965–5913

Pediatric Mental Health, Pediatric Projects, P.O. Box 571555, Tarzana, CA 91357; 800–947–0947

Pediatrics for Parents, P.O. Box 1069, Bangor, ME 04402–1069; 207–942–6212

Practical Homeschooling, c/o Home Life, P.O. Box 1250, Fenton, MO 63026–1850; 800–346–6322

PTA Today, National PTA, 330 North Wabash Avenue, Chicago, IL 60611–3690; 312–670–6782

Sesame Street Parents Magazine, Children's Television Workshop, P.O. Box 55518, Boulder, CO 80322–5518

The Single Parent, Parents Without Partners, Inc., 401 North Michigan Avenue, Chicago, IL 60611; 312–644–6610

Stepfamilies, Stepfamily Association of America, 215 Centennial Mall South, Suite 212, Lincoln, NE 68508; 402–477–7837

Teaching K-8, P.O. Box 54808, Boulder, CO 80322–4808; 800–678–8793

Totline, Warren Publishing House, P.O. Box 2250, Everett, WA 98203; 800–773–7240

Twins Magazine, P.O. Box 12045, Overland Park, KS 66282–2045; 800–821–5533

Understanding Our Gifted, Open Space Communications, Inc., P.O. Box 18268; Boulder, CO 80308–8268; 303–444–7020

Welcome Home, (for mothers who choose to stay at home), 8310A Old Courthouse Road, Vienna, VA 22182

Well-Centered Child, Willow Tree Publications, P.O. Box 428, Naperville, IL 60566–9725; 800–453–7148

Work & Family Life, 2301 Mound Road, Jacksonville, IL 62650; 800–278–2579

Working Mother, P.O. Box 5240, Harlan, IA 51593–2740; 800–627–0690

*Young Children, National Association for the Education of Young Children, 1509 16th Street NW, Washington, DC 20036–1426; 800–424–2460

*Zero to Three, National Center for Clinical Infant Programs, P.O. Box 25494, Richmond, VA 23260–5494; 800–899–4301

AUDIOVISUALS

Fast becoming the format of choice for many parents, the market has exploded in recent years with increasingly more affordable information on videotape for parents. Just as the presence of videotape collections in libraries has attracted new constituencies to the library, this format has great potential for reaching the nonreading parent in the community. At the same time, it can appeal to the working parent with limited time who prefers information in a faster, more entertaining format. Agency professionals can use videos for group presentations and one-on-one consultation with their clients. Audiocassettes are less popular but can be helpful for working parents or professionals who commute or for the ever beleaguered car-pooling parent.

The quality of videotape material is improving but is still quite "spotty," with both excellent and poor treatments available at equally dear prices. When previewing, consider the following criteria:

accuracy and currency of the information
technical quality/appeal of the presentation
suitability for intended audience
cultural/social limitations of the presentation
length/ability to hold viewer's attention

Both *Booklist* and *Library Journal* review audiovisual material, often including titles appropriate for family support collections. But the *Video Rating Guide for Libraries*, published by ABC-CLIO (130 Cremona Drive, Santa Barbara, CA 93117; 805–968–1911) is the standout reviewing source for videotapes. Every issue of this quarterly publication includes rated reviews of titles under "Home Economics & Family Living" and elsewhere that would make wonderful additions to parent/professional collections. Jordan and Stackpole's *Audiovisual Resources for Family Programming* (Neal-Schuman, 1994) offers the most comprehensive resource directory available on audiovisual materials for parents and family professionals. And don't overlook your local experts as advisors. The social workers, early childhood teachers, nurses, psychologists, etc., with whom you will be increasingly networking around family issues, can be good sources of recommendations for video purchases. Ask them for suggestions or enlist their help in previewing videos for possible purchase. These subject specialists are well qualified to evaluate for both subject content and audience appeal.

There are many distributors of video material suitable for parent/professional collections. Don't hesitate to speak to the company's sales representative if the price is beyond your reach. They sometimes have some latitude to strike a "deal," especially if you are planning to purchase a number of titles from the same source. Also inquire about any consortium buying opportunities in your area. A number of video distributors nationwide have made available greatly reduced price offerings to public libraries in New York State when purchases are routed through this consortium. Similar buying opportunities may be available elsewhere.

Cambridge Parenting & Family Life (P.O. Box 2153, Charleston, WV 25328–2153; 800–468–4227) has assembled in a single catalog a very extensive collection of video titles for parents at reasonable prices. Other good sources of videotapes for parent/professional collections are listed below.

AIMS Media, 9710 DeSoto Avenue, Chatsworth, CA 91311–4409; 800–367–2467

Altschul Group Corporation, 1560 Sherman Avenue, Evanston, IL 60201; 800–421–2363

American Academy of Pediatrics, P.O. Box 927, Elk Grove Village, IL 60009–0927; 800–433–9016

Boys Town, 13603 Flanagan Boulevard, Boys Town, NE 68010; 402–498–1111

Cambridge Parenting & Family Life, P.O. Box 2153, Charleston, WV 25328–2153; 800–468–4227

Chip Taylor Communications, 15 Spollett Drive, Derry, NH 03038; 800–876–CHIP

Churchill Media, 6901 Woodley Avenue, Van Nuys, CA 91406–4844; 800–334–7830

Coronet/MTI, P.O. Box 4649, Columbus, OH 43216; 800–621–2131

Educational Productions, 7412 SW Beaverton Hillsdale Highway, Portland, OR 97225; 800–950–4949

ETR Associates, P.O. Box 1830, Santa Cruz, CA 95061–1830; 800–321–4407

Family Communications, 4802 Fifth Avenue, Pittsburgh, PA 15213; 412–687–2990

Fanlight Productions, 47 Halifax Street, Boston, MA 02130; 617–524–0980

Films for the Humanities & Sciences, P.O. Box 2053, Princeton, NJ 08543–2053; 609–275–1400

Injoy Productions, 3970 Broadway, Boulder, CO 80304; 303–447–2082

International Childbirth Education Association, P.O. Box 20048, Minneapolis, MN 55420; 800–624–4934

KidSafety of America, 4750 Chino Avenue, Chino, CA 91710; 800–524–1156

Kidsrights, 10100 Park Cedar Drive, Charlotte, NC 28210; 800–892– KIDS

Learner Managed Designs, P.O. Box 3067, Lawrence, KS 66046; 913–842–9088

Media Projects, 5215 Homer Street, Dallas TX 75206; 214–826–3863

PBS Video, 1320 Braddock Place, Alexandria, VA 22314–1698; 800–344–3337

Polymorph, 118 South Street, Boston, MA 02111; 800–370–3456

Research Press, P.O. Box 9177, Champaign, IL 61826; 217–352–3273

Sunburst Communications, 39 Washington Avenue, Pleasantville, NY 10570; 800–431–1934

United Learning, 6633 West Howard Street, Niles, IL 60648; 800–424–0362

Universal Health Communications, 1200 South Federal Highway, Boynton Beach, FL 33435; 800–229–1UHA

Vida Health Communications, 6 Bigelow Street, Cambridge, MA 02139; 617–864–4334

VERTICAL FILE

Arranged by subject in file drawers, this offers the best way to organize ephemeral materials like pamphlets, articles, reports, etc. If your library maintains several vertical files, or if your children's department has both a vertical file for children and one for parents, you may want to consider having special vertical file labels printed or using different colors (label or file folder) to distinguish the collections. Again, this is an aid in keeping the collection organized and also reinforces the identity of the family support collection.

For limited collections with limited budgets, building a solid vertical file can be a good way of having information readily available for parents on a wide variety of subjects without investing a great deal of money. Many national organizations provide extensive amounts of information free of charge for the asking. The "ready reference" tools listed under the reference section above list organizations on every conceivable subject of interest to parents. A selected listing of agencies and organizations that focus on family support is provided in Appendix G. Using a preprinted postcard or form letter, send for their free information and use this as the beginnings of your vertical file. Many of the subject specific ordering sources listed above also include good vertical file source material. Feinberg and Deerr's *Running a Parent/Child Workshop: A How-To-Do-It Manual for Librarians* (Neal-Schuman, 1995) includes an excellent list of sources of free and inexpensive materials for parent collections as well as a vertical file subject heading list for both beginning and extensive collections.

Unless you are using the vertical file as a replacement for a well-rounded book collection, the vertical file should be weeded regularly and reflect essentially current information, especially on those topics where information is scarce. Long before there were books on the Americans With Disabilities Act, fragile x, shaken baby syndrome, or facilitated communication, there were articles and pamphlets available on these topics. This is where the vertical file can be most useful. Because this kind of information is not at all appealing to the browser, however, it often goes overlooked unless the librarian draws the parents' attention to it.

FREE HANDOUT COLLECTION

These are inexpensive (and sometimes free) brochures that are ordered in bulk quantities and made available free for the taking to parents. They can be put out in attractive displays, and regularly rotated to encourage frequent browsing and allow for different subjects to be featured. They are great reinforcers to give out in conjunction with parenting programs. Everyone loves the idea of getting something for free, so this is a real goodwill booster. Information in brochure or flyer format, particularly those using illustrations, large print, and limited text, is often more suitable for limited literacy audiences and more apt to be taken home by nontraditional library users. Use the source list of free handouts by Feinberg and Deerr, cited above, and don't overlook the publication divisions of your state health department, department of social services, and department of alcohol and substance abuse as good places to start.

Some sources: *National Education Association* (P.O. Box 509, West Haven CT 06516; 203–934–2669); *Reading is Fundamental* (600 Maryland Avenue, SW, Suite 600, Washington, DC 20024–2520; 202–287–3220); *National Information Center for Children and Youth With Disabilities* (P.O. Box 1492, Washington, DC 20013–1492; 800–695–0285); and *American Academy of Child and Adolescent Psychiatry* (3615 Wisconsin Avenue NW, Washington, DC 20016; 202–966–7300). These sources provide reproducible masters with permission to duplicate, another good alternative.

These "free handouts" should also include brochures from local family support services like child care centers, mothers centers, parenting programs, domestic violence resources, health clinics, early intervention programs, and community recreation facilities. Most agencies welcome the exposure and will send quantities for your display rack free of charge. This is a wonderfully inexpensive way to make the library the connecting point between the parent and all of those community resources that parents may very much need but be totally unaware of. It also reminds the health and human service providers that libraries are the information centers for families and they may begin to envision other ways of connecting with you on behalf of families.

COMMUNITY INFORMATION FILE

Whether a Rolodex, card file, book directory, or sophisticated computer database, the children's librarian needs to have a mechanism for helping families to locate local community resources and services. The library may take responsibility for developing and maintaining this file; provide leadership in making this a community-wide, coalition-building endeavor; or simply make available within the library an already existing resource file developed elsewhere. Access to these "people" resources and services is a critical piece of the family support collection, augmenting the material resources and elevating the librarian's role as the community information specialist for families.

SPECIAL AUDIENCES

LIMITED LITERACY AUDIENCES

Making available information for parents with limited reading ability is particularly challenging. Look at your family support collection/area as a whole and see if you have included:

- Books on parenting topics written at a low reading level
- Videotapes and audiocassettes for parents
- Free handouts with parenting information in simple, single sheet flyer/brochure formats
- Books that may not be specifically designated "low literacy" but that have limited text and/or larger print and rely heavily on illustrations and or photographs for visual cues—e.g., Barron's board books for parents: *Your Baby: Basic Care and First Aid* (Hauppauge, NY: Barron's, 1987) and *Your Baby: The First Twelve Months* (Hauppauge, NY: Barron's, 1989); and Laurie Krasny Brown's *Baby Time* (NY: Random House, 1989) and *Toddler Time* (NY: Little Brown, 1990).
- Posters featuring simple parenting tips displayed around the children's room/family support collection area

LOW LITERACY RESOURCES

New Readers Press (Box 888, Syracuse, NY 13210; 800–448–8878) publishes a half dozen or more titles for parents written at a very basic reading level as well as a low literacy parent education curriculum, "Let's Work It Out."

Contemporary Books (Department AB95, Two Prudential Plaza, 180 North Stetson Avenue, Chicago, IL 60601–6790: 800–621–1918) publishes two series of high-interest, low-level readers for parents on common parenting issues and concerns—"Let's Read Together" and "Stories for Parents." Specify their basic skills catalog.

The *National Committee for the Prevention of Child Abuse* (200 State Road, South Deerfield, MA 01373–0200; 800–835–2671) puts out a series of very simple parenting brochures such as "Would You Like to Wear the Red or Blue Socks" and "Splash Water on Your Face."

Pueblo Distribution Center (649 Main Street, Groveport, OH 43125; 800–858–5222) publishes a set of thirty child management cards in both English and Spanish on topics such as crying, thumb-sucking, and toilet training, with limited text and written at a very basic level.

Two poster sets with limited text—"Constructive Play for Very Young Children" and "Positive Child Guidance: Tips for Better Caregiving"—are available from *J. Weston Walch*, P.O. Box 658, Portland, ME 04104–0658; 207–772–2846.

There are several good series for teen parents, a group which would also benefit from a limited text approach: the Franklin Watts "Teen Guide" Series and the Morning Glory Press "Teens Parenting" Series.

Jan Thurling's *Serving Families With Limited Resources*, listed at the end of Chapter 11; is helpful in identifying other materials for this audience.

CULTURALLY DIVERSE AUDIENCES

All libraries need to look critically at their family support collections/areas to see if they've created both an environment and a collection that reflect the cultural diversity of their communities and send a welcoming message to all families. Look at such things as the area's artwork and posters, the collection as a whole, the items selected for display, free handout material, and the families portrayed in the videos for parents. Has an attempt been made to reflect cultural diversity in these materials? If there is a significant non-English speaking population, are there materials in other languages available? Has attention been drawn to their existence?

This is admittedly not an easy task as most commercially available parenting material in either print or video format seems to be targeted at white, middle-class families. It therefore becomes even more important to locate those materials that will bring some balance to the collection. The following materials and/or sources will be of assistance.

James Comer's *Raising Black Children* (New York: Plume, 1992); Marita Golden's *Saving Our Sons: Raising Black Children in a Turbulent World* (New York: Doubleday, 1995); and Darlene and Derek Hopson's *Different and Wonderful: Raising Black Children in a Race-Conscious Society* (New York: Simon and Schuster, 1992).

Center for the Improvement of Child Caring (11331 Ventura Boulevard, Studio City, CA 91604–3147; 800–325–CICC) is the publisher of two culturally specific parent education curricula, *Effective Black Parenting* and *Los Ninos Bien Educados*.

African-American Images (1909 West 95th Street, Chicago, IL 60643; 800–552–1991) is a source of books and other materials for both children and parents, including a well-known series of books for parents and professionals by Jawanza Kunjufu.

That's My Child: Tips for African American Parents is a pamphlet published by the Black Task Force on Child Abuse and Neglect, Diocese of Brooklyn, 191 Joralemon Street, Brooklyn, NY 11201; 718–722–6000.

Highsmith's Multicultural Bookstore (P.O. Box 800, Fort Atkinson, WI 53538–0800; 800–558–2110) catalog, a resource for African Americans and other multicultural books and materials for adults and children.

Developing Cross-Cultural Competence: A Guide for Working With Young Children and Their Families is an excellent source from Paul H. Brookes Publishing Company (Box 10624, Baltimore, MD) for staff development around multicultural awareness and sensitivity.

National Black Child Development Institute (1023 15th Street NW, Washington DC 20005; 202–387–1281) is the publisher of two newsletters focusing on the health and welfare of African American children and families as well as print resources and several posters for this audience.

Working With African American Families: A Guide to Resources, is published by the Family Resource Coalition, 200 South Michigan Avenue, Chicago, IL 60604; 312–341–0900.

Many videos put out by the *Altschul Group Corporation* (1560 Sherman Avenue, Evanston, IL 60201; 800–421–2363), particularly the "Lily" Series, work well with multiculturally diverse audiences. This series and many other Altschul titles on parenting issues are also available in Spanish.

Other videos featuring culturally diverse families: *From the Crib to the Classroom,* stressing the importance of parents' involvement in their child's education, is available from PLAN Inc., 1332 G Street, SE, Washington, DC 20003; 202–547–8903; *Shaking, Hitting, and Spanking: What To Do Instead* is available from Family Development Resources, 3160 Pinebrook Road, Park City, UT 84060; the *Growing Together Series* for teen parents is available from American Guidance Service, 4201 Woodland Road, Circle Pines, MN 55014–9989; *Babies Are People Too,* describing infant and toddler development and behavior and narrated by Maya Angelou, is available from Churchill Films, 6901 Woodley Avenue, Van Nuys, CA 91406–4844; 800–334–7830. Previewing is often the only way of evaluating for multicultural appropriateness prior to purchase.

Distributors of Spanish language parenting books include: *Distribuidora Norma, Inc.* (P.O. Box 195040, Hato Rey, PR 00919–5040; 809–788–5050) *Bilingual Publications* (270 Lafayette Street, New York, NY 10012; 212–431–3500) *Hispanic Book Distributors* (1665 West Grant Road, Tucson, AZ 85745; 602–882–9484) *SBD Spanish Book Distributor* 13410 SW 81st Street, Miami, FL 33183; 305–382–1835; and *Lectorum Publications* (137 West 14th Street, New York, NY 10011; 212–929–2833).

Madera-Cinevideo (525 East Yosemite Avenue, Madera, CA 93638; 800–828–8118) is a distributor of Spanish language videos, some on parenting topics.

MELD, 123 North Third Street, Minneapolis, MN 55401; 612–332–7563) publishes "Nueva Familia," a low literacy Spanish language series of books for parents, as well as parenting audiotapes and guides in the Hmong language.

National Maternal and Child Health Clearinghouse (8201 Greensboro Drive, McLean, VA 22102–3810; 703–821–8955) publishes free information for parents and professionals including a number of brochures and pamphlets in Spanish, Chinese, Korean, Laotian, Tagalog, Samoan, and Vietnamese.

Family Development Resources (3160 Pinebrook Road, Park City, UT 84060; 800–688–5822) is the publisher of "Multicultural Parenting Education Guides," which highlight parenting values and practices, roles, and traditions in families from fourteen different cultures.

ACCESS ENHANCERS: MARKETING FOR MAXIMUM UTILIZATION

Access enhancers refer to the various ways of packaging, presenting, and guiding people to information in the family support collection in order to increase access, awareness, and utilization of materials. There are many creative and fun approaches, and librarians traditionally love finding better ways to lead people to the resources they have so painstakingly assembled. As your family support collection grows and develops, consider adding additional access enhancers to enliven, enrich and draw attention to this great library resource.

BIBLIOGRAPHIES AND BOOKLISTS

Librarians are familiar with these most traditional means of highlighting collections and subject areas within collections. Repeated requests may indicate that a handy bookmark listing or more lengthy annotated list is in order (e.g., New Baby on the Way; Siblings; Off to School; Helping Children Cope With Death; Children's Fears, etc.). The most successful lists combine books and other resources for parents with read-aloud suggestions for the child.

FAMILY SUPPORT COLLECTION BROCHURE

Designed to highlight all the components of the collection available to families, this brochure "pulls it all together" for parents. The librarian may not have the in-person opportunity to point out all the great resources assembled for parents so this is the chance to get it all down in one neat handout. This is great to have available for families new to the community, to give out to new parents through the local hospital, or to distribute through another form of library promotion to new parents. Some libraries follow birth announcements and send welcome letters and information packets to new parents at home. Provide the school district, pediatricians, and local agencies offering family services within your area with supplies of this brochure and encourage them to urge families to utilize the library. And don't assume "regulars" are thoroughly familiar with all you have to offer; marketing should be ongoing and diverse. Take nothing for granted.

KITS

Kits allow libraries to assemble a variety of materials on a specific theme or with a specific focus and package them together so they're attractive and easy to use. Target particular audiences and eliminate the time-consuming task of material selection, hoping that the best resources are on the shelf at the moment. Kits can be developed to welcome the new baby in the community, for sick-at-home kids looking for quiet activities to occupy them, or for grandparents with visiting grandchildren. The possibilities are endless.

There are two types of kits used by libraries. Some kits, designed to circulate, are packaged in sturdy plastic, cloth, or mesh bags with handles or in plastic or heavy-duty cardboard containers. Others are intended to be kept permanently by the patron. These can be packaged in large paper envelopes and printed with colorful logos, illustrations, and decorative borders for eye-catching appeal. The cost factor must be considered when determining the contents of the giveaway kits but some libraries do include a paperback or board "first book" to welcome the new baby or complimentary box of crayons along with activity sheets or coloring book in "Get Well Kits."

An *Infant Kit*, a giveaway for expectant and new parents, might include information such as the following.

> prenatal care and new baby care
> infant development and infant stimulation activities
> local childbirth preparation classes
> breastfeeding
> library programs for new parents, infants and toddlers
> nursery rhymes to stimulate early language development
> local "Mommy and Me" programs and parent support groups
> bibliography of resources for new parents
> bibliography of the very earliest books for infants
> local maternal child health and nutrition programs
> early intervention services
> parenting tips
> safety information
> developmental milestones in the early years
> welcoming letter from library

Most of this information can be gathered relatively inexpensively by requesting brochures from local services and programs; developing or utilizing already existing library publications; and ordering bulk quantities of free or low-cost pamphlets from state health and social service departments and other state agencies, the cooperative extension service, and manufacturers of baby products like Gerber, Johnson & Johnson, and Beech-Nut. The contents of the giveaway kits can be regularly reviewed and rotated as new items are identified.

Circulating kits, which are borrowed but returned by the patron, can be quite creative. The following are two examples of circulating kits.

The *Hospital Kit*, targeted to parents of children entering the hospital, containing:

- Picture books on the "going to the hospital" theme for parents to read aloud to young children
- Pamphlets designed for parents to help their child with this experience (available from ACCH, 7910 Woodmont Avenue, Rockville, MD 20814–3015; 301–654–6549)
- Video for children on the hospital experience (e.g., Mister Rogers)
- Hands-on activities to do in the hospital (e.g., "Fuzzy Felt Hospital" or "The Hospital Game" (available from *Pediatric Projects*, Box 571555, Tarzana, CA 91357–1555; 818–705–3660)

The *Family Day Care Kit*, targeted to family day care home providers but equally useful for the center-based provider or early childhood teacher, might contain:

- Picture books and "big books" on a specific theme (i.e., farm animals, families, colors, teddy bears, or the seasons)
- Felt board and felt board story figures
- Hand puppet
- Music audiocassette or storybook video
- Fingerplays
- Suggestions for developmentally appropriate activities

LOCAL DIRECTORIES AND SOURCEBOOKS

The library can be very helpful to parents by organizing and maintaining current information on local resources. The following suggestions aim to build a good collection of current information.

- Collect listings or brochures on local things to do and places to go with young children
- Assemble a looseleaf binder assembling local day camp brochures for parents to review
- Compile a directory of local nursery schools and child care centers

- Develop a family recreation sourcebook arranged in looseleaf binders with see-through plastic pockets for information on museums, amusement parks, and places of interest for children within a day's trip of the library

These are just a few examples of the kinds of information the library might gather and maintain for families. It's a great service as well as "access enhancer."

REFERENCES

Siegel, Elinor. "Bringing Up Baby by the Book." *Publishers Weekly* (June 14, 1991): 18–24.

13 INTERNET RESOURCES: FAMILIES ONLINE

This annotated listing of Internet resources was compiled by Jennifer L. Brown of the San Antonio Public Library.

Patrons requiring immediate state-of-the-art information may find Internet resources, aimed at families and professionals who work with families, their format of choice. This listing of resources for parents and families on the Internet includes Gopher and World Wide Web sites. The entries (in alphabetical order) are organized as follows: name of resource, address (either a Gopher site, including the path, or a Uniform Resource Locator (URL) to a World Wide Web (WWW) location), and a brief description of content. Due to the constantly changing nature of the Internet, some of these resources may disappear as new ones become available. The best way to use the Internet is to constantly search for new sources.

ADOLESCENCE DIRECTORY ON-LINE (ADOL)

URL address: http://education.indiana.edu/cas/adol/adol.html
The Adolescence Directory On-Line is a collection of electronic resources to information regarding adolescent issues and secondary education. It is intended to be used by parents, educators, researchers, health practioners, and teens. It contains links to electronic resources for the following topics: mental health issues, health risk factors, education, lesson plans, and resources for teachers and teens.

ADMINISTRATION FOR CHILDREN AND FAMILIES (ACF)

URL address: http://www.acf.dhhs.gov/
The ACF, part of the U.S. Department of Health and Human Services, brings together in one organization the broad range of federal programs that address the needs of children and families. This WWW site provides access to information on the programs and services of the ACF, the organizational structure of the ACF, ACF press releases, and links to other related Internet resources.

CATALOG OF FEDERAL DOMESTIC ASSISTANCE

Gopher address: gopher.rtd.utk.edu
Choose Federal Government Information/ Catalog Federal Domestic Assistance/Search the CFDA.src
The Catalog of Federal Domestic Assistance is a directory of federal programs, projects, service, and activities which provide assistance or benefits to the American public. It contains financial

and nonfinancial assistance programs administered by departments and establishments of the federal government. This site allows a keyword search of the catalog leading to information about the various programs.

CHILDREN NOW

URL address: http://www.dnai.com/~children/children_now.html
Children Now is a nonpartisan policy and advocacy organization for children. It provides materials that build partnerships among policymakers, the private sector, parents, service providers, and individuals in an effort to improve the lives of children.

CHILDREN, YOUTH, AND FAMILY CONSORTIUM CLEARINGHOUSE

URL address: http://fscn1.fsci.umn.edu/cyfc/
Choose Children, Youth and Family Clearinghouse
The CYF Clearinghouse contains practical research-based information of interest to parents, educators, and human service providers. It includes resources on the following topics: adoption, infants and children, families with special needs, parenting and families, youth at risk, and children's rights.

CYFERNET—CHILDREN, YOUTH, AND FAMILY EDUCATION RESEARCH NETWORK

URL address: http://www.cyfernet.mes.umn.edu:2400/
Choose CYFERNet or
URL: gopher://gopher-cyfnet.mes.umn.edu/
CYFERNet is the electronic children, youth, and family information system operated jointly by the Cooperative Extension System Children, Youth and Family Network, and the National Agricultural Library. It offers information about four national networks focused on improving the status of at-risk families. The national networks are Child Care, Family Resiliency, Science and Technology, and Collaborations. CYFERNet presents the projects, research, and participants of the networks as well as information on other youth at risk programs.

CONSUMER INFORMATION CENTER (CIC)

URL address: http://www.gsa.gov/staff/pa/cic/cic.htm
The Consumer Information Center distributes federal consumer information to the public. This site offers a number of electronic publications on parenting (located under the heading "Children").

D.O.S.A. PARENTING HOME PAGE

URL: http://www.mbnet.mb.ca:80/~ahawkins
This page contains many resources for parenting. There are question and answer forums, discussion groups, links to other Internet parenting resources, and information on books and parenting strategies.

FACTS FOR FAMILIES

URL: http://www.psych.med.umich.edu/web/aacap/factsFam
Facts for Families is a set of forty-six information sheets providing concise and up-to-date material on issues to educate parents and families about psychiatric disorders affecting children and adolescents. The sheets, published by the American Academy of Child and Adolescent Psychiatry, include information on issues such as mental depression, children and divorce, child abuse, suicide, television violence, learning disabilities, and many other topics.

FAMILY WORLD

URL address: http://family.com/homepage.html/
Family World is a collaboration of over forty monthly parenting publications. It contains monthly activity calendars (broken down by region in the country) for parents and children; monthly features on health, home technology, family activities, recreation and

travel, and parenting tips; the Parent's Forum for parents to exchange questions, advice, and anecdotes; information on products of interest to parents; education resources; and links to other related resources.

FATHERNET

Gopher address: tinman.mes.umn.edu:80/11/FatherNet
FatherNet is an electronic continuation of issues raised during "Family Re-Union III: The Role of Men in Children's Lives," a national conference on family policy. This resource includes the conference proceedings as well as research on men and children, a father's resource center, a discussion group, and related newsletters.

KIDS AND PARENTS ON THE WEB

URL address: http://www.halcyon.com/ResPress/kids.htm
This WWW site contains links to more than 500 resources with information for education and family use. Some of the topics included are adoption, consumer information, disabilities, education, educational television and radio, health and social services, and parenting.

KIDSPEACE: THE NATIONAL CENTER FOR KIDS IN CRISIS

URL address: http://good.freedom.net:80/kidspeace
KidsPeace's mission is to end the emotional pain of America's kids in crisis by preventing child abuse, promoting the emotional well-being of children, and restoring childhood to kids in crisis. This resource provides access to parenting research and parenting tips.

METUCHEN PSYCHOLOGICAL SERVICES' HOME PAGE

URL: http://www.castle.net/~tbogen/mps.html
This page contains links to various mental health resources on

the Internet. Included in the resources are the following topics and organizations: Alcoholic Anonymous and related organizations, codependency, addiction, divorce, attention deficit disorder, families, depression, anxiety, abuse, grief, and cancer.

NATIONAL NETWORK FOR COLLABORATION (NNCO)

Gopher address:
gopher://gopher-cyfernet.mes.umn.edu:4242/hh/Coalitions
Choose CYFERNet/Collaboration
The National Network for Collaboration provides technical assistance in building collaborations at the community level through the state and national level. Its purpose is to foster collaboration and citizen participation to improve the lives of children, youth, and families. NNCO is a self-directed team of eleven Land Grant Universities from around the United States.

NATIONAL PARENT INFORMATION NETWORK (NPIN)

URL address: http://ericps.ed.uiuc.edu/npin/npinhome.html
NPIN is a project of the ERIC Clearinghouses on Elementary & Early Childhood Education. Its purpose is to provide information and to foster electronic communication among parents and those who work with them. It contains resources for parents and parent educators, access to ERIC Digests and Bibliographies, news for parents, and access to Parents AskERIC.

ASKERIC AND PARENTS ASKERIC

URL address: http://ericps.ed.uiuc.edu//npin/paskeric.html
Parents AskERIC is an Internet-based information service that responds to questions on child development, child care, parenting, and child rearing. To send a question to Parents AskERIC, send an e-mail message with the question to: *askeric@ericir.syr.edu.* A response will generally include the results of a short search of the ERIC database and sometimes will include a referral to other Internet resources, a short list of other organizations or information providers that can be contacted for information, or the complete text of a relevant article.

PARENT AND COMMUNITY INVOLVEMENT RESOURCES AT THE U.S. DEPT. OF EDUCATION

Gopher address: gopher://gopher.rbs.org
Choose Internet Resources for the National Education Goals/ Goal 8-Parental Participation/
Parent and Community Involvement Resources
This Gopher site provides Internet resources for the National

Education Goals. This particular link contains information on parent involvement in education, including the Family Involvement Initiative. It provides access to publications dealing with helping children succeed in various educational disciplines.

PARENTING RESOURCES (FROM PEDINFO, A PEDIATRICS WEBSERVER)

URL: http://www.lhl.uab.edu/pedinfo/Parenting.html
A collection of resources for parents and families on the Internet. The resources included range from support groups to health information.

PARENTS HELPING PARENTS (PHP)

URL: http://www.portal.com/~cbntmkr/php.html
PHP is a parent-directed family resource center for children with any kind of special need. This particular PHP WWW site contains links to resources concerned with parenting and special needs.

PARENTSPLACE.COM

URL: http://www.parentsplace.com/index.html
This "Parenting Resource Center on the Web" provides information to parents on a variety of topics. There is an online shopping resource containing catalogs, products, and services for parents. There are also reading rooms providing access to newsletters, book excerpts, and other resources for parents.

UNITED NATIONS CHILDREN'S FUND (UNICEF)

Gopher address: gopher://hqfaus01.unicef.org
The UNICEF Gopher contains information on the work of UNICEF, including its major programs in child survival, development, and child advocacy. The site provides access to full-text UNICEF publications, information about UNICEF, press releases, and other information.

U.S. DEPARTMENT OF EDUCATION PUBLICATIONS

URL: http://www.ed.gov/pubs/parents.html
This resource contains electronic versions of popular pamphlets and brochures designed to address parents' concerns about their

children's education published by the U.S. Department of Education. The pamphlets available are: the OERI "Helping Your Child Series," ERIC Parent Brochures, "Summer Home Learning Recipes," "Preparing Your Child for College," and "The Student Guide" (information about federal student financial aid).

LISTSERVS

PARENTING

An Internet discussion group on topics related to parenting children (including child development, education, and care) from birth to adolescence. It is run through the ERIC Clearinghouse on Elementary and Early Childhood Education. To subscribe, send an e-mail message to: *marjordomo@uxl.cso.uiuc.edu.* In the body of the message, type: subscribe PARENTING (your e-mail address)

FATHERNET LISTSERV

A listserv discussion group for comments on fathers and fathering issues. This is associated with FatherNet. To subscribe, send an e-mail message to: listserv@vml.spcs.umn.edu. In the body of the message, type: subscribe father-l (your e-mail address) (your name)

DADVOCAT

A listserv for fathers of children with disabilities. The mission is to share information, inquiries, ideas, and opinions on matters pertaining to the experiences of fathers of special needs children. To subscribe: send an e-mail message to: *listserv@ukcc.uky.edu.* In the body of the message, type: sub dadvocat (your name)

FREE-L

An electronic conference for the exchange of information regarding the issues of father's rights. To subscribe, send an e-mail message to: *listserv@indycms.iupui.edu.* In the body of the message, type: sub free-l (your name)
There may be other listservs suggested by the Gopher and World Wide Web sites.

During 1993 and 1994 the Onondaga County Public Library in Syracuse, New York provided an opportunity for parents; health care professionals, including a pediatrician; and a child development specialist to communicate through the listserv PIRLTALK.

The experience showed that the electronic format is a necessary extension of library service and could be adapted to replicate any of the model library-based family support services previously discussed in Chapter 5. While the urban executive may seek reference help from librarians during the noon hour, the harried parent may find midnight the perfect time to formulate their reference query. The next day the monitor of the electronic reference service can answer using a multitude of resources on the Internet. The future holds an unlimited range of technologies to offer from text to graphics to real-time interactive video. Perhaps even more exciting is the power of parent-to-parent support that is potentially available through electronic means. It is libraries and librarians that must take the leadership role in connecting parents, caregivers, agencies, and organizations. The electronic collaborations will offer new opportunities for public libraries to revolutionize family services.

INDEX TO APPENDIXES

APPENDIX C: SERVICES, SURVEYS, AND EVALUATION FORMS

Figure C-1: Whole Services Worksheet: Internal Review Form
Figure C-2: Whole Services Worksheet: External Review Form
Figure C-3: Family Service Self-Assessment Questionnaire
Figure C-4: Quality Indicator Assessment Tool
Figure C-5: Parent's Evaluation of Toddler Story Hour
Figure C-6: Parent/Child Workshop Evaluation Form
Figure C-7: Program Registration Survey
Figure C-8: In-Service Evaluation Form

APPENDIX D: PUBLICITY MATERIALS

Figure D1a–D1b: PIRL Brochure
Figure D-2: Flyer on New Mothers Discussion Group
Figure D-3: Flyer on Family Resource Fair
Figure D-4: Flyer on Parent Connections
Figure D-5: Flyer on Kids' Answer Place
Figure D-6: Flyer on Parents Anonymous
Figure D-7: News Release on Infant/Toddler Screening
Figure D-8: Flyer on Nursery School Fair
Figure D-9: Flyer on Project Link
Figure D-10: Flyer on Parent and Child Workshop (English Version)
Figure D-11: Flyer on Parent and Child Workshop (Spanish Version)
Figure D-12: Resource Professionals for Parent and Child Workshop (Spanish)
Figure D-13: News Release on Library/Head Start/Museum Partnership

APPENDIX E: SELF STUDY FOR CHILDREN'S LIBRARIAN

APPENDIX F: PARENT SATISFACTION SURVEY

APPENDIX G: PARENT EDUCATION AND SUPPORT CHECKLIST

APPENDIX H: NATIONAL AGENCIES AND ORGANIZATIONS

APPENDIX A: COALITION BUILDING

Figure A-1: Coalition Inventory Form

COALITION INVENTORY FORM

Name of Agency or Organization	
Address	
Phone # **Contact** **Person**	
Date of Initial Contact: **by phone** **by mail** **meeting**	
Mission of Agency or Organization	
List of pamphlets or publications (attach samples)	
Information or Service Needs of Agency Identified	
Formal Collaborations with other groups	
Follow - up	

Figure A-2: Survey for Family Focus Center

SURVEY FOR FAMILY FOCUS CENTER

Name of Agency   **Contact Person**   **Phone number**

1. What is your agency's target population?

2. What services does your agency provide?

Localities/sites of such services

3. Do you offer educational programs and/or workshops? If so, on what topics?

4. Do you specifically address prevention or early intervention of developmental disabilities?
          Yes _____   No _____   If so, in what way?

5. What do you see as currently unaddressed or underaddressed prenatal educational issues?

6. If the library program were able to address those issues, what do you think might be the best approach?

How many of your clients are currently in need of such education or information?

How could your agency facilitate its attendance at our library prenatal classes?

7. What techniques or incentives have you found most helpful in promoting good turnouts for workshops or educational programs?

8. Would anyone in your agency be willing to do a workshop for the library prenatal series?

Name _____ **Availability** _____
Topic(s) _____

REPRINTED COURTESY OF CRANDALL PUBLIC LIBRARY, GLENS FALLS, NY

Figure A-3: Sample Recruitment Letter

January 5, 1990

Ann Campo
YMCA Family Services Division
6 Unity Drive
Centereach, NY 11720

Dear Ann,

As per our conversation of the phone, I am writing to confirm the meeting for professionals interested in participating in the development of a Family Resource Coalition. The first meeting of the Coalition will be held at the _____Library on May 19, 1990 from 9:30 a.m. - 11:30 a.m. It is vital for your organization to be represented because you do such an outstanding job for the families in our community.

This meeting offers an opportunity for you to share materials and network with other local service providers, parents and professionals who work with families. Please consider sending one or two people to represent your agency. Individuals may distribute brochures, information or flyers concerning your agency and be available to discuss what it is you do best.

Please complete and return the enclosed form or bring it with you to the meeting. For any questions contact myself or Mary Smith at 585-9393. Looking forward to working with you on this exciting venture.

Very truly yours,

John Dawnwood
Youth Services Consultant

Figure A-4: Sample Recruitment Letter

May 24, 1995

John Williams, M.A.
Director, Prevention Education
Long Island Association for Aids Care
SUNY Health Science Center
Stony Brook, NY 11790

Dear John,

As per our conversation, I am writing to invite you to attend a meeting of professionals who are concerned about AIDS prevention and education. We hope to form a coalition of agencies and organizations who are concerned about AIDS and wish to share their expertise and knowledge about community resources committed to this health issue.

The first meeting of our coalition will be held at the _____Library on Tuesday, May 16, 1995 at 9:30 a.m. We look forward to meeting you and your participation in the development of this network.

Very truly yours,

Mary Smith
Children's Librarian

Figure A-5: Recruitment Letter for Parent Educator's Network

Suffolk Coalition for Parents & Children

"...Because children are our most precious resource"

Mailing Address: Middle Country Public Library,
101 Eastwood Blvd., Centereach, NY 11720

Dear Coalition Member,

As you know, the Suffolk Coalition for Parents and Children is a networking organization that focuses on the needs of Suffolk's families through bi-monthly programs and information sharing. The strength of the Coalition lies in its diversity and breadth of representation.

Some members of the Coalition who work specifically in the area of parent education have expressed the need for a parent educator's network which would serve as a professional development support group and could exist as a special interest sub-group within the Coalition.

This parent educator's network would provide an opportunity for members to:
*meet each other, share information about their programs, purpose, process, staff, resources and types of parents served;
*identify resources that could reinforce and strengthen their on-going parenting education efforts;
*determine ways to communicate to parents and others the types and sources of parenting education available;
*identify parenting education needs which can be met by modification of some programs, cooperative programming or unified support for the development of new programs.

If you are interested in working towards the development of such a group, please return the tear-off at the bottom and join us on Wednesday, February 13, 1992 at 3:00 P.M. in the main meeting room of the Middle Country Public Library, 101 Eastwood Blvd, Centereach.

Looking forward to hearing from you.

Sincerely

Barbara Jordan
Head of Children's Services
Middle Country Public Library

Nancy Olsen-Harbich
Human Development Specialist
Cornell Cooperative Extension

- -

_____I am interested in developing a Parent Educator's Network and <u>will attend</u> the meeting on February 13.

_____I am interested in developing a Parent Educator's Network but I am unable to attend the meeting.

Figure A-6a: Recruitment Letter for Family Resource Fair

Suffolk Coalition for Parents & Children

"...Because children are our most precious resource"

Mailing Address: Middle Country Public Library,
101 Eastwood Blvd., Centereach, NY 11720

Dear Colleague,

The Suffolk Coalition for Parents and Children in cooperation with the Suffolk Family Education Clearinghouse and Suffolk County's Youth Bureau/Office for Children is jointly sponsoring a FAMILY RESOURCE FAIR on May 9th, 1990 9:30-12:30 at the Middle Country Public Library on 101 Eastwood Blvd. in Centereach.

It is really vital for your organization to be represented because you do such an outstanding job for Suffolk County. This day offers an opportunity for you to share materials and network with other service providers, parents and professionals. Would you kindly consider sending one or two people to represent your agency who might distribute brochures, information or flyers and be available to discuss what it is you do best?

We at the Library will provide tables and any audio-visual requirements you may have.

Please complete the attached and return it. This is a don't miss event so please, plan on coming!

Feel free to call myself or Barbara Jordan at 585-9393, ext. 220 if you need more information. Looking forward to working with you in the near future, I remain

Sincerely yours

Harriet Chomet
Resource Fair Coordinator

HC/cb

Figure A-6b: Registration Form for Family Resource Fair

FAMILY RESOURCE FAIR

PLEASE COMPLETE THIS FORM AND RETURN BY FEBRUARY 23, 1990

Organization/Agency Name: _____

Contact Person: _____ Title: _____

Address: _____ Phone: _____

_____ We will bring materials and attend.

_____ We will be sending the following people (person) to
offer information about our agency:

        NAME: _____

        NAME: _____

_____ We are able to send materials to the Fair but cannot
attend.

_____ We cannot participate on that date.

Audio-visual requirements:

        Screen _____

     Slide Projector _____

    16mm Movie
       Projector _____

   VCR/Television _____

       Other _____

RETURN THIS FORM TO: Suffolk Family Education Clearinghouse
                    Middle Country Public Library
                    101 Eastwood Blvd.
                    Centereach NY 11720
                    Phone: 585-9393 ext. 220

Figure A-7a: Recruitment Letter for Public Hearing

PUBLIC HEARING

SEARCHING FOR SOLUTIONS
The Challenge of Diminishing Resources for
Children and Families in Suffolk County

REQUEST FOR SPONSORSHIP

A public hearing on the state of children and families in Suffolk County is being planned for the morning of March 20, 1992 at the Middle Country Public Library. Entitled **SEARCHING FOR SOLUTIONS: The Challenge of Diminishing Resources for Children and Families in Suffolk County**, this public hearing will be addressed to local legislators and policy makers.

We are asking for your organization's sponsorship of this hearing. This would include lending your organization's name to the list of sponsors, providing testimony at the hearing, and, possibly, participating in the overall organization of the event. Initially suggested by the Suffolk Coalition's Planning Committee meeting last June, the hearing is currently being organized by the Coalition's Advisory Board, Child Care Council of Suffolk, Family Service League of Suffolk County, Suffolk County Youth Bureau, Children's Librarians' Association of Suffolk County, and Brookhaven Youth Bureau. All major youth and family organizations are being solicited to lend their support and participation to this hearing.

It is envisioned that this hearing will address the major issues facing Suffolk's families today. Infant mortality, health care, teen pregnancy, child abuse, child care, AIDS, parent support, substance abuse, family workplace issues, school aid cuts, transportation, homelessness and poverty are some of subjects to be addressed through written and oral testimony. Beyond expanding awareness of the state of Suffolk's children and families, one of our goals will be to alert legislators and policy makers that we are willing to work as a team in our efforts to confront these issues. Breaking down bureaucratic barriers, coordinating resources, looking at long term solutions, and streamlining services can only be accomplished if we all join forces and work together. Another goal will be to produce a written document of the testimonies that will be made available for public distribution. A third goal, depending on availability of business support, will be to produce a video document that can be edited for public viewing and media coverage of the issues.

Please fill out the enclosed form today and lend your support to this hearing. SEARCHING FOR SOLUTIONS can only succeed with the help of the entire community.

Figure A-7b: Registration Form for Public Hearing

PUBLIC HEARING
ON THE STATE OF CHILDREN AND FAMILIES
IN SUFFOLK COUNTY

SPONSORSHIP FORM

CONTACT: _____

ORGANIZATION: _____

ADDRESS: _____

CITY, STATE: _____ ZIP:_____

PHONE NUMBER: _____

SIGNATURE OF RESPONDER: _____

DATE: _____

Please return form by January 31, 1992:

Suffolk Coalition for Parents and Children
c/o Middle Country Public Library
101 Eastwood Blvd
Centereach, NY 11720-2745

Figure A-8: Suffolk Coalition for Parents and Children Mailing List

AGENCIES AND ORGANIZATIONS

This list of agencies and organizations is provided as an aid to professionals who are looking for potential members of networks.

All About Me Preschool
Alternatives Counseling Center
American Red Cross
Amityville Schools
Apple Institute
Association for Children With Learning Disabilities
    Kramer Learning Center
The Atrium
Audiology & Communication Services
Babylon Consultation Center
Babylon Public Library
Babylon Town
Babylon Youth Institute
Bay Shore Day Care
Bay Shore-Brightwaters Public Library
Bayport-Blue Point Public Library
Bayville Public Library
Bellport Area Community Action Committee
Bellport Area Community Center
Bellport Head Start
Bellport Middle School
Better Living Resources
Better Parenting
Big Brother/Big Sister of Nassau
Birthright
Brentwood Public Library
Brentwood School District
Brentwood Youth Development Corp.
Bretton Woods Elementary School
Bridgehampton School
Brighter Tomorrows
Brookhaven Country Preschool
Brookhaven Free Library
Brookhaven Hospital
Brookhaven Opportunity Center
Brookhaven Town
Building Block Developmental Pre-School
CAPS (Child Abuse Prevention Services)
Catholic Charities
Cayuga Elementary School
Center for Family Resources
Center Moriches High School
Center Moriches Library
Central Brook Head Start

Central Islip Healthy Neighborhood Project
Central Islip High School
Central Islip Public Library
Childbearing Family Alliance
Child Care Council of Suffolk, Inc.
Child Safety Services of America
Children's Community Head Start
Children's House
Cleary School for the Deaf
Cold Spring Harbor Central School District
Colonial Youth and Family Services
Commack-Half Hollow Hills Community Youth Agency
Commack Middle School
Commack Public Library
Community Mediation Center
Community Programs Center
Community Services Program of Suffolk County
Comprehensive Home Care Services
Comsewogue Public Library
Comsewogue School District
Comsewogue Youth Club
Concepts, Inc.
Connetquot Central School District
Connetquot Public Library
Convenor Project
Copiague High School
Copiague Youth Council
Cornell Cooperative Extension of Suffolk County
Council for Exceptional Children
Curriculum Planning Instructional Services
Developmental Disabilities Institute
Deer Park Community Center
Deer Park Public Schools
EAC Developmental Learning Program
EAC/ERASE/PEER Program
EAC Supervised Visitation
Eagle Drive Elementary School
Early Childhood Center, Coram
East End Committee on Family Violence and Child Abuse
East End Counseling Project/Alternatives
East Hampton High School
East Hampton Human Services
East Islip Public Library
East Islip School District
East Quogue Unified School District
Eastern Suffolk BOCES (Board of Cooperative Education Services)
Economic Opportunity Council of Suffolk, Inc.
Emma S. Clark Memorial Library
E.R.A.S.E. (Education, Rehabilitation and Support Enforcement)
Family Counseling Services
Family Service League
Floyd Memorial Library
Forest Brook Learning Center
For Our Children and Us
Foster Grandparent Program
Good Samaritan Hospital
Grumman Corporation
Half Hollow Hills Central School District
Half Hollow Hills Community and Youth Agency
Half Hollow Hills Community Library

Figure A-8: Suffolk Coalition for Parents and Children Mailing List (cont'd)

Harborfields Public Library
Harborview Psychological Services
Harry Chapin Inn
Hauppauge School System
Headstart, Flanders
Health and Welfare Council of Nassau County
Health House
Hope House Ministries
Horizons Counseling Center
HUGS
Human Connections Learning and Counseling Center
Huntington Coalition for the Homeless: *Haven House*
Huntington High School
Huntington NOW
Huntington Public Library
Huntington Town
I Can Do That Workshops/Seminars
IGHL (Independent Group Home Living)
Interfaith Nutrition Network
International Lactation Consultant Association
Islip Community Nursery School
Islip Public Library
Islip Schools
Islip Town
Jack & Jill Day Nursery
Jeanne's Junior Jungle
Jericho Union Free School District
Jewish Community Services of Long Island
Joseph Edgar School
Just Kids
Legal Aid Society of Suffolk Cty,Inc.
Kings Park Central School District
League of Women Voters
La Leche League
L.I. Advocacy Center Inc.
L.I. Association for AIDS Care (LIAAC)
L.I. Association for Children with Learning Disabilities
L.I. Cares
L.I. Cottage of Designs Ltd.-Studio
L.I. Council of Churches
L.I. Head Start Child Developement Services, Inc.
L.I. Housing Partnerhsip, Inc.
L.I. Lutheran Services
L.I. Regional Health Education Resource Center
L.I. School for Gifted
L.I. Self-Help Clearinghouse
L.I. Veteran's Center
L.I. Women's Coalition
L.I. Youth For Christ
L.I. Youth Guidance, Inc.
Light House Counseling Center
Lindenhurst Memorial Library
Little Flower Children's Service
Little Peoples' Day Care
Little Red School House
Longwood Public Library
Longwood School District
Love'M
Madonna Heights Services
March of Dimes

Marie Coleman Nelson Referral Service
Marion St. School
Mary Clarkson
Massapequa Library
Mastics-Moriches-Shirley Community Library
Mather Memorial Hospital Outreach Center
Mental Health Association in NYS
Mental Health Association in Suffolk County
Mental Health Consultants for Professionals
Mercy Center Ministries, Inc.
Middle Country Central School District
Middle Country Public Library
Mid Suffolk NOW
Miller Place School District
The Ministries at Coram
Minority AIDS Education Project
Mothers' Center Development Project
Mothers Center of Suffolk
Mothers' Group (Hope Lutheran Church)
Mothers of Young Children
Mulligan School
Nassau County Department of Health
Nassau Law Services
Nassau Library System
New Beginnings
Newsday
New York Hospital
North Babylon Public Library
North Fork Women's Resource Center
Northport-E. Northport School District
Northport E. Northport Public Library
North Suffolk Mental Health Center
NYS Commission for the Blind
NYS Council on Children and Families
NYS Department of Health
NYS Department of Labor
NYS Division For Youth
NYS Education Department/L.I. Regional Office
NYS Technical Assistance Resource Network
Ocean Avenue School
Oceanside Unified School District
Office of the County Executive
The Opportunity Pre-School
Options for Community Living
Orton Dyslexia Society
Our Lady of Queen Martyrs Parish
Our Savior Lutheran Church
Outreach Project
Parent-Child Home Program-Oyster Bay
Parent Connections
Parent Networking (The Net Result)
Parents and Friends of Lesbians and Gays (P-FLAG)
Parents Division, Long Island ASPO
Passages Counseling Center
Patchogue-Medford Library
Patchogue Medford School District
Patchogue-Medford Youth Services
Pathways for Learning
Pederson-Krag Center
People Counseling

Figure A-8: Suffolk Coalition for Parents and Children Mailing List (cont'd)

Plainview/Old Bethpage Public Library
Planned Parenthood of Suffolk County
The Preschoolers Place
Project Care
Project Empower/American Red Cross
Project Fresh Start
Project Independence
Pronto of Long Island
Rainbow Chimes Day Care Center
Rainbow Program
Rall Elementary
Rauch Foundation
RESPONSE Hotline
Resurrection House
The Retreat, Amagansett
Riverhead Free Library
Robert Frost Junior High School
Rocky Point School District
Roger's Memorial Library
RSVP Program
Sachem Central School District
Sachem Public Library
Sachem Teen Center
Safe Kids Coalition of Suffolk County
Sagamore Children's Psychiatric Center
Sag Harbor Unified School District
Sagtikos Educare Center
Salvation Army
Saxton PTA
Sayville Public Schools
Schneider Children's Hospital
SCOPE (Suffolk County Office for Professional Education)
Seafield Center
Selden Centereach Community Coalition
Selden-Centereach Youth Assoc.
Self-Help Community Services
Shelter Plus
Shinnecock Indian Health Services
Shoreham-Wading River Public Library
Shoreham-Wading River School District
Smithtown Central School District
Smithtown Cooperative Nursery School
Smithtown Library - Nesconset Branch
Smithtown Youth Bureau
SNAP (Suffolk Network on Adolescent Pregnancy)
Society of St. Vincent DePaul
South Country Central School District
South Country Drug & Alcohol Prevention Center
South Country Library
South Fork Community Health Imitative
South Huntington Public LIbrary
South Huntington Union Free School District
South Oaks Hospital
South Shore Community Organization
Southold Free Library
Southside Hospital
St. Boniface Day Care
St. Charles Hospital
St. Joseph Outreach/CCD

St. Joseph's College
St. Joseph's Mothers Group
St. Patrick Outreach
St. Peter the Apostle R.C. Church
Suffolk Coalition for PADD
Suffolk Community Council, Inc.
Suffolk Community Development Corp
Suffolk Cooperative Library System
S.C. Attorney's Office
S.C. for Vietnam Veterans' Children
S.C. Coalition for the Prevention of
    Alcoholism & Drug Dependencies
S.C. Courts
S.C. Department of Alcohol & Substance Abuse
S.C. Department for the Aging
S.C. Department of Health
S.C. Department of Labor
S.C. Department of Social Services
S.C. Division of Mental Health Serv.
S.C. Girl Scouts
S.C. Legislature
S.C. Mental Health Association
S.C. Office of Handicapped Services
S.C. Perinatal Coalition, Inc.
S.C. Police Department
S.C. Veterans Services Agency
S.C. Women's Services
S.C. Youth Bureau
Suffolk District PTA
SUNY (State University of New York)
SYNERGY
Syosset High School
Syosset Public Library
Three Village Central School District
Three Village Community and Youth Services
Three Village Parents Group
Tot-Saver CPR - Children's Safety
Tri-Community Health Center
La Union Hispanica
UCP (United Cerebral Palsy)
United Way of Long Island
University Hospital
Vanderbilt Elementary School
Variety Preschoolers Workshop
VESID
Veterans Administration Medical Center
VIBS (Victims Information Bureau of Suffolk,Inc.)
Wantagh Public Schools
West Babylon Jr. High
West Babylon Public Library
West Islip Day Care Center
West Islip Youth Enrichment (YES)
Western Suffolk BOCES
William Floyd School District
Wyandanch School Board
YMCA of Long Island
YM-YWHA of Suffolk
Youth and Family Counseling
Youth Enrichment Services

Figure A-9: List of Meeting Topics

A List of Suggested Topics for Coalition Meetings

The following list of topics and issues have been presented at the bi-monthly meetings by members of the Coalition and are provided as ideas for those involved in planning or organizing networks and coalitions. Sample agendas are also provided as a guide to presentation content.

Adolescence and AIDS
Advocacy of Human Resources
AIDS and Children
Anger Control for Parents and Children
Battering During Pregnancy: Early Identification and Intervention
Child Abuse Prevention Programs (Joint Program with Western Suffolk Coalition
              on Child Abuse and Neglect)
Child Advocacy
Childhood Stress, Depression and Suicide
Children as Caregivers
Children in Poverty
Children Infected and Affected by AIDS
Children of Addictions
Children of Divorce
Children with Mentally Ill Parents: Some Perspective, Intervention Strategies
              and Program Models
Colloquim on National Family Policy
Courts and the Family
Day Care and Maternal Employment
Educating Students and Parents About Alcohol and Other Drugs
Empowering Families and Youth: Getting Ready to Share the Power
Families of Children with Chronic Illness
Families of Vietnam Veterans: Issue and Concerns
Helping Parents with Life Planning for Their Children
Homosexuality and Youth
Improving Working Relations with Child Protective Services
Inclusion
Infant Mortality
Information and Referral in Suffolk County
Intergenerational Programs
Legal Rights of Children Within the School Setting
Listen! Parents of Children with Special Needs Speak Out
Mental Health Services for Youth
Model Parent Education Programs
Multicultural View of Child Rearing
Navigating the System After Abuse is Reported (Joint Meeting with
              Western Suffolk Coalition on Child Abuse)
Peer Leadership
Preventing Youth Violence
Restructured Families
Serving Multicultural Population
Structuring a Competent Child Abuse Interview
Suicide and Children

Figure A-10: Sample Meeting Agenda

Suffolk Coalition for Parents & Children

"...Because children are our most precious resource"

Mailing Address: Middle Country Public Library,
101 Eastwood Blvd., Centereach, NY 11720

TO: Member of the Suffolk Coalition for Parents and Children
FROM: Lynda Yenerall

MEETING NOTICE

DATE: Tuesday January 18, 1994
TIME: 9:30 A.M. - 12:00 noon
PLACE: Middle Country Public Library
          101 Eastwood Blvd
          Centereach NY 11720

CHILDREN INFECTED AND AFFECTED BY AIDS

Lynda Yenerall, M.A.
Director of Prevention Education
L.I. Association for AIDS Care
385-2451

Margherita Proscia, M.S.
Special Educator in Early Intervention
St. Charles Educational & Therapeutic Center
474-1297

Peggy Melendez, R.N.
Dept. of Pediatrics
Health Sciences Ctr.
Suny at Stony Brook
444-1313

Robyn Berger, C.S.W.
Associate Educator - Women's Programs
L.I. Association for AIDS Care
385-2451

A PANEL OF FAMILY MEMBERS WILL ALSO PARTICIPATE

Figure A-11: Sample Meeting Agenda

Suffolk Coalition for Parents & Children

"...Because children are our most precious resource"

Mailing Address: Middle Country Public Library,
101 Eastwood Blvd., Centereach, NY 11720

TO: Members of the Suffolk Coalition for Parents and Children
FROM: Barbara Baskin and Veronica Murtha

MEETING NOTICE

DATE: Tuesday November 13, 1990
TIME: 9:30 a. m. - 12:00 noon
PLACE: Middle Country Public Library
              101 Eastwood Blvd.
              Centereach NY 11720

COURTS AND THE FAMILY

Mary Werner
Suffolk County District Attorney's Office
Family Crime Bureau
Criminal Courts Building
Evan K. Griffins Drive
Riverhead, NY 11901
548-4270

Eileen Behar
FOCUS
For Our Children & Us Inc.
550 Old Country Road
Hicksville, NY 11801
433-6633

Paul McCrann
Acting Administrator
Family & Child Services Administration
S. C. Dept. Of Social Services
Box 2000
Hauppauge, NY 11788
468-2935

Anne Martin
Supervisor - DAS
PINS Diversion Program
S.C. Dept of Probation
Veterans Memorial Highway
North Complex, Building 15
Hauppauge, NY 11788

360-4746

Introduction and panel moderator - Dr. Beverly Birns
Dept. of Child and Family Studies • SUNY Stony Brook 632-7689

Figure A-12: Sample Meeting Agenda

Suffolk Coalition for Parents & Children

"...Because children are our most precious resource"

Mailing Address: Middle Country Public Library,
101 Eastwood Blvd., Centereach, NY 11720

TO: Members of the Suffolk Coalition for Parents and Children
FROM: Barbara Jordan, Veronica Murtha, and Sharon Breen

MEETING NOTICE

DATE: Wednesday November 9, 1988
TIME: 9:30 a.m. - 12:00 noon
NOTE: CHANGE OF MEETING PLACE
PLACE: Middle Country Public Library
         Main Building
         101 Eastwood Blvd.
         Centereach NY 11720

CHILDHOOD DEPRESSION, STRESS, AND SUICIDE

Clifford Bennett
Director of Special Education
Patchogue Medford School District
241 South Ocean Avenue
Patchogue, NY 11772
758-1000 ext. 1039

Remani Ninan, M.D.
Child Psychiatrist
Sagamore Children's Center
Melville, NY 11747
471-6400 ext. 14

Jean Richards
Suffolk County Mental Health Association
Support Group for Families of the Mentally Ill
298-4267 or 298-4433

George Andreozzi
Asst. for Special Services
Smithtown Central School District
26 New York Avenue
Smithtown, NY 11787
361-2225

Sister Patricia Smyth
Associate Director
Hope House Ministries
PO Box 358
Port Jefferson, NY 11777

Roseann Miceli
Coordinator of Community Education
RESPONSE
PO Box 300
Stony Brook, NY 11790

BUSINESS MEETING
A Suffolk Coalition Board meeting will follow at 12:15 $4.00 per person lunch. RSVP Board meeting only. Lois Casa 585-9393 ext. 342

Figure A-13: Sample Meeting Agenda

Suffolk Coalition for Parents & Children

"...Because children are our most precious resource"

Mailing Address: Middle Country Public Library,
101 Eastwood Blvd., Centereach, NY 11720

TO: Member of the Suffolk Coalition for Parents and Children
FROM: Linda Milch, Sheila Fleming and Margaret Sampson

MEETING NOTICE

DATE: Tuesday September 20, 1994
TIME: 9:30 am - 12:00 noon
PLACE: Middle Country Public Library
         101 Eastwood Blvd
         Centereach NY 11720
         585-9393 Ext. 220

PERSPECTIVES ON INCLUSION
Welcome & Introductions
Linda Milch

Part 1: ***Perspectives on Early Childhood Inclusion***
Policy and Practice • *Carol Nash, NYS Developmental Disabilities Planning Council*
Dialogue Among Parents Professionals and Administrators • *Sheila Fleming, LI Head Start*
  Disabilities Service Coordinator, Anita Gresich, LI Head Start, Teacher; Sheila Grey, Parent
Margaret Sampson, Moderator
Part 2: ***Perspectives on Inclusion: School Age***
Legal Perspectives on Inclusion • *Alyse Middendorf, Protection & Advocacy Coordinator for the*
  Developmentally Disabled Long Island Advocacy Center
Parents Speak Up Inclusion in the School and Community • *Linda Carroll, LI Safe (Schools Are For*
  Everyone);Ed Hand, Co-Chair Suffolk LI Family Support Consumer Council; Susan Platkin,
  Northport SEPTA
Margaret Sampson, Moderator
Part 3: ***Perspectives on Inclusion: Transition***
From School to Work in the Community • *Donna Gary Donovan, Just Kids; Michelle Sampson,*
  Student, Shoreham-Wading River High School Life Skills Program

Figure A-14: Sample Meeting Agenda

Suffolk Coalition for Parents & Children

"...Because children are our most precious resource"

Mailing Address: Middle Country Public Library,
101 Eastwood Blvd., Centereach, NY 11720

TO: Members of the Suffolk Coalition
for Parents and Children
FROM: Meryl Cassidy

MEETING NOTICE

DATE: Tuesday, May 16, 1995
TIME: 9:30 A.M. - 12:00 NOON
PLACE: Middle Country Public Library
101 Eastwood Blvd.
Centereach, NY 11729

COMMUNITY SUPPORTS FOR DIVORCED SEPARATED AND BLENDED FAMILIES

Karen Knoeble, CSW
Banana Splitz Program
Westhampton Beach
Elementary School

Roberta Karant, PhD
Children Cope With Divorce Program
Family Service League

Helen Gronus
Senior Case Manager
New Beginnings
Islip Town Dept of Human Services

Pamela Gittler, CSW
Private Therapist Specializing in
Stepfamily Support

Moderator: Meryl Cassidy, ACSW
Family Service League

Figure A-15: Sample Meeting Agenda

Suffolk Coalition for Parents & Children

"...Because children are our most precious resource"

Mailing Address: Middle Country Public Library,
101 Eastwood Blvd., Centereach, NY 11720

TO: Members of the Suffolk Coalition for Parents and Children
FROM: Jane Corrarino Suffolk County Executive's Office for Children

MEETING NOTICE

DATE: Wednesday January 11, 1989
TIME: 9:30 A.M. - 12:00 noon
PLACE: Middle Country Public Library
         Main Building
         101 Eastwood Blvd
         Centereach, NY 11720

CHILDREN IN POVERTY

Dr. Rose Pinckney
Chief Deputy Commissioners
Suffolk County Dept of Special Services
220 Rabro Drive East
Hauppauge NY 11787

Bessie Urquhart, RN-MA
Director
Public Health Nursing
Suffolk County Dept of Health Services
225 Rabro Drive East
Hauppauge NY 11787

John Chicherio
Director
Long Island Cares, Inc.
PO Box 1073
West Brentwood NY 11717

Sandra Ruiz
Director
Suffolk County Executive's Office for Children
65 Jetson Lane
Central Islip NY 11722

Betty-Jean Wrase
Assistant Director
Child Welfare Training Program
School of Social Welfare
SUNY Stony Brook NY 11794

Edna Negron
Reporter
Newsday
Pinelawn Road
Melville NY 11747

APPENDIX B: GRANT INFORMATION

Figure B-1: Grant Concept Form

GRANT CONCEPT FORM

1. **Working Title:** _____

2. **Is this a new idea/new to your institution/expansion of a program?**

3. **Literature search completed   yes _____   no _____   (attach).**

4. **Briefly describe project and need.**

5. **Collaborating agencies, organizations, individuals.**
   (Names, phone numbers, address, e-mail, contact made)

6. **How will the outcomes be measured?**

7. **What are the plans for the project after the grant funding period?**

8. **Funding range needed.**

9. **In-kind support available.**

10. **Length of funding needed.**

11. **Financial summary.**

ADAPTED FROM: GRANT CONCEPT FORM, SHARON AKKOUL, ONONDAGA COMMUNITY COLLEGE

Figure B-2: Sample Request for Funding Letter

TO A REAL ESTATE DEVELOPER IN THE COMMUNITY

Dear Ms. LaRosa,

*(Open with a graphic child abuse story from the local newspaper.)*In 1996 the Children's Collaborative Network will be launching its most innovative program to date - the Family Respite Program. Child abuse is an ever increasing problem *(use a strong statistic)* and the Family Respite Program will reduce the incidence of child abuse and give help to families throughout this community.

In order to launch this program we need your property at 222 Main Street. The site of a former day care center, 222 Main Street has the perfect space for children to play, adults to receive counseling and our staff of three social workers from three different community agencies to provide information and referral. There is additional space for community resources, a children's library, and a kitchen.

Your willingness to provide this space rent free for three years will ensure that:
*the program will be launched without the excessive financial burden of monthly rent.
*the program can seek a stable funding stream while demonstrating its success in the community.
*the program will be named for your real estate company to acknowledge the essential contribution you made to the success of this project.

The Children's Collaborative Network will be responsible for:
*all insurance and liability that accompanies use of the property.
*renovation, repair and daily maintenance to the property.
*seeking funding for a fair and equitable rent to begin in year four of the project.
*naming the program for your company and using that name in all publicity and presentations related to the project.

As this year's convener for the Children's Collaborative Network, I will be contacting you in the next week for a detailed discussion of the project and our proposal to use 222 Main Street for the project site. I am enclosing a list of the current and active membership of the Children's Collaborative Network as well as a proposed budget for the respite project. As you can see the project will initially begin with in-kind contributions from over 20 agencies, organizations, businesses and community groups.

This project will change the lives of children and parents. I know you will want to join all of us in making that difference.

Sincerely,

Figure B-3: Sample Request for Funding Letter

TO COMPUTER STORES AND WHOLESALERS
(INDIVIDUALIZE EACH LETTER)

Dear Mr. Smith,

What could be a better picture than a mother and child working together on a computer? The Community Library and the New York State Job Service are planning an innovative family and workplace literacy program that uses computers and preschool software to empower economically and educationally disadvantaged families with new skills, new opportunities and an important "jump-start" on getting children ready for school.

Your one-time gift of a 486 computer with CD-ROM will make an important difference in the lives of over 100 families during 1996. Each mom and tot pair will visit the library for two one hour sessions per week. During the sessions moms and tots will enjoy the computer while developing computer literacy skills. The moms and tots will also visit the job service site where moms will learn word processing and tots will attend story times or other library sponsored programs. Computers at the job service site were purchased through a grant from the New York State Department of Labor but they do not have the graphic and audio capability needed to run today's preschool software. The library needs at least 4 computers to serve the more than 100 families eligible for this program in 1996.

Your gift would be tax deductible and your donation would be recognized in all news releases and presentations related to this project. A plaque would be placed on the computer as a continued reminder to the community of your generous spirit and interest in family service. The computers would be available to all families whenever they are not in use for the Moms and Tots Program.

This project will make a difference in the educational success of children and the ability of young mothers to get workplace skills and gain confidence in using state-of-the art equipment. We will be calling you to set up an appointment and we look forward to having the opportunity to further describe this project.

Sincerely,

(signed by both agency representatives.)

Figure B-4: Sample Request for Funding Letter

A LETTER TO AN INSURANCE COMPANY THAT PRIDES ITSELF IN MANAGED CARE FOR CHILDREN.

Dear Mr. Jones,

The Community Library and the Department of Social Services are creating a resource center, THE FAMILY ROOM, to ensure that families have the information they need to address everyday problems, to improve communication between parents and children, and to help with tough family and community issues. Your one time financial support of $2500 would enable us to purchase signs which are needed to heighten awareness and improve the visibility of the THE FAMILY ROOM and a video playback unit to allow on-site viewing of information videos.

We know that your insurance company has made an important commitment to young children and families in this community. The need for the THE FAMILY ROOM was identified by the staff of more than 50% of all service programs in this community. It will be a valuable and on-going resource used by parents, caregivers, agency representatives, children and young adults.

A room at the Community Library will be dedicated for this project. The library will contribute $5000 for new books and videos. The library and the Department of Social Services will jointly staff the room and make presentations to community and parent groups as well as visit schools to promote THE FAMILY ROOM.

Any contribution made by your company is tax deductible. Your company would be recognized in all news releases, printed materials and presentations. We would be proud to have a permanent acknowledgement of your company in the form of a placque at the door of the room.

We will be contacting you in two weeks and look forward to meeting with you to discuss your interest in this project and your commitment to families in this community.

Sincerely,

(signed by both agency representatives)

Figure B-5a: Request for Funding

February 23, 1995

John Wingate
Commissioner of Social Services
Suffolk County Department of Social Services
3085 Veterans Memorial Highway
Ronkonkoma, NY 11779

Dear Commissioner Wingate,

Enclosed is a request for funding for further development of the Suffolk County Information and Referral Database. This proposal outlines the next step or building block towards a comprehensive computerized listing of services.

As you know, Middle Country Library and members of the Suffolk Coalition for Parents and Children have been working on this project since 1991. The recent transfer of 4000 records to our on-line computer system has been completed and we are now pursuing various avenues of funding to add to and update the already extensive database.

Our first major goal is to add and update entries based on the Suffolk Community Council's Directory published in 1989 and to provide the Council with a current listing in a word processing format that they can produce in paper copy for wide distribution. The proposal we are submitting covers all costs to produce the data base in a word processing format for the Council. The Council will submit a proposal for producing the paper copies.

In the meantime, we will work with your Response Unit to facilitate access and regular use of the database on-line. They can provide us with critical feedback in assessing the database for content and currency.

We look forward to working with you and your staff on this interagency endeavor that has long range implications for maximizing access to human services in our county.

Very truly yours,

Sandra Feinberg
Director

cc: Ruth Kleinfeld, Director, Suffolk Community Council

Figure B-5b: Budget for Information and Referral Database

SUFFOLK COUNTY INFORMATION & REFERRAL DATABASE "BUILDING BLOCK" PROPOSAL FOR DEVELOPMENT

A. EXPANSION OF DATABASE

Surveying, coding and data entry of approximately 325 agencies/programs, governmental entities, etc. included in the last edition of Suffolk Community Council's print directory of Community Resources that are not currently in the database.

325 @ $25 per entry $8125

B. CAPACITY FOR PRINT DIRECTORY PRODUCTION

Purchase of software component that would allow downloading of data into a word processing program for purposes of paper directory production.

$7500

C. DATABASE ACCESS ENHANCEMENTS

Additional port to handle greater volume using system to ensure quick dial-up access to database. Includes port, modem, line installation and annual line charges.

$3125

TOTAL COST $18,750

FUTURE DEVELOPMENT

1) Additional entries at the request of Commissioner's Response Unit @ $25 per added entry.

2) Dedicated port/terminals for DSS Response Unit and JOBS program.

3) Assistance towards annual maintenance of database.

Figure B-6: Letter of Support for Information and Referral Database

LONG ISLAND'S UNITED WAY

819 Grand Boulevard
Deer Park, II, NY 11729-3766
516 593-6400 • Fax 516 593-6439

April 7, 1995

Ms. Sandra Feinberg
Computerized Information & Referral Database Project
c/o Middle Country Public Library
101 Eastwood Boulevard
Centereach, NY 11720-2745

Dear Ms. Feinberg,

On behalf of United Way of Long Island, I am pleased to inform you that our Board of Directors at its March 23rd meeting approved a motion to support the further development of the Suffolk Coalition for Parents and Children's *Computerized Information & Referral Database Project.*

We recognize that the participation of strongly committed organizations is critical to the Project's success. We will continue to provide the services of our Director of First Call for Help to the Project's Steering Committee and offer any technical assistance needed as the Project works to make the database more comprehensive and reach new users.

United Way believes that an *Island-wide* computerized database of human care resources will be of great assistance to its First Call for Help Information and Referral program as well as to its member agencies. We look forward to future collaborations to achieve this goal.

Sincerely,

Robert L. Wendt

Robert L. Wendt
Chairman
First Call for Help Committee

Figure B-7: Letter of Support for "Train the Trainer Institutes"

November 7, 1994

Steve Held
Executive Director
Just Kids Early Childhood Learning Center
PO Box 12
Middle Island, NY 11953

Dear Steve,

I am very pleased to write this letter in support of Just Kids proposal for funding to develop and deliver training programs for the New York State Early Intervention Program. It is an exciting and innovative approach to reaching families and providing them with information and support. My staff and I are committed to your idea and would be most pleased to work with you on the presentation of the "Train the Trainer Institutes," the development of materials for parents, librarians and early childhood educators, and the implementation of the grant under Part B, representing the Long Island region.

The Middle Country Public Library is a recognized leader in New York State in the development of parent resources, early childhood programming, and information and referral services in the public library setting. Our library initiated the Parent/Child Workshop (a model library-based family support program) in 1979 and has since mentored over 30 libraries statewide in the development of this early intervention program. We conducted the statewide training for the participants of the "Parenting Centers in Public Libraries" grants under the sponsorship of the Developmental Disabilities Planning Council in 1992/1993. We are a founding member of the Suffolk Coalition for Parents and Children and have provided space and support for the Coalition's bi-monthly informational meetings since 1981. The library was instrumental in starting the Librarians Alliance for Parents and Children, and the Parent Educators Network in Suffolk County and is the recipient of a Rauch Foundation grant to replicate the Parent/Child Workshop in public libraries in Nassau County.

As an adjunct professor at C.W. Post School of Library and Information Studies, I have developed a course in library-based family support services. I have also co-authored the *Parent/Child Workshop: A How-To-Do-It Manual* to be published by Neal-Schuman Publishers in January 1995, and have recently signed a contract to publish another manual entitled *Serving Families and Children Through Partnerships*. Barbara Jordan, Coordinator of the library's Suffolk Family Education Clearinghouse, will also be directly involved in the development of our proposal. She is the chief editor of the library's publication, *Audiovisual Resources for Family Programming,* and is currently serving as Vice President of the Family Resource Coalition of New York State.

Thank you for inviting us to participate in your proposal. We are committed to working with the Just Kids staff as well as the other professionals you have garnered for implementation of your proposal should you be awarded this grant.

Sincerely,

Sandra Feinberg,
Director

Figure B-8: Proposal Overview of PIRL

PROPOSAL OVERVIEW

The PIRL (PARENT INFORMATION RESOURCE LIBRARY)

The Onondaga County Public Library System was chartered by the New York State Board of Regents to serve residents and public libraries in Onondaga County. The system is composed of a Central Library in downtown Syracuse, 8 city branches, 2 satellites, one bookmobile, 20 independent libraries in Onondaga County, and 3 independent libraries in Oswego County. During the past decade, the Onondaga County Public Library System has administered grant-funded projects to serve the functionally illiterate, the disabled community, non-English speaking families, older adults and the economically disadvantaged.

The purpose of this project is to make available to parents, prospective parents, caregivers, and agency personnel a comprehensive one-stop source for information and referral needs. The intent of the PIRL is to promote information and library resources as tools to help prevent the occurrence of developmental disabilities, to assist in early intervention, and to empower families with children having developmental delays and disabilities.

The services of the PIRL will include a multi-media, multi-cultural collection for adults of all reading and learning levels. An information and referral database of community resources and programs will be available. Under the direction of the Project Director, Onondaga County Public Library System's Coordinator of Children's Services, a health educator will develop the multi-media collection, will create the database, and will provide a resource directory that samples the PIRL holdings for individuals and agencies. The health educator will also provide training for Onondaga County Public Library staff, provide public information programs at non-traditional outreach sites, and hold regular consultation sessions at the PIRL.

The PIRL will be established through a task force of Onondaga County Public Library staff, Onondaga County representatives who provide prevention, parenting and family support services, and PIRL clients. The task force will assist in planning, implementation, and evaluation of the PIRL.

The PIRL will be based at the Central Library of the Onondaga County Public Library System. Special attention will be given to the near west and southwest areas of the city of Syracuse through mini-collections at the Southwest Community Center Library and the Mundy Branch Library, the location for the Neighborhood Based Initiative. Promotion of the PIRL will include open house events, speaking engagements, a wide distribution of a simple handbill, and press releases to the media. Quantitative and qualitative evaluation will be on-going through all phases of the project for continuous reassessment. The total funds requested from the Developmental Disabilities Planning Council are $50,000.

Figure B-9: Sample Project Description for Meeting Mother Goose

"Meeting Mother Goose" funded by Library Services and Construction Act Title I Onondaga County Public Library, Syracuse, NY

"Meeting Mother Goose" is designed to encourage, support and train children's librarians to serve children 0-3 years of age and their parents with developmentally appropriate story hour programs and book collections. A series of 3 training programs covering language development, child development and library programs for babies and toddlers will be presented in Onondaga County for approximately 34 children's librarians. The first two programs will be presented by local early childhood specialists. The third program will be presented by Jane Marino, co-author of <u>Mother Goose Time.</u> In addition librarians from neighboring library systems will be invited to attend the training.

The Central Library, 5 urban branches and 6-10 suburban and rural libraries in Onondaga and Oswego Counties will be given toddler and Mother Goose story time book and music collections. The Coordinator of Children's Services and two other experienced children's librarians will assist the 22 libraries in the development of a toddler, Mother Goose or baby story time series or in the improvement of an existing series.

Figure B-10a: Support Materials for Information and Referral Database

Computerized I&R Database Project

If you are excited about revolutionizing the delivery of I&R service in Suffolk County, read on...

☐ The Project _____

The **Computerized Information and Referral Database**, a directory of health and human services and resources for individuals and families, includes information on more than 4000 agencies and programs in the Suffolk County/Long Island area. No other database currently exists of this magnitude. It is the most accessible and detailed computerized directory currently in development and our goal is to make it the most comprehensive as well. Each entry contains a description of services, addresses, phone numbers, contact persons, office hours, eligibility, and geographic service areas. The database can be instantly searched by agency name, subject, or keyword and limited by geographic area or by combining search terms. It is available on-line via modem for maximum accessibility.

This database was initiated by a consortium of public and private community agencies in Suffolk County and through the support of the Suffolk Coalition for Parents and Children. The Suffolk County Youth Bureau, Suffolk County Department of Social Services, and Suffolk County Department of Health Services have provided critical financial support and professional leadership to this initiative (see timeline attached). Middle Country Public Library is the Central Manager for the project and the ongoing development of the database is guided by a Steering Committee (see attached list). The Steering Committee is actively seeking funding for its maintenance.

The intent of the **Computerized Information & Referral Database** is to have one, comprehensive, shareable, up-to-date and consistent database of local community resources that is centrally updated and available countywide. Individuals and families and the human service personnel working to assist them need access to current information about available community resources and services. The advantages of a computerized database include easy updating, consistency of information, ease of access through in-depth indexing and keyword search capability, and the avoidance of duplication of effort by having the labor intensive task of data collection and maintenance handled centrally. Index terms are based on the *Info Line Taxonomy of Human Services* which has been accepted as the national standard by the Alliance of Information and Referral Systems (AIRS).

Figure B-10b: Support Materials for Information and Referral Database

Computerized I & R Database Project
Steering Committee

Brookhaven Town Youth Bureau
Cornell Cooperative Extension of Suffolk
Family Service League of Suffolk
Middle Country Public Library
Patchogue-Medford Public Library
Suffolk Community Council
Suffolk Cooperative Library System
Suffolk County Department of Social Services
Suffolk County Health Department

Suffolk County Inter-Agency Coordinating Council
Suffolk County Labor Department
Suffolk County Women's Services
Suffolk County Youth Bureau
United Way First Call For Help
Victim's Information Bureau

AGENCIES WHO HAVE PARTICIPATED IN THE DEVELOPMENT OF THIS PROJECT

BROOKHAVEN YOUTH BUREAU
CHILD CARE COUNCIL OF SUFFOLK, INC.
CORAM HEALTH CENTER
HEALTH AND WELFARE COUNCIL OF NASSAU COUNTY
HEALTH HOUSE
ISLIP HOTLINE
KINGS PARK HOTLINE/KINGS PARK PSYCHIATRIC
  CENTER
LONG ISLAND HOUSING PARTNERSHIP, INC.
LONG ISLAND SELF HELP CLEARINGHOUSE
MASTICS-MORICHES-SHIRLEY COMMUNITY LIBRARY
MIDDLE COUNTRY CENTRAL SCHOOL
MIDDLE COUNTRY PUBLIC LIBRARY
RESPONSE
SCOPE
SMITHTOWN CENTRAL SCHOOL DISTRICT
SUFFOLK COMMUNITY COUNCIL
SUFFOLK COOPERATIVE LIBRARY SYSTEM
SUFFOLK COUNTY DEPARTMENT OF HEALTH/
  BUREAU OF PUBLIC HEALTH NURSING
SUFFOLK COUNTY DEPARTMENT OF HEALTH/SOCIAL
  WORK DEPARTMENT

SUFFOLK COUNTY DEPARTMENT OF HEALTH/
  SPEAKER'S BUREAU
SUFFOLK COUNTY DEPARTMENT OF SOCIAL
  SERVICES
SUFFOLK COUNTY DEPARTMENT OF SOCIAL
  SERVICES/CHILD PROTECTIVE SERVICES
SUFFOLK COUNTY DEPARTMENT OF SOCIAL
  SERVICES/FAMILY AND CHILD SERVICE BUREAU
SUFFOLK COUNTY DEPARTMENT OF SOCIAL
  SERVICES/WELFARE MANAGEMENT UNIT
SUFFOLK COUNTY EXECUTIVE'S OFFICE OF
  MANAGEMENT AND RESEARCH
SUFFOLK COUNTY MENTAL HEALTH DEPARTMENT
SUFFOLK COUNTY OFFICE FOR WOMEN
SUFFOLK COUNTY YOUTH BUREAU/OFFICE FOR
  CHILDREN
UNITED WAY OF LONG ISLAND
VICTIM'S INFORMATION BUREAU

Figure B-10c: Support Materials for Information and Referral Database

POSITION STATEMENT

COMPUTERIZED INFORMATION, RESOURCE AND REFERRAL DATA BASE POSITION STATEMENT 1989

The goal of this project is to develop a computerized on-line data base of services to families and children in Suffolk County. This data base will include a comprehensive listing of human service and health agencies, referral services, speakers bureaus and specialized resources.

Among the many advantages of this data base are the following:

(1) ACCESSIBILITY AND ENHANCEMENT OF REFERRAL SERVICES: Information and referral services throughout the county will have access to the data base and contribute to it. For those with a computer, the data base will be accessible either on-line through a modem or through a copied disk.

(2) EASY UPDATING: Updating will be done through one source, thereby increasing efficiency, consistency, and accuracy. This would be in marked contrast to each agency performing independently its own updating--a labor intensive, time consuming, and duplicative task.

(3) COORDINATION OF RESOURCES AND NEEDS ASSESSMENT: This data base will provide a simple method for defining what resources and services are available in Suffolk County and where gaps in services exist.

(4) EASY GENERATION OF DIRECTORIES: Print outs of the current service listings can be easily generated, tailored to the specific needs of organizations and groups.

(5) CROSS REFERENCING CAPABILITY: A computerized system allows data to be sorted by geographic areas, fees, ages served, and other commonly requested sub-categories of information.

(6) CONSISTENCY: A single, county-wide taxonomy defining human care services will be established.

This pro ect is being developed with the help and support of many agencies currently involved in providing information and referral services. Most of them are still using card files and are looking for a computerized system. This is an opportune moment in the development of these services to look at coordinating our efforts to produce a more comprehensive and accessible system.

The committee is made up of a variety of professionals who have had experience in setting up service directories, organizing and running hotlines, locating and training professionals serving families, dealing with classification systems, and providing a variety of educational, health, and human services in Suffolk County. The committee also has the technical expertise of librarians and social service professionals who have used computers to adapt their own files for information and referral. Together, the committee will be able to create a computerized data base to meet the growing need for information, resource sharing, cooperative programming, and improved access to services for families, children and youth.

Figure B-11: Proposed Workplan for Early Intervention Project

Proposed Workplan for Early Intervention Project

The Agencies envision offering six series of Parent/Child Workshops over a period of twelve months. Each series will be six weeks long and be offered at three different time slots each week. While parents are interacting with their child using library materials, qualified resource people will be available to answer questions, provide referrals, and to offer reassurance about developmental issues. The sixth session will be provided by an early intervention team from the DOH who will provide screenings for developmental delays and disabilities and as appropriate, will offer infant monitoring questionnaires to participating families.

Our goal for this project is to achieve the following measurable outcomes:

1. Enroll and support active participation of at least 200 "at risk" families in a library-based early intervention service project (Parent/Child Workshop) by:

a) Retaining the present Workshop Coordinator, Jane Moss, a professional librarian; hiring a librarian trainee or early childhood specialist as project assistant; and providing 10 hours per week of clerical assistance.

b) This coordinator will work through local community agencies, such as the Department of Health, the Family Health Center, WIC, and the Newburgh City School System to attract "at risk" families to the Workshops.

2. Maintain and develop links to community agencies that are already serving this population by:

a) Enrolling qualified resource people to participate in individual sessions.

b) Supporting and developing the understanding that the Department of Health and the Public library share many of the same goals and objectives of the participating agencies.

3. Help this population improve their parenting skills by:

a) Social and verbal interaction between parent and child.

b) Pointing out and reinforcing the value of daily interaction between parent and child by reading and playing together.

c) Providing qualified resource people who will interact with the individual parents and share relevant information on topics such as speech, nutrition, play, child development and physical fitness.

d) Stimulating the development of language and gross motor skills by providing age appropriate toys and materials displayed in a highly accessible manner.

e) Expanding and adjusting our current parenting collection to better reflect this population's needs and interests. Seeking to provide the best in multi-media information as well as high interest/low reading level and English as a second language materials.

f) Providing access to the Department of Health Early Intervention System for Children with developmental delays and/or disabilities.

Figure B-12: Evaluation Strategies for Ready, Set, Read Project

"Ready, Set, Read: Family Literacy for Family Child Care Providers" funded by the Central New York Community Foundation. Onondaga County Public Library, Syracuse, NY.

Quantitative Measures
1. Number of contact hours per family child care provider.
2. Number of family child care providers and the children in their care registering for library cards.
3. Retention of family child care providers in the home-based educational program.

Qualitative Measures
1. Interviews by librarian assistants to determine attitudes about books and libraries before and after the home-based educational program.
2. Written impressions of the librarian assistants on the quality of home visits and the reactions of the family child care provider and children.

Figure B-13: Interagency Partnership Agreement for Museum/Head Start/Library

INTERAGENCY PARTNERSHIP AGREEMENT

MUSEUM/HEAD START/LIBRARY
FEBRUARY 24, 1995

This agreement, entered into the 24th day of February, 1995 by and between **Explorations V Children's Museum,** *hereinafter referred to as "Museum",* **Haines City Center of the East Coast Migrant Head Start Project,** *hereinafter referred to as "Head Start Center", and the* **Bartow Public Library,** *hereinafter referred to as "Library".*
While meeting at the Florida Invitational Conference for Libraries, Head Start and Museums, the parties agree to the following:

1. Create a Portable Museum Display, hereinafter referred to as the Display, for the purpose of informing participants and visitors to the Head Start Center and the Library of the opportunities and programs offered by and at the Museum.
      A. The Display will be designed and created by the Museum, and will hold Museum Brochures, Workshop, Programming and Event Schedules/ Flyers, Photos, and a Handout for the children to take home as an activity. This Handout will be geared to children up to age seven, and will be redeemable upon return to the Museum for a Museum gift (pencil or sticker).
      B. The Head Start Center and the Library agree to pick up the Display upon notification of its completion, and to set up and maintain the Display in a favorable, high traffic location.
      C. The Head Start Center and the Library agree to photocopy all documents for the display as demand warrants, to maintain the Display in a well-stocked, neat, orderly, and complimentary condition. In event of wear & tear or damage, the Head Start Center and the Library will return the Display to the Museum for replacement.
      Timeline: By 4/1/95, the Museum will construct the Display and will contact the Head Start Center and the Library for pick up by 4/15/95, to be displayed immediately thereafter.
      Evaluation: The Head Start Center and the Library will track by count the Display Handouts as they exit their facilities to measure the utilization and effectiveness of the Display, and the Museum will track by count the Display Handouts returned to the Museum for redemption.

11. Include Head Start Center children/parents/coordinators and Library participants in Museum outreach programs, Magical Mondays and Terrific Tuesdays.
      A. Head Start Center and Library have agreed to encourage their participants to utilize the Museum program, Magic Mondays, a program geared toward children ages 1½–3 and their caregivers, which offers age-appropriate creative fun, songs, games, crafts, and storytelling.
      B. Head Start Center has agreed to transport small groups of Head Start Center participants to Terrific Tuesdays—a Museum program geared toward children ages 2–5 and their caregivers, which focuses on caregiver/child development and relationships. Terrific Tuesdays are conducted once/month on the second Tuesday, from 9:30am to 11:00am. Head Start Center has agreed to register participants in advance according to Museum enrollment requirements. The Library has agreed to encourage participants to utilize this program.
      C. The Museum has designated the Head Start Center a recipient of a donated Family Membership, which will allow program participants to register for programs as Museum members, allowing discounted fees, effective 2/95.

Figure B-13: Interagency Partnership Agreement for Museum/Head Start/Library (cont'd)

INTERAGENCY PARTNERSHIP AGREEMENT (cont'd.)

Timeline: Head Start Center has agreed to target April 12, 1995 as the Initial Terrific Tuesday program to attend. Entitled "Trash to Treasures" Sharon Gray, workshop presenter, shares inexpensive ways to create educational tools for children from items readily available in the home.

Evaluation: The Museum has agreed to design a survey form for program participants to measure the effectiveness of the program, and the Head Start Center has agreed to communicate to the Museum any undocumented participant comments or anecdotes.

III. Sharing of Resources

A. The Head Start Center has agreed to provide Hispanic translation services to the Museum upon request as services are available by the Head Start Center.

B. The Library has agreed to provide a program presenter for the Head Start Center or the Museum on selected topics, i.e: storytelling, library skills, literacy.

C. The Head Start Center has agreed to provide a program presenter for the Library or the Museum on selected topics, i.e: parent training, child development.

Timeline: Effective immediately.

Evaluation: Program presenters will be evaluated by program participants.

Figure B-14: Memorandum of Agreement Between Head Start and Library

MEMORANDUM OF AGREEMENT

This agreement is between the City of Oakland Head Start Program and the Oakland Public Library regarding special programs and related materials and services to be provided by the Library for the benefit of Head Start children, parents and teachers.

ADMINISTRATION
The library hereby designates Julie Odofin, Coordinator of Children's Services as its liaison to the Library for purposes of administering the agreement.

Any change, amendment to, or other variation from this agreement shall be in writing and duly signed by authorized representatives of the parties.

Any dispute arising between the parties during the course of the agreement, if it cannot be resolved informally, shall be decided by arbitration. Each party shall appoint an arbitrator who together shall select a third arbitrator to serve on an arbitration panel. The dispute shall be resolved by the panel under the rules of the American Arbitration Association, with a majority of two votes necessary for resolution. This agreement may be canceled by either party upon 30 days written notice to the other party.

TERM OF AGREEMENT
The term of this agreement is from October 1, 1994–September 30, 1995, or commencing on the notification of Award of Books for Wider Horizons Grant or on whichever one comes first.

LIBRARY SERVICES AND MATERIALS
The Library shall, at reasonable times to be agreed upon by the parties:
1. Provide at least 176 literacy focused programs, each last approximately 40 minutes for children at 8 Head Start sites (morning and afternoon sessions) between October 1, 1994–September 30, 1995,
2. Provide (1) literacy/library focused program for Head Start parents at Head Start centers lasting approximately 15 hours,
3. Provide (1) library/literacy focused program for Head Start teachers, parents, and children at main library's site lasting approximately 15 hours,
4. Provide special, long term (four week) book loan arrangements for Head Start sites and families,
5. Provide one (1) special orientation program at the Library for Head Start teachers in family literacy and the related use of library resources.
6. Provide library consulting services for Head Start Teachers not to exceed 15 hours in book selection for Head Start classes and to assist Head Start in expanding on books/topics used in its program.
7. Provide tutoring services as applicable for Head Start parents in need of literacy services.
8. Provide special notice and invitation to Head State classes and families concerning regular library activities for children which would be applicable to the children's ages and interests, such as storytimes, special children's programs, etc.
9. Provide books and materials to Head Start children, parents, and teachers which will be deposited in each Head Start Center.
10. Provide literacy events and activities during Head Start's monthly visit to neighborhood libraries.

HEAD START SERVICES AND MATERIALS
Head Start shall, at reasonable times to be agreed upon by the parties:
1. Provide transportation for Project staff and Volunteers to present weekly reading programs at Head Start Sites.

Figure B-14: Memorandum of Agreement Between Head Start and Library (cont'd)

MEMORANDUM OF AGREEMENT (cont'd.)

3. Reimburse the Library for books and other materials deposited in each center.
4. Provide two to four volunteer to be trained by library staff to assist with the Head Start Library program.
5. Provide a set, dedicated and agreed upon time for programs specified herein with no other activities scheduled that would interfere with the programs.
6. Provide childcare while parents receive literacy tutoring from Second Start/Families for Literacy.

PAYMENT
Head Start shall pay the Library $10,000 for the children's books and learning materials to be purchased for purpose of developing permanent book collections in 8 Head Start Centers.

FEDERAL FUN REQUIREMENTS APPLICABLE
All federal regulations pertaining to equal employment opportunity, wages, non-discrimination in employment, and other requirements found in the Code of Federal Regulations with respect to recipients of federal funds are applicable.

Dated: June 2, 1994
Signed

Director, Oakland Public Library   Director, Oakland Head Start

APPENDIX C: SERVICES, SURVEYS, AND EVALUATION FORMS

Figure C-1: Whole Services Worksheet: Internal Review Form

WHOLE SERVICES WORKSHEET

INTERNAL REVIEW

RESOURCES	Strengths	Weaknesses	Barriers
Staff			
Collection			
Physical Space			
Special Activities/ Programs			

created by Lindsay Ruth (Ruth and Feldman, "The Whole Service Approach," SLJ, May 1994.)

Figure C-2: Whole Services Worksheet: External Review Form

WHOLE SERVICES WORKSHEET

EXTERNAL REVIEW

STRENGTHS	Agency A	Agency B	Agency C
Staff			
Collection			
Physical Space			
Special Activities/ Programs			

created by Lindsay Ruth (Ruth and Feldman, "The Whole Service Approach," SLJ, May 1994.)

Figure C-3: Family Service Self-Assessment Questionnaire

Family Service Self-Assessment Questionnaire

1.   **The greatest strengths of our family service are:** _____
_____
_____

    What do you think family members would say? _____
_____
_____

    What do you think other service providers would say? _____
_____
_____

2.   **We need to work on the following in order to have a more comprehensive, family-centered, and commmunity-based family service program that is coordinated among providers:** _____
_____
_____

    What do you think family members would say? _____
_____
_____

    What do you think other service providers would say? _____
_____
_____

Adapted from "Self-Assessment and the Change Process: Applications in Early Intervention," Madison: Waisman Center UAP, University of Wisconsin.

Figure C-4: Quality Indicator Assessment Tool

QUALITY INDICATOR ASSESSMENT TOOL

CS=CURRENT STATUS:
1=a strength; 2=needs strengthening;
3=not a strength, would like 4=not a priority

I=IMPORTANCE:
1=very important; 2=important;
3=somewhat important; 4=not important

Quality Indicator

WORKING WITH PARENTS	CS	I
1. Provide parent(s) with pertinent information on programs and services. _____		
2. Give parents written materials about the library._____		
3. Establish rapport, giving ample opportunity for parent(s) to ask questions. _____		
4. Interact with families in a manner that is respectful of individual and cultural diversity._____		
5. Offer parent(s) choices in programs for their children and themselves. _____		
6. Assist parents in obtaining information and services that the library cannot provide. _____		
7. Utilize good communication skills (e.g.active listening, questioning, checking of understanding) to develop partnerships with parents._____		
9. Facilitate parent(s) participation in planning for new library services and evaluating existing services. _____		
10. Ensure that parent(s) can participate in all programs available for their children. _____		
11. Share information, knowledge and skills with families to help them become more knowledgeable, skilled and confident._____		
12. Provide services that reflect parent's preferences for type, location, duration, and frequency. _____		
13. Offer parent(s) choices about level of participation in services._____		
14. Offer parent to parent services not only parent-child services. _____		
15. Minimize procedures and policies that block parent and child participation. _____		
16. Have written policies and plans that support family centered philosophy and practice. _____		

WORKING WITH OTHER AGENCIES	CS	I
1. Share information about formal and informal services for families. _____		
2. Participate in the coordination of services. _____		
3. Work collaboratively to address service gaps. _____		
4. Recognize that parent(s) assume or want to assume responsibility for the services they need. _____		
5. Strengthen information and referral service to address family needs. _____		
6. Provide services that reflect the agency need for information. _____		
7. Offer agencies choice in their level of participation._____		
8. Minimize policy and procedure that block agency participation. _____		

Adapted from Self Assessment and the : hange Process: Applications in Early Intervention," Waisman Center UAP, University of Wisconsin, Madison.

Figure C-5: Parent's Evaluation of Toddler Story Hour

Parent's Evaluation - Toddler Story Hour

We would appreciate your comments about this program in order to help evaluate its worth and to help determine whether it should be continued.

Time of Day:	Too early _____	Too late _____	OK _____
Length:(each program)	Too short _____	Too long _____	OK _____
Length:(series)	Too short _____	Too long _____	OK _____
Place:	Too small _____	Too many distractions _____	OK _____
Size of group:	Too large _____	OK _____	

Program and materials used:

        Not enough planned _____   Too much planned _____

        Child not interested in stories   _____

        Child not interested in activities   _____

        Stories, activities too old for child   _____

        Stories, activities too young for child   _____

        Stories, activities OK   _____

Would you attend this program again? _____

Why or why not? _____

_____

Would you recommend this program to a friend or neighbor?   Yes _____   No _____

Did you find this program helpful in selecting library materials for your child? Yes _____   No _____

Since you both began participating in the program, have you noticed any changes in your child:

Long attention span	Yes _____	No _____
Greater interest in looking at books	Yes _____	No _____
Greater interest in listening to stories at home	Yes _____	No _____
Greater enjoyment and interest in coming to the library	Yes _____	No _____
Greater rapport with other children	Yes _____	No _____
Greater rapport with adults outside the family	Yes _____	No _____

Do you have any comments you would like to add? _____

_____

_____

Reprinted with permission of Upper Merion Township Library, King of Prussia, PA

Figure C-6: Parent/Child Workshop Evaluation Form

Parent/Child Workshop Evaluation Form
Middle Country Public Library

I. GENERAL INFORMATION

Name _____

Date _____

Child's Age _____

II. COMMUNITY RESOURCES

A. Did you feel the resource people were a necessary and valuable part of the workshop?
  1. Speech pathologist: yes __ no __ did not attend session _____
  2. Librarian, books and reading: yes ____ no _____ did not attend session _____
  3. Child behavior specialist: yes ___ no ___ did not attend session _____
  4. Nutritionist: yes ____ no ___ did not attend session _____
  5. Movement specialist: yes __ no __ did not attend session _____

B. Comment if you were specifically affected from contact with any of the resource people.
_____

C. Were you made aware of other local parenting groups or playgroups, i.e., Direction Center, Child Care Council, Parents Anonymous, etc.?
yes _____ no _____

III. MATERIALS

A. Did you check out any parenting materials provided in the workshop?
yes _____ no _____
B. Did you check out any children's books or materials provided in the workshop?
yes _____ no _____
C. Did you take any of the free handouts?
yes ____ no _____
D. What were your child's favorite toys? _____
E. Do you have any toy suggestions? _____

IV. GENERAL REACTION AND FUTURE PROGRAMS

A. Your general reaction to the workshop is _____
_____
B. What did you like best? _____
C. What did you like least? _____
D. Would you be interested in Parenting Workshops (adults only)   yes ___ no ___
Topics? _____

Figure C-7: Program Registration Survey

PROGRAM REGISTRATION SURVEY

Adult _____

I prefer Fall registration in:
      late August_____
      Early September_____

I found registration today:
      satisfactory_____
      unsatisfactory_____

Do you prefer registration for both
Departments on the same day?
      yes_____
      no_____
      does not apply _____

Children _____

I prefer Fall registration in:
      late August_____
      Early September_____

I found registration today:
      satisfactory_____
      unsatisfactory_____

Do you prefer registration for both
Departments on the same day?
      yes_____
      no_____
      does not apply_____

Comments: _____
_____
_____
_____

Thank you for taking the time to fill out the survey. We appreciate your input.

(optional)   Name _____
                Phone # _____

MIDDLE COUNTRY PUBLIC LIBRARY

Figure C-8: In-Service Evaluation Form

IN-SERVICE EVALUATION FORM

In-Service Date: Presentation Title:
Presenter:

Please answer the following questions by circling the appropriate answer:

Prior to this in-service
did you refer clients to the library? yes no rarely
did you recognize the library's role in
family service? yes no somewhat
Did today's presentation give you reasons to refer
your clients to the library? yes no somewhat
Examples:

Are there library services that could help you do
your job better? yes no
Examples:

Are you interested in working with the
library in the area of family service? yes no

Was the presentation informative? yes no somewhat
clear? yes no somewhat

Is there more information you would like? yes no

Name: (optional) _____
Phone: (optional) _____

APPENDIX D: PUBLICITY MATERIALS

Figure D-1a: PIRL Brochure

PIRL

...a unique place with information to meet the needs of parents and caregivers.

PIRL offers information on:

- pregnancy
- discipline
- health
- general parenting
- child development
- nutrition
- parenting children with special needs

BORROW, BROWSE OR CALL!

PIRL offers the following features:

- books
- pamphlets
- videos
- community information
- video viewing

Hazard Branch Hours:
Mon., Wed., Fri. & Sat. 9–5
Tues.& Thurs. 9–9
Summer hours may vary

This publication was supported by a grant from the New York State Developmental Disabilities Planning Council.

PARENT INFORMATION RESOURCE LIBRARY

at
HAZARD BRANCH
Onondaga County Public Library
1620 West Genesee Street
Syracuse, New York
468-1628

Figure D-1b: PIRL Brochure

PIRL
(Parent Information Resource Library)

In 1992, the Onondaga County Public Library was one of five libraries to receive a grant from the New York State Developmental Disabilities Planning Council to create a library-based parenting center. The purpose of this project is to make available to parents, prospective parents, caregivers and agency personnel a comprehensive one-stop source for information and referral needs.

PIRL—a unique place, a library within a library.

The PIRL is located in a separate room on the main floor of the Hazard Branch Library, Onondaga County Library and has been designed for the comfort and convenience of parents and caregivers. For any young children of PIRL visitors, there are toys, picture books and a playpen available. The private space is perfect for browsing the book collection or viewing videos on site.

All of PIRL's materials (videos and books) may be borrowed at Hazard or transferred to a city branch or suburban library.

Please call 468-1628 for any additional videos and books, and for information available through PIRL.

Figure D-2: Flyer on New Mothers Discussion Group

Children's Services Department
Middle Country Public Library

New Mothers Discussion Group

A Five-Week Program for first-time new mothers and babies, birth to eleven months. The goal of this program is to give new mothers confidence in their parenting skills and reduce their sense of isolation.

The topics to be covered by the group are as follows:

October 17   *Postpartum:* sharing the birthing experience, the experiences of the first month at home with the baby and how parents' life styles have changed.

October 24   *Growth/Development/Play:* discussion will focus on child development in the first 12 months and the importance of play to the baby.

October 31   *Nutrition:* overview of healthy nutrition and the feeding experience of the infant.

November 7   *Safety:* discussion of safety factors in selecting baby equipment, toys and the potential safety hazards in baby's home environment.

November 14   *Mother Goose Nursery Rhymes Program.*

For more information call the Children's Services Department at 585-9393.

Middle Country Public Library
101 Eastwood Boulevard
Centereach, NY 11720

Figure D-3: Flyer on Family Resource Fair

FAMILY RESOURCE FAIR

SAVE THE DATE – PARTICIPATE!

A DAY OF
INFORMATION AND NETWORKING
For Professionals and Parents

Wednesday, May 9, 1990
9:30 - 12:30 pm

Middle Country Public Library
101 Eastwood Blvd., Centereach, NY 11720
585-9393, ext. 220

• • Caring People Sharing Information About Suffolk's Resources • •

Programs for Youth	Family Services
Children's Services	Substance Abuse: Prevention
Bilingual Agencies	& Treatment
Health Services	School Based Programs

This Year's Opportunity to Meet Face-to-Face and Under One Roof

Co-Sponsors
Suffolk Coalition for Parents and Children
Suffolk Family Education Clearinghouse
Suffolk County Youth Bureau/Office for Children

Figure D-4: Flyer on Parent Connections

Middle Country Public Library
is pleased to announce
the formation of:

"Parent Connections"
A Support Group and Workshop Series
for Parents of Young Children
with Special Needs

Workshops will be held on Monday evenings from 7:00pm–9:00pm at the Cultural Center in the Early Childhood Room on the following dates:

January 23	March 13	April 24
February 6	March 27	May 8
February 27	April 10	May 22

Parenting a child with special needs is rewarding, but can sometimes present parents with special challenges. Often, parents feel alone, and isolated from friends and other family members.

You are not alone in these feelings and experiences! Come and join our group, and learn strategies to reduce stress, increase coping and communication skills, and meet your need for support. Attendance at all sessions is not mandatory.

— — — — — — — — — — — — — — Registration Form — — — — — — — — — — — — — — — —

Please return by **January 20, 1995** to: Middle Country Public Library, Children's Services Dept.,
101 Eastwood Blvd., Centereach, NY 11720-2745
Attention: Margaret Sampson, 732-1478

_____ I would like join "Parent Connections"

Name: _____ Phone (day) _____

Address: _____ Phone (evening) _____

_____

Figure D-5: Flyer on Kids' Answer Place

Kids' Answer Place

WHO: •Children, teens and concerned adults

WHAT: •Information about tough family and community issues such as AIDS, adoption, death, divorce, conflict resolution and substance abuse. Over 700 videos and books pulled together provide improved access.

WHERE: •Children's World, Level 4, Central Library

WHEN: •All regular Central Library hours (Monday, Thursday, Friday and Saturday 9–5, Tuesday and Wednesday 9–8:30).

WHY: •To help families and child care professionals find information and facilitate communication around difficult issues.

HOW: •Funds from: Blue Cross, New York State, Onondaga County

Figure D-6: Flyer on Parents Anonymous

Help and Support for Parents Under Stress ..... *because parenting is the hardest job in the world.*

Parents Anonymous might be the answer for you.

Parents Anonymous, a professionally lead support group, meets weekly at the Cultural Center in Selden, for parents needing help coping with the stresses of parenthood. Also open to non-residents.

*** For more information call**
24 hour helpline: 265-3311

Figure D-7: News Release for Infant-Toddler Screening

NEWS RELEASE - INFANT-TODDLER SCREENING

FOR FURTHER INFORMATION:

Mastics-Moriches-Shirley
Community Library
Children's & Parents' Services
(516) 399-1511 Ext. 266
October 8, 1991

FOR IMMEDIATE RELEASE

INFANT-TODDLER SCREENING

Do you have questions about your infant or toddler's development? Are you concerned about how he or she is:

Learning to talk?
Learning to walk?
Understanding things?
Eating or sleeping?
Playing and exploring?
Relating to you and others?

If so, you are invited to the MASTICS-MORICHES-SHIRLEY COMMUNITY LIBRARY on Thursday, November 7th, between 9:00 a.m. - 4:00 p.m. Developmental screenings will be provided by Just Kids Diagnostic and Treatment Center for children ages birth through two.

The library is located on William Floyd Parkway in Shirley. Please call 399-1511, Ext. 262 to make an appointment.

Figure D-8: Flyer on Nursery School Fair

Nursery School Fair

Sponsored by

Children's Services Department

Representatives from area nursery schools and preschool programs will be available to answer your questions.

DATE: Saturday, January 27, 1996
.TIME: 10:30 - 12:00
PLACE: Main Library

This program is open to the general public and no pre-registration is required.

Middle Country Public Library
101 Eastwood Boulevard
Centereach, NY 11720
585-9393

Figure D-9: Flyer on Project Link

Project Link: The Library, Family Day Care, Parent/Child Connection

Attention

Family Home Daycare Providers

The Middle Country Public Library has received a grant from the New York State Education Department to develop and circulate storytime kits to family home day care providers in the Middle Country District.

Each kit will contain books, a video, a puzzle or puppet and activities to use with the children in your care.

Special programs will also be offered at the library for family day care providers, for parents and children together.

Interested? Call the library at 585-9393 ext. 362.

Middle Country Public Library
101 Eastwood Blvd.
Centereach, NY 11720
585-9393

Figure D-10: Flyer on Parent and Child Workshop (English version)

Parent and Child Workshop

Play and Learn at the Newburgh Free Library

A special invitation for families with children from ages birth to 3 years who have not previously attended Library pre-school programs.

- •Spend time with your child
- •Play together
- •Create art, make music & enjoy books
- •Meet new people at the Library

Community professionals will be on hand to answer questions about your child's speech and hearing, fitness, nutrition and behavior.

These six-week programs are held Wednesdays or Fridays, from 10:30am to 11:30am. PROGRAMS BEGIN April 26, 1995.

Come to the Library to register, weekdays from 9:00am to 5:00pm. REGISTRATION BEGINS APRIL 3, 1995. For further information, contact the Youth Services Department at 561-1985.

Newburgh Free Library • 124 Grand St. • Newburgh, NY 12550 • 561-1985

Figure D-11: Flyer on Parent and Child Workshop (Spanish version)

Taller Para
Niños Y Padres

Jueguen y aprendan
en La
Biblioteca de Newburgh

Una invitación especial para familias con niños recien nacidos hasta 3 años de edad, que no han asistido a un programa pre-escolar en las bibliotecas.

- **Pase un bien tiempo con su niño**
- **Jueguen juntos**
- **Crean arte, toquen musica y compartan libros (tenemos libros en Español.)**
- **Conozca nuevas personas.**

Professionales de la comunidad estarán presente para contestar sus preguntas sobre el desarollo de la comunicación, el habla y el audio, la habilidad fisica, la nutrición y el comportamiento.

Este programa es de 6 semanas - Miercoles y Viernes Horario: de 10:00 am a 11:00am. EL PROGRAMA COMENZARA EL 18 DE ENERO. Pueden registrarse en la Biblioteca, de Lunes a Viernes de 9:00am - 5:00pm.

Para mas información, comuniquese con los Servicios Juveniles al: 561-1985

Biblioteca de Newburgh • 124 Calle Grand • Newburgh, NY 12550

Figure D-12: Resource Professionals for Parent and Child Workshop

Taller Para Niños Y Padres

Jueguen y aprendan en La
Biblioteca de Newburgh

Lista del Programa

Seman 1	Orientación/Salud & Sequridad Teddy Bear Time (Tiempo de Ositos)	Equipo Padres/Niños Community Health Outreach
Semana 2	Nutrición Pancake	Cornell Cooperative Extension (EFNEP)
Semana 3	Desarollo del Language Head, Shoulders, Knees & Toes (Cabreza, Umbros, Rodillas & Dedos)	Arden Hill Hospital
Semana 4	Habilidad Fisica & Moviemento Hokey Pokey	Maternal Infant Services Network
Semana 5	Arte & Juego Two Little Feet (Dos Piesesitos)	Mount St. Mary College
Semana 6	Evaluación	Orange County Dept. of Health (Dept. de Salud)

Para mas información, comuniquese con los Servicios Juveniles al: 561-1985

Biblioteca de Newburgh • 124 Calle Grand • Newburgh, NY 12550

Figure D-13: News Release on Library/Head Start/Museum Partnership

June 8, 1995

NEWS RELEASE

Library/Head Start/Discovery Center Museum Partnership Begins

ROCKFORD—"Reading can immunize against failure," said Virginia Mathews of the Center for the Book in the Library of Congress as she coordinated a regional workshop April 27-29 in St. Paul, MN. One hundred library, museum and Head Start representatives were selected to attend the workshop hosted by the Minnesota Center for the Book. Rockford was the only community in Illinois to send a complete three-person team, with representatives from Head Start, the Discovery Center Museum and Rockford Public Library.

The purpose of the workshop was to forge friendships, share experiences and plan for future partnerships. Special emphasis was put on planned cooperation, which makes programs better, broadens the base for effective collaborations and brings continuing commitment from all the groups.

As a result of the workshop, City of Rockford Head Start, Discovery Center Museum and Rockford Public Library are beginning a partnership of new dimensions as Head Start runs its very first summer program.

The summer pilot project will take the Library and Discovery Center Museum to Head Start classrooms three times in June and July with thematic programs designed to support Head Start's High Scope curriculum. High Scope encourages young children to make plans for learning based on their own interests and curiosity. Bubbles, Camping and Water are this summer's themes.

Discovery Center Museum will bring wonderful experiential learning activities to children in half-hour sessions. The Library will follow with engaging stories and language play. Project organizers hope to spark children's curiosity, and want children to know that books can satisfy curiosity in unique ways.

The ultimate purpose of the partnership is to work together toward lifelong learning, to encourage family involvement and to develop informal community-based services to support family literacy and learning. Goals are specific—to help children have a better start at school and to encourage more reading activities in homes. They involve helping families to become better teachers of their children and to recognize the poser of learning.

"Not only can this partnership build family literacy, it can also build family social competency," says Granada Williams, Interim Executive Director of City of Rockford's Human Services.
The Library, Discovery Center Museum, and Head Start will begin a different collaborative venture this fall, targeting parents of families served by Head Start. "We believe the enthusiasm, good ideas, and new understanding gained this summer will carry well into a lasting future relationship," Williams said.

For more information, contact Granada Williams, 987-5782

APPENDIX E: SELF STUDY FOR CHILDREN'S LIBRARIAN

SELF STUDY FOR CHILDREN'S LIBRARIAN

It is important for children's librarians or professionals assigned to work with children in the library, particularly with regard to those who work with young children and families, to identify their own strengths and weaknesses. To assist in this self-study process, the following tool is provided. It is intended that the librarian/professional will complete the checklist and, if desired, share the information with people who can assist in obtaining technical assistance and training to enhance those skills that need improvement, and to offer assistance to others in areas where the librarian feels competent.

THE SELF STUDY IS DIVIDED INTO EIGHT SKILL AREAS:

Program and Service Strategies
Program Development and Implementation
Materials and Collections Development
Family Involvement
Support Staff
Administrative Aspects
Interagency Cooperation
Self-Development

THE TOOL LISTS FOUR POSSIBLE REACTIONS:

⬆ HELP! Help is needed as soon as possible. This is something I can learn but I need education and training.

⬆ NEED MORE: No emergency, but perhaps a workshop or conference could help fill this gap in knowledge and skill. Seek help from an experienced colleague.

⬆ OK: No technical assistance is needed. I can and do an adequate job.

⬆ COMPETENT: I feel competent in this area and could serve as a mentor and potential resource to other librarians.

After reading the skill, check the box which best reflects your "level" of need. After you have marked all the items, review the needs assessment and circle the item you would like to work on first. Outline a plan of self-training, research the topic and read relevant materials, talk to colleagues that you feel could provide advice and guidance, and look for training opportunities.

Adapted from: Gaetz, Joan and others. *To Be the Best That We Can Be: A Self-Study Guide for Early Childhood Special Education Programs and Staff.* Poulsbo, WA: Educational Services District 114, Marine Science Center and Oak Harbor School District, 1987.

PROGRAM AND SERVICE STRATEGIES

Help!
Need More
Okay
Competent

	H	N	O	C	COMMENTS
State the philosophy and long range goals of the early childhood and family support programs in the library					
Justify the program strategy that you utilize within each early childhood/parent program.					
Effectively use resources to help plan your program content.					
Structure the physical setting to meet the needs of young children and their parents/caregivers.					
Design and implement appropriate schedules and program content.					
Cooperatively plan and carry out programs with staff members, parents, and other related professionals.					
Apply program/service strategies to meet the needs of young children and their families individually.					
Apply program/service strategies to meet the needs of young children and their families in groups.					
Modify program/service strategies to serve children with special needs and their families.					
Describe strategies to educate children in the least restrictive environment.					
Develop and use a system for evaluating the effectiveness of your program/service.					
Effectively use the expertise of other library professionals in program planning for young children and their families.					
Implement an effective communication system to share information and concerns with staff.					
Other needs and concerns related to program/service strategies:					

PROGRAM DEVELOPMENT AND IMPLEMENTATION

Help! — Need More — Okay — Competent

	H	N	O	C	COMMENTS
Perform a task analysis of a long term goal.					
Describe the steps leading to the development of a program or service.					
Understand child development at all stages so that library programs and policies can reinforce the child's growth.					
Produce a written outline and summary of the program or service.					
Select activities and resources from professional materials and children's collection that best meet the needs of the intended audience.					
Describe the various elements that affect an individual's learning style.					
Modify program/service content to accommodate children with special needs.					
Effectively organize group activities for children, birth through age 8, and their parents.					
Provide opportunities and follow-up activities to reinforce specific program/service.					
Use ongoing evaluation to improve program/service.					
Provide appropriate supervision and management of other staff.					

Other needs and concerns related to program development and implementation:

MATERIALS AND COLLECTIONS DEVELOPMENT

Help! *Need More*
Okay Competent

	H	N	O	C	COMMENTS
Select appropriate commercially produced materials for an early childhood program/service.					
Produce "staff-made" materials to facilitate the achievement of program objectives.					
Effectively *develop* materials which foster independence in learning (learning packets, kits, stations, handouts for home use, etc.)					
Effectively use technology with young children and parents.					
Select, order and catalogue materials for young children and their families.					
Train support staff and parents to use materials effectively.					
Modify materials to make them accessible to children with special needs.					
Evaluate the appropriateness of materials used in programs.					

Other needs and concerns related to materials and collections development:

FAMILY INVOLVEMENT

H = Help!
N = Need More
O = Okay
C = Competent

	H	N	O	C	COMMENTS
Communicate with parents regarding their child's reading interests					
Understand the "parent as teacher" role and its relationship to library service					
Understand the "family centered" approach to library service					
Have knowledge of cultural issues relevant to the population served					
Develop your own rationale for involving families in the program.					
Define the staff's responsibilities and the program's resources in implementing a parent involvement component.					
Initiate and maintain effective communication with the child and his/her family.					
Identify factors in the home that have a positive effect on the child's academic performance.					
Train parents in the process of parenting as it applies to their child's education, particularly with regard to literacy, language development, computer literacy, creativity and independent learning.					
Promote positive parent/child interactions.					
Model appropriate discipline techniques to use with young children.					
Develop creative strategies to encourage participation from all family members.					
Evaluate the effectiveness of involving families in programs.					
Other needs and concerns related to family involvement:					

Help! = H
Need More = N
Okay = O
Competent = C

SUPPORT STAFF

	H	N	O	C	COMMENTS
Justify the need for a family service program.					
Help recruit, interview and place volunteers/support staff appropriately according to needs and abilities.					
Orient new assistants to the program.					
Delegate effectively and in an orderly and gradual manner.					
Provide training opportunities for support staff.					
Facilitate positive interpersonal communication among staff.					
Manage staff time efficiently throughout daily program.					
Implement an effective communication system to relay instruction to and receive information from staff.					
Assess the performance of assistants.					
Other needs and concerns related to support staff:					

ADMINISTRATIVE ASPECTS

	H	N	O	C	COMMENTS
Demonstrate knowledge of standards, guidelines and roles regarding public library service to young children and families.					
Demonstrate knowledge of budget and funding sources for early childhood and parent education services.					
Maintain appropriate internal records relating to the administration of early childhood and parent programs/services.					
Use effective communication strategies with the library administration.					
Other needs and concerns related to adminstrative aspects:					

INTERAGENCY COOPERATION

Help! = **H**elp!
Need More = **N**eed More
Okay = **O**kay
Competent = **C**ompetent

	H	N	O	C	COMMENTS
Exchange program and referral information with other community agencies.					
Understand the referral process as it relates to the role of information and referral in a public library setting, particularly regarding families and young children.					
Identify all agencies in the community who work with young children and families.					
Develop an awareness of public and private agencies providing educational, recreational, and informational services to young children and their families.					
Develop an awareness of local family support programs.					
Develop a channel to disseminate information on library programs to the general public.					
Provide relevant information to the child and his/her family.					
Assist staff in other departments within the library in understanding the goals and functions of the library's early childhood and parent programs.					
Understand the laws concerning child abuse and the services that are provided to help young children and their families with abuse problems.					
Understand the meaning of advocacy as it relates to young children and their families.					
Help coordinate and cooperate with agencies to improve services to the child and his/her family.					
Cooperatively develop programs with other agencies.					
Participate on interagency task forces, coalitions, agency boards, etc. that advocate and work for children and families.					
Integrate library service with other services to families within the community.					

Other needs and concerns related to inter-agency cooperation:

SELF-DEVELOPMENT

H = Help!
N = Need More
O = Okay
C = Competent

	H	N	O	C	COMMENTS
Understand the basic needs of human beings.					
Act relaxed and comfortable with parents and children.					
Maintain good eye contact, often getting down to child's eye level.					
Speak with a voice that is gentle, quiet, calm, and firm sending messages that are direct and clear.					
Use a special voice for talking with young children.					
Exhibit a clean, healthy professional appearance and wear clothes appropriate to the day's work.					
Listen carefully and respectfully to children and parents.					
Exhibit a high tolerance for variety of noise and movement and don't expect order every moment.					
Touch children often with movements that soothe, guide, redirect, reassure, reinforce.					
Identify factors which you need to consider for personal self-growth.					
Examine your personal attitudes towards being a librarian.					
Describe qualities of an effective early childhood and family support professional.					
Analyze professional behavior to understand its impact on child and parent behaviors.					
Create a positive atmosphere that promotes learning.					
Describe stages of librarian development.					
Evaluate your performance in program and service delivery.					
Secure resources to aid you in staff development.					

APPENDIX F: PARENT SATISFACTION SURVEY

PARENT SATISFACTION SURVEY*

Please indicate how satisfied you are with services you receive from your child's program. For each item put a check to show how strongly you agree or disagree with that statement. Your response to each statement is important - any unanswered items have a negative effect on the final score.

GOAL I - PROGRAM AND STAFF RESPONSIVENESS	STRONGLY DISAGREE	DISAGREE	AGREE	STRONGLY AGREE
The library staff listens and responds to my concerns, questions, and ideas.	SD	D	A	SA
The staff gives me information that is clear and useful.	SD	D	A	SA
The library's services and programs focus on my child's needs.	SD	D	A	SA
I am satisfied with my child's experiences when he/she participates in library activities.	SD	D	A	SA
I feel that the library's programming for children includes important learning for me.	SD	D	A	SA
The information and assistance I get fits into our family's needs. I am informed of a variety of choices for my child and my family.	SD	D	A	SA

Comments: (Please comment if you've checked any items SD or D) _____

_____

_____

_____

_____

GOAL II - GROWTH IN KNOWLEDGE AND SKILLS FOR FAMILIES	STRONGLY DISAGREE	DISAGREE	AGREE	STRONGLY AGREE
Because of my family's participation in library programs...				
...I am more able to look at my child and see what he/she is learning to do.	SD	D	A	SA
...I have learned about child development, parenting and family literacy from library programs.	SD	D	A	SA

GOAL II - cont'd.	STRONGLY DISAGREE	DISAGREE	AGREE	STRONGLY AGREE
...I enjoy teaching my child more.				
	SD	D	A	SA
...I know what my child needs to learn.				
	SD	D	A	SA
...I am aware of how ordinary activities are part of my child's learning and development.				
	SD	D	A	SA
...I feel more confident about how my family and I are helping our child.				
	SD	D	A	SA
...I am more aware of how to help my child's development.				
	SD	D	A	SA
...I can feel confident about the library as a family information place.				
	SD	D	A	SA

Comments: (Please comment if you've checked any items SD or D) _____

_____

_____

_____

GOAL III - UTILIZATION OF COMMUNITY RESOURCES	STRONGLY DISAGREE	DISAGREE	AGREE	STRONGLY AGREE
Because of my library use:				
...I know more about community agencies, services, and programs that can help my child or my family.				
	SD	D	A	SA
...I get help from staff when I want referrals to other programs or people to work with me, my child, or my family.				
	SD	D	A	SA
...I now have contact with services and programs in the community which may help my child or my family.				
	SD	D	A	SA
...I am able to get information that is important to the health and happiness of my family and child.				
	SD	D	A	SA

Comments: (Please comment if you've checked any items SD or D) _____

_____

_____

_____

GOAL IV - BUILDING A SUPPORT SYSTEM

	STRONGLY DISAGREE	DISAGREE	AGREE	STRONGLY AGREE

Because of my use of the library...

...my partner/my family are more involved in my child's learning.

SD	D	A	SA

...I have made friends and my child has made friends of other children helping me help my child.

SD	D	A	SA

...staff helped the people I know be more caring and understanding of my child.

SD	D	A	SA

...the library staff are caring and understanding.

SD	D	A	SA

...I have gotten support from other parents.

SD	D	A	SA

...I feel less alone as the parent of my child.

SD	D	A	SA

...staff are willing and able to help my family and friends when we have concerns or questions about my child.

SD	D	A	SA

Comments: (Please comment if you've checked any items SD or D) _____

_____

_____

_____

My child is ___ years ___ months old.

Signature (optional) _____

THANK YOU FOR GIVING US THIS FEEDBACK!

*Adapted from *The Project Dakota Parent Satisfaction Survey,* developed by JoAnne Kovach and Robert Jacks, Project Dakota, Inc., Eagan, MN: June 1989.

APPENDIX G: PARENT EDUCATION AND SUPPORT CHECKLIST

PARENT EDUCATION AND SUPPORT CHECKLIST

Parent education and support programs are one means of supporting and strengthening families. The goal of such programs is to provide parents with the information, skills, and support they need to raise their children and foster an environment that will enable children to develop to their full potentials. Parent education and support programs offer settings where parents can access concrete services such as quality child care, employment and training programs and medical services while also providing opportunities for informal support networks to develop among parents. In addition, parent education and support programs can provide a range of support services to enhance a parent's growth and development, including nutrition, personal health and hygiene, and substance abuse and alcohol prevention.

Parent education and support program models vary according to the populations being served, the communities in which they are based, the staff offering the service, and the particular needs and concerns of the families in the program. New York State, while recognizing the importance and value of allowing for flexibility in local program design, is also working to ensure a standard of quality for parenting services offered throughout the state.

The following checklist represents recommended basic elements of a parent education and support program. It was developed through a state-level review of numerous effective and validated programs, followed by the identification of the successful characteristics of these programs. It is intended to help local providers infuse high-quality parenting services into their program settings and should be used as a self-assessment tool for providers currently delivering services.

The checklist contains program characteristic that are organized into three major areas: Participant, Administration and Policy, and Staff. To use this checklist, compare your program to each of the characteristics below and identify ways your program could be improved or modified to reflect the elements of a high quality parent education and support program.

The Parent Education and Support Checklist was produced by the Interagency Work Group on Parent Education and Support as part of New York Parents. Permission for reprint granted by Gail Koser, New York State Council on Children and Families, Corning Tower Building, Albany, NY.

PARTICIPANT

YES NO WAYS TO IMPROVE

☐ ☐

Parents are offered education, opportunities and information to enhance the development of parental skills, self-confidence and competence on fostering an environment that will help their children develop to their full potential. The following topics might be offered to parents:

_____ child development
_____ family communication skills
_____ discipline and problem-solving techniques
_____ infant and toddler care
_____ health, nutrition and safety (e.g., immunization, poison control and
         Nutrition for Life curriculum)
_____ self esteem enhancement
_____ parent as a child's first teacher and preparing your child for school
_____ family literacy
_____ alcohol/substance abuse prevention
_____ parenting a child with special needs
_____ child abuse and neglect prevention (e.g., anger control, stress
         management)
_____ family and community resources (e.g., health, social services
         and mentoring)
_____ adolescent development
_____ family recreation activities

YES NO WAYS TO IMPROVE

☐ ☐

Parent education information is offered through a variety of learning opportunities, such as:

_____ workshops/classes
_____ discussion groups
_____ facilitated parent/child activities
_____ home visits
_____ parent weekend retreat
_____ family literacy activities
_____ newsletters
_____ peer mentoring relationships
_____ films/videos/television/radio
_____ written materials
_____ roleplaying
_____ videotaping

PARTICIPANT	YES	NO	WAYS TO IMPROVE
Parents have access to high-quality child care. Parallel programming is available for children while parents attend parent education and support activities.	☐	☐	
A procedure has been developed that enables parents to identify their needs regarding childbearing information and problem areas where support is desired.	☐	☐	
Linkages to crisis intervention services are available to families where appropriate.	☐	☐	
Program has increased parental awareness of community resources and services and has facilitated necessary referrals.	☐	☐	
Parents are offered parent training on developing effective participation, decision making, and advocacy skills on behalf of their family.	☐	☐	
Parents are offered supports and services to enhance their personal growth and development. The service might include: _____ *personal health and hygiene* _____ *mental health* _____ *nutrition* _____ *alcohol and substance abuse prevention* _____ *life and human management skills* _____ *education (e.g. GED, Adult Basic Education, English as a Second Language)* _____ *training and employment*	☐	☐	
Parents have access to transportation in order to attend parenting activities.	☐	☐	
Parents are provided with print, audio, and video materials, and suggestions for educational activities that can be used at home.	☐	☐	
Parents are offered follow up and consultation regarding at-home activities.	☐	☐	
Parents have opportunities for informal support activities, such as social events, drop-in hours, warm lines, and family recreation events.	☐	☐	
Parents have access to health and developmental screening for children of are given appropriate referrals.	☐	☐	

PARTICIPANT

	YES	NO	WAYS TO IMPROVE
Families are offered opportunities to be involved in the program on several levels, such as paid employees, volunteers and observers.	☐	☐	
Home visits are available to families when appropriate.	☐	☐	
Families participate in the planning, policymaking, and evaluation of the program.	☐	☐	

ADMINISTRATION AND POLICY

	YES	NO	WAYS TO IMPROVE
Program has written policies and procedures developed with staff and parent participation that describe in detail the implementation of parent education and support services.	☐	☐	
The written policies and procedures are evaluated and revised annually by parents and staff.	☐	☐	
An adequate budget and resources have been dedicated to support ongoing parent education and support activities and children's activities.	☐	☐	
Adequate space for parent education and support activities is provided.	☐	☐	
Program provides a welcoming, comfortable, and family-friendly atmosphere for parents.	☐	☐	
Program ensures flexibility in scheduling and operating hours to reflect the needs and employment patterns of the families being served.	☐	☐	
Families have choices regarding the activities/services in which they wish to participate.	☐	☐	
Information is exchanged with families on a regular and continuing basis.	☐	☐	
Program responds in a timely manner when feedback from families is negative and responds to families' suggestions and requests.	☐	☐	

ADMINISTRATION AND POLICY

	YES	NO	WAYS TO IMPROVE
All program materials reflect the diversity of the language and culture of the families in the program.	☐	☐	
Families are recruited through sensitive outreach and recruitment strategies. Such as:	☐	☐	
_____ *program is located in a family-friendly setting*			
_____ *program as been integrated into the community settings where families are already accessing services (libraries, ACCESS sites, JOBS programs, schools)*			
_____ *program delivers positive messages regarding the universal benefit of parent education and support services*			
Families participate in the planning, policy making and evaluation of the program.	☐	☐	

STAFF

	YES	NO	WAYS TO IMPROVE
Program ensures that staff reflect the racial, ethnic, and cultural heritage and values of the families served.	☐	☐	
Staff are selected because of prior education, training or experience in working with families in a manner that focuses on family strengths.	☐	☐	
Program ensures that administrative and program staff receive pre-service and in-service training to enhance their ability to work effectively and in partnership with families and staff.	☐	☐	
Staff receive adequate and on going supervision, support, and validation.	☐	☐	
Adequate time is allotted for program planning.	☐	☐	
Families are involved in staff training sessions.	☐	☐	

APPENDIX H: NATIONAL AGENCIES AND ORGANIZATIONS

NATIONAL AGENCIES AND ORGANIZATIONS

This list of national agencies and organizations is provided for purposes of identifying potential partners in the collaborative process. Their publications, research services and local affiliate contacts will help in a librarian's efforts to build networks, develop programs and collections, and broaden services to encompass the family.

AMERICAN FAMILY SOCIETY (AFS)
5013 Russett Rd.
Rockville, MD 20853
Kenneth Wayne Scott, President
301-460-4455

AMERICAN FOSTER CARE RESOURCES (AFCR)
P.O. Box 271
King George, VA 22485
Jacob R. Sprouse Jr., Director
703-775-7410

AMERICAN MOTHERS, INC. (AMI)
6145 Jochums Dr.
Tucson, AZ 85718
Mary Dorr, President
602-299-0666

AMERICAN SELF-HELP CLEARINGHOUSE
St. Clares-Riverside Medical Center
Denville, NJ 07834
201-625-7101

ASSOCIATION FOR CHILDHOOD EDUCATION INTERNATIONAL (ACEI)
11501 Georgia Ave., Suite 315
Wheaton, MD 20902
Gerald Odland, Executive Director
301-942-2443   800-423-3563

ASSOCIATION FOR CHILDREN FOR ENFORCEMENT OF SUPPORT (ACES)
723 Phillips Ave., Suite J
Toledo, OH 43612
Geraldine Jensen, President
419-476-2511   800-537-7072

ASSOCIATION FOR CHILDREN WITH RETARDED MENTAL DEVELOPMENT (A/CRMD)
162 5th Ave., 11th Floor
New York, NY 10010
Ida Rappaport, Executive Director
212-741-0100   800 WOW-ACRM

ASSOCIATION FOR CHILDREN WITH DOWN SYNDROME (ACDS)
2616 Martin Ave.
Bellmore, NY 11710
Fredda Stimell, Executive Director
516-221-4700

ASSOCIATION FOR THE CARE OF CHILDREN'S HEALTH (ACCH)
7910 Woodmont Ave., Suite 300
Bethesda, MD 20814
William Sciarilli, Sc.D., Executive Director
301-654-6549

ASSOCIATION OF MATERNAL AND CHILD HEALTH PROGRAMS (AMCHP)
1350 Connecticut Ave. NW, Suite 803
Washington, DC 20036
Catherine Hess, Executive Director
202-775-0436

BIG BROTHERS/BIG SISTERS OF AMERICA
230 N. 13 St
Philadelphia, PA 19107
Thomas M. McKenna, Executive Director
215-567-7000

CENTER FOR FAMILY SUPPORT (CFS)
386 Park Avenue South
New York, NY 10016
Alice Dick, Executive Director
212-481-1082

CENTER FOR THE STUDY OF PARENT INVOLVEMENT (CSPI)
JFK University
370 Camino Pablo
Orinda, CA 94563
Daniel Safran Ph.D., Director
510-254-0110

CENTER ON HUMAN POLICY (CHP)
200 Huntington Hall, 2nd Floor
Syracuse, NY 13244-2340
Steven Taylor, Ph.D., Director
315-443-3851

CHILD LIFE COUNCIL (CLC)
7910 Woodmont Ave., Suite 310
Bethesda, MD 20814
Susan Salisbury-Richards, Contact
301-654-1343

CHILD WELFARE LEAGUE OF AMERICA (CWLA)
440 1st St. NW, Ste. 310
Washington, DC 20001
David S. Liederman, Executive Director
202-638-2952

CHILDREN'S CREATIVE RESPONSE TO CONFLICT PROGRAM (CCRC)
c/o Fellowship of Reconciliation
523 N. Broadway
Box 271
Nyack, NY 10960
Priscilla Prtuzman, Coordinator
914-358-4600

CHILDREN'S DEFENSE FUND
25 E St. NW
Washington, DC 20001
Marian Wright Edelman, President
202-628-8787   800-CDF-1200

CHILDREN'S RIGHTS COUNCIL (CRC)
220 Eye St. NE
Washington, DC 20002
David L. Levy, President
202-547-6227

COUNCIL FOR LEARNING DISABILITIES (CLD)
P.O. Box 40303
Overland Park, KS 66204
Kirsten McBride, Executive Secretary
913-492-8755

DEPRESSION AFTER DELIVERY (DAD)
P.O. Box 1282
Morrisville, PA 19067
Nancy Berchtold, Executive Director
215-295-3994   800-944-4773

EPIC - Effective Parenting Information for Children
State University College at Buffalo
Cassety Hall - Room 340
1300 Elmwood Ave
Buffalo, NY 14222

FAMILIES AND WORK INSTITUTE (FWI)
330 7th Ave., 14th Floor
New York, NY 10001
Ellen Galinsky, Co-President
212-465-2044

FAMILY ACTION SECTION (FAS)
c/o Dr. Charles Hennon
260 McGuffey Hall
Miami University
Oxford, OH 45056
Dr. Charles Hennon, Section Chair
513-529-4900

FAMILY RESEARCH COUNCIL (FRC)
700 13th St., Suite 500
Washington, DC 20005
Gary Bauer, President
202-393-2100

FAMILY RESOURCE COALITION (FRC)
200 S. Michigan Ave.
Chicago, IL 60604
Judy Langford-Carter, Executive Director
312-341-0900

FAMILY SERVICE AMERICA (FSA)
11700 W. Lake Park Dr.
Milwaukee, WI 53224
Geneva B. Johnson, CEO & President
414-359-1040   800-221-2681

FATHERHOOD PROJECT (FP)
c/o Families and Work Institute
330 7th Ave., 14th Floor
New York, NY 10001
James A. Levine, Director
212-268-4846

FORMULA
P.O. Box 39051
Washington, DC 20016
Carol Laskin, Executive Officer
703-527-7171

FOSTER GRANDPARENTS PROGRAM (FGP)
1100 Vermont Ave NW, 6th Floor
Washington, DC 20525
Rey Tejada, Program Director
202-606-4849

FOUNDATION FOR GRANDPARENTING (FG)
Box 326
Cohasset, MA 02025
Arthur Kornhaber, M.D., Founder & President

GRANDPARENTS RAISING GRANDCHILDREN
(GRG)
P.O. Box 104
Colleyville, TX 76034
Barbara Kirkland, Chairman
817-577-0435

GRANTMAKERS FOR CHILDREN, YOUTH, AND
FAMILIES (GCYF)
c/o Council on Foundations
1828 L St. NW
Washington, DC 20036
Mary Leonard, Contact
202-466-6512

GUARDIAN ASSOCIATION (GA)
P.O. Box 1826
Pinellas Park, FL 34664
Patricia Johnson, Executive Officer
813-448-0730

INSTITUTE FOR AMERICAN VALUES (IAV)
1841 Broadway, Suite 211
New York, NY 10023
David Blankenhorn, President
212-246-3942

INSTITUTES FOR THE ACHIEVEMENT OF HUMAN
POTENTIAL (IAHP)
8801 Stenton Ave
Philadelphia, PA 19118
Glen J. Doman, Chairman
215-233-2050

INTERRACIAL FAMILY ALLIANCE (IFA)
P.O. Box 16248
Houston, TX 77222
Jane Archie, President
713-454-5018

JACK AND JILL OF AMERICA (JJA)
346 Commerce St.
Alexandria, VA 22314
Barbara B. Hofman, Executive Secretary
703-683-9663

JOINT CUSTODY ASSOCIATION (JCA)
10606 Wilkins Ave.
Los Angeles, CA 90024
James A. Cook, President
310-475-5352

LA LECHE LEAGUE INTERNATIONAL (LLLI)
P.O. Box 1209
Franklin Park, IL 60131-8209
Mary Lawrence, Contact
708 455-7730   800 LA LECHE

LEARNING DISABILITIES ASSOCIATION OF
AMERICA (LDA)
4156 Library Rd.
Pittsburgh, PA 15234
Jean Petersen, Executive Director
412-341-1515

LEGAL SERVICES FOR CHILDREN (LSC)
1254 Market St., 3rd Floor
San Francisco, CA 94102
Christopher Wu, Executive Director
415-863-3762

MISS MOM/MISTER MOM
535 Oliver St.
Moab, UT 84532
Tina L. Lopez, Executive Director
801-259-5090

MOTHERS AT HOME
8310-A Old Courthouse Rd.
Vienna, VA 22182
Cathy Myers, President
703-827-5903

MOTHERS' NETWORK
875 Avenue of the Americas, Suite 2001
New York, NY 10001
Mr. Silver, President
212-239-0510

NATIONAL ACADEMY OF COUNSELORS AND
FAMILY THERAPISTS (NACFT)
8038 Camellia Ln.
Indianapolis, IN 46219
Anthony T. Palisi, Ed.D., Executive Director
317-898-3211

NATIONAL ASSOCIATION FOR FAMILY DAY
CARE (NAFDC)
1331-A Pennsylvania Ave. NW, Suite 348
Washington, DC 20004
Deborah Eaton, Pres.
602-838-3446   800-359-3817

NATIONAL ASSOCIATION FOR THE EDUCATION
OF YOUNG CHILDREN
1509 16th St. NW
Washington, DC 20036
202-232-8777

NATIONAL ASSOCIATION OF CHILD CARE RE-
SOURCE AND REFERRAL AGENCIES
(NACCRRA)
1319 F. St. NW, Suite 606
Washington, DC 20004
Yasmina Vinci, Contact
202-393-5501

NATIONAL ASSOCIATION OF COUNSEL FOR
CHILDREN (NACC)
1205 Oneida St
Denver, CO 80220
Alice Arnold, Director
303-322-260

NATIONAL ASSOCIATION OF MOTHERS' CENTERS
336 Fulton Ave.
Hempstead, NY
Lorri Stepian, Co-Director
516-486-6614   800-645-3828

NATIONAL CENTER FOR LEARNING
DISABILITIES (NCLD)
381 Park Ave. S., Suite 1420
New York, NY 10016
Shirley C. Cramer, Contact
212-545-7510

NATIONAL CENTER FOR YOUTH WITH
DISABILITIES (NCYD)
University of Minnesota
Adolescent Health Program
Box 721
420 Delaware St. SE
Minneapolis, MN 55455
Nancy A. Okinow, Executive Director
612-626-2825   800-333-6293

NATIONAL CHILD SUPPORT ADVOCACY
COALITION (NCSAC)
P.O. Box 420
Hendersonville, TN 37077-0420
Beth Bellino McKinney, Executive Director
800-84-NCSAC

NATIONAL COALITION AGAINST DOMESTIC
VIOLENCE (NCADV)
P.O. Box 18749
Denver, CO 80218
Rita Smith, Program Coordinator
303-839-1852

NATIONAL COUNCIL ON CHILD ABUSE AND
FAMILY VIOLENCE (NCCAFV)
1155 Connecticut Ave. NW, Suite 400
Washington, DC 20036
Alan Davis, President
202-429-6695 800-222-2000

NATIONAL COUNCIL ON FAMILY RELATIONS
(NCFR)
3989 Central Ave. NE, Suite 550
Minneapolis, MN 55421
Mary Jo Czaplewski Ph.D., Executive Director
612-781-9331

NATIONAL COMMITTEE FOR THE PREVENTION
OF CHILD ABUSE
332 S. Michigan Ave., Suite 1600
Chicago, IL 60604-4357
312-663-3520

NATIONAL COUNCIL ON FAMILY RELATIONS
3089 Central Ave. NE, Suite 550
Minneapolis MN 55421

NATIONAL FOSTER PARENT ASSOCIATION
(NFPA)
Information and Services Office
26 Kilts Dr.
Houston, TX 77024
Gordon Evans, Director
713-467-1850

NATIONAL INFORMATION CENTER FOR CHIL-
DREN AND YOUTH WITH DISABILITIES (NICHCY)
P.O. Box 1492
Washington, DC 20013
Carol Valdiviesco, Director
703-893-6061   800-999-5599

NATIONAL ORGANIZATION OF CIRCUMCISION
INFORMATION RESOURCE CENTERS (NOCIRC)
P.O. Box 2512
San Anselmo, CA 94979
Marilyn Fayre Milos, R.N., Executive Director
415-488-9883

NATIONAL ORGANIZATION OF MOTHERS WITH
TWINS CLUBS (NOMOTC)
P.O. Box 23188
Albuquerque, NM 87192-1188
Lois Gallmeyer, Executive Secretary
505-275-0955

NATIONAL ORGANIZATION OF SINGLE MOTHERS
P.O. Box 68
Midland, NC 28107-0068
704-888-9354

NATIONAL VACCINE INFORMATION CENTER
512 Maple Ave. W, Suite 206
Vienna, VA 22180
Kathryn Williams, Contact
703-938-DPT3

PARENTS ANONYMOUS (PA)
675 W. Foothill Blvd., Suite 220
Claremont, CA 91711-3416
Linda Faber, Pres.
909-621-6184

PARENTS CHOICE FOUNDATION (PCF)
P.O. Box 185
Newton, MA 02168
Diana Huss Green, Editor-in-Chief
617-965-5913

PARENTS, FAMILIES, FRIENDS OF LESBIANS AND
GAYS (PFLAG)
1012 14th St. NW, Suite 700
Washington, DC 20005
Sandra Gillis, Exec. Dir.
202-638-k4200

PARENTS HELPING PARENTS (PHP)
535 Race St., Suite 140
San Jose, CA 95126
Florene M. Poyadue, R.N., Executive Director
408-288-5010

PARENTS OF CHILDREN WITH DOWN
SYNDROME (PODS)
c/o The Arc
11600 Nebel St.
Rockville, MD 20852
301-984-5792

PARENTS SHARING CUSTODY (PSC)
595 The City Dr., Suite 202
Orange, CA 92668
Marvin Chapman, Vice President
714-385-1002

PARENTS WITHOUT PARTNERS (PWP)
401 N. Michigan Avenue
Chicago, IL 60611-4267
K.M. Bell, Executive Director
312-644-6610   800-637-7974

PAUL ANDREW DAWKINS CHILDREN'S PROJECT
(PADCP)
P.O. Box 11008
Fayetteville, NC 28303
Paul Andrew Dawkins, Founder & Executive Director
919-868-6538

SINGLE MOTHERS BY CHOICE
P.O. Box 1642
Gracie Square Station
New York, NY 10028
212-988-0993

SINGLE PARENT RESOURCE CENTER
141 West 28 St
New York, NY 10001
212-947-0227

SOUTHERN EARLY CHILDHOOD ASSOCIATION
(SECA)
P.O. Box 56130
Little Rock, AR 72215
Jane Alexander, Administrative Services Director
501-663-0353

STEPFAMILY ASSOCIATION OF AMERICA (SAA)
215 Centennial Mall S., Suite 212
Lincoln, NE 68508
William F. Munn, Executive Director
402- 477-7837   800-735-0329

STEPFAMILY FOUNDATION (SF)
333 West End Ave.
New York, NY 10023
Jeannette Lofas, President
212 877-3244   800 SKY-STEP

YOUNG WOMEN'S CHRISTIAN ASSOCIATION OF
THE UNITED STATES OF AMERICA
(YWCA-USA)
726 Broadway
New York, NY 10003
Dr. Prema Matillai, Exec. Dir.
212-614-2700

INDEX

COLOPHON

Sandra Feinberg has devoted the past twenty-five years to public library service. It is this experience that she brings to her present position as director of the Middle Country Public Library. Feinberg is an advocate for improving the quality of life for children and families. She oversees a district of 56,000 people which circulates more than one million items annually and operates with a current budget of over $6 million. A passionate believer in the ability of public libraries to be family-oriented community institutions, she has been a frontrunner in the development of innovative programs and services for children and parents. In collaboration with many colleagues in other disciplines, Feinberg founded the Suffolk Coalition for Parents and Children in 1980. This organization has grown into a network of over 1,500 professionals, still providing ongoing opportunities for education, advocacy, and information sharing on behalf of children and families on a bi-monthly basis. Sandra Feinberg continues to be a leader in the development of programs and services for public libraries. She is the coauthor of *Running a Parent/Child Workshop: A How-To-Do-It Manual for Librarians* (Neal-Schuman Publishers, 1994) and *Parenting Bibliography* (Scarecrow, 1994) and an adjunct professor at the Palmer School of Library and Information Science at Long Island University. She lives in Stony Brook, New York with her husband and two sons.

Sari Feldman has focused her entire career on public library service. She has worked with library users of all ages and has particular expertise in youth services. As head of the Onondaga County Central Library she administers a major urban public library in New York State which serves a population of almost half a million users. Her ability to work in partnership with other community groups and agencies as well as in a consistently successful fund development and grant writing program has contributed to a revitalization of library service in the Syracuse community. She initiated the Onondaga County Public Library Projects PIRL (Parent Information Resource Library) and Ready, Set, Read. Feldman has also been an adjunct faculty member of the Syracuse University School of Information Studies for the past twelve years. In 1995 she received the Syracuse University Vice President's Award for Teacher of the Year. She has encouraged hundreds of MLS students to share her passion for public libraries and to become advocates for youth services. Feldman has presented numerous workshops and lectures and has written for professional journals. She is the coauthor of *Drugs: A Multimedia Sourcebook for Young Adults* (Neal-Schuman Publishers, 1980). She lives in Syracuse, New York, with her husband and two daughters.